Harvest of a Dialogue

Reflections of a Rabbi/Scholar on a Catholic Faculty

by

Hayim G. Perelmuter

Edited by

Dianne Bergant, C.S.A.

and

John T. Pawlikowski, O.S.M.

KTAV Publishing House, Inc.

1997

Library of Congress Cataloging-in-Publication Data

Perelmuter, Hayim Goren.
　　Harvest of a dialogue : reflections of a rabbi/scholar on a Catholic faculty / edited
by Dianne Bergant and John T. Pawlikowski.
　　　　p.　　cm.
　　Includes bibliographical references.
　　ISBN 0-88125-570-X (alk. paper)
　　　　1. Judaism—20th century. 2. Judaism—Relations— Christianity. 3. Christianity
and other religions—Judaism. I. Bergant, Dianne. II. Pawlikowski, John. III. Title.
BM45.P46 1997
296'.09'24—dc21　　　　　　　　　　　　　　　　　　　　　　　　　　　　97-3093
　　　　　　　　　　　　　　　　　　　　　　　　　　　　　　　　　　　　　　CIP
　　　　　　　　　　　　　　　　　　　　　　　　　　　　　　　　　　　　　　r97

Manufactured in the United States of America

Harvest of a Dialogue

Reflections of a Rabbi/Scholar on a Catholic Faculty

For Jon Nilson

~~For~~ a beloved friend and
long-time partner
in the "dialogue"

With affectionate
greetings & respect,

Hayim Perelmuter

12/5/97

Contents

The Contributors

This volume was occasioned by Catholic Theological Union's celebration of Rabbi Hayim Perelmuter's eightieth birthday, to recognize his long ministerial service at K.A.M.-Isaiah Israel Congregation in Chicago and his more than a quarter-century of service to CTU as Chautauqua Professor of Jewish Studies. The event took place at the Catholic Theological Union on April 24, 1994.

The publication was made possible by grants from the Anna Gamble Foundation, the Charles and Morris Shapiro Foundation, the Elias Family Foundation and the Catholic Theological Union.

Acknowledgements

The editors wish to acknowledge permission from the following publishers/publications to reprint writings by Dr. Perelmuter.

Journal of Reform Judaism for "When Sacrifice Became Prayer" (chap. 3), "Once a Pun a Preacher" (chap. 4), and "Gershom Scholem: Jewish Revolutionary of Our Age" (chap. 6).

Hebrew Union College Press for "Introduction to David Darshan" (chap. 5) from Dr. Perelmuter's volume *Shir Ha-Ma'alot l'David and K'tav Hitnazzelut l'Darshanim* (1984).

Paulist Press for "From Prophet to Preacher" (chap. 7) and "Christianity and Judaism as Siblings" (chap. 8) from Dr. Perelmuter's volume *Siblings: Rabbinic Judaism and Early Christianity at their Beginnings* (1989).

Deutscher Taschenbuch Verlag for "After Emancipation: Jews and Germans," written by Dr. Perelmuter as an added chapter for his translation of *Von Kanaan nach Israel: Kleine Geschichte des jüdischen Volkes* by Emil Bernard Cohn (1986).

The Liturgical Press for "Rabbinical Tradition on the Role of Women" (chap. 12) from *Women and Priesthood: A Call to Dialogue from the Faculty of the Catholic Theological Union*, edited by Carroll Stuhlmueller, C.P. (1978), and "'Do Not Destroy'— Ecology in the Fabric of Judaism" (chap. 13) from *The Ecological Challenge: Ethical, Liturgical and Spiritual Resources*, edited by Richard N. Fragomeni and John T. Pawlikowski (1994).

INTRODUCTION

Remarkable Person, Remarkable Era

John T. Pawlikowski, O.S.M.

This has been a remarkable period in Catholic–Jewish Relations. After centuries of stereotyping and persecution of Jews rooted in a theology of Jewish displacement from the covenant for the supposed murder of the Messiah Catholicism entered upon a dramatically new path with the passage of Vatican II's *Nostra Aetate*. This document not only rejected the basis for the long-dominant displacement theology of Judaism but laid the foundations for a whole new understanding as well by underscoring the continuance of the covenantal relationship with God on the part of the Jewish people and the inherent bonding between Christians and Jews through that covenant. Subsequent Vatican documents in 1974 and 1985 built upon, and amplified, the basic themes of Vatican II, stressing the need to come to understand Jews as they define themselves (1974 document) and highlighting the profound ties of Jesus and his Apostles to the Jewish community of his day, to Pharisaism in particular (1985 document). And statements from the U.S.

Catholic Bishops have addressed the issue of eliminating anti-semitism from preaching, liturgy, and passion plays.

Meanwhile, in the scholarly community equally remarkable developments have taken place. Major revolutions have occurred, in fact are still in process, regarding the Church's approach to the Hebrew Scriptures, to the Jewishness of Jesus and to Paul's links with the Jewish community. More and more Catholicism is coming to value the Hebrew Scriptures in their own right as a continuing source of revelational meaning for the Church, to understand that any divorce of Jesus and his teaching from a profoundly Jewish context distorts the meaning of the gospels, and increasingly to recognize that Paul may well have retained continuing ties to Judaism to a far greater degree than previously acknowledged.

In this remarkable period Catholic Theological Union has been enriched by the presence on its faculty of a remarkable person—Rabbi Hayim Goren Perelmuter. Respected as colleague, teacher and scholar, Rabbi Perelmuter retains as well that pastoral sense which many have come to know during his long years of service to Isaiah Israel and K.A.M.-Isaiah Israel Congregations. He has contributed in many ways to the growth of Catholic-Jewish understanding here at CTU, in the Cluster of theological schools in Hyde Park and internationally through his writings and lectures.

Rabbi Perelmuter's classes, his special lectures in other professors' classes, and his Sabbath experience seminars have introduced Christian students to Jewish mysticism, rabbinic thought, Jewish liturgy (in theory and practice) and other aspects of the Jewish tradition. His influence has also extended beyond CTU and Hyde Park to the Pacific Lutheran Theological Seminary at the Graduate Theological Union in Berkeley, California, where he taught for a number of years, to Luzern, Leuven, Lublin, Cracow, Jerusalem, and elsewhere. Through his writings he has also enhanced Christian-Jewish understanding with the translation and updating of *This Immortal People* and his groundbreaking work *Siblings* which became a bestseller and has has contributed to the changing paradigm shift in our understanding of the original relationship between the early Church and Judaism. His leadership in the Paul and Jewish Responsa project also represents another major contribution to the developing scholarship in this area. I can also mention his contribution on the Jewishness of Jesus and Paul in the May 1994 issue of *New Theology Review* as well as several essays in CTU faculty volumes, including *The Ecological Challenge: Ethical, Liturgical, and Spiritual Responses,* ed. by Richard Fragomeni and John T. Pawlikowski (Liturgical Press, 1994).

This commemorative volume gathers together a representative sample of Rabbi Perelmuter's writings over the years. The range of the collection shows the breadth of his interest and vision, from the condition of American Jewry to Prayer to Christian-Jewish Relations to contemporary issues such as the role of women and the ecological crisis. In all of these pieces, while his focus is often present-day, his resources are rabbinic and mystical. Sections from his two most important works, his study of David Darshan and his volume on the original split between Christianity and Judaism, clearly show both his scholarly depth and his pastoral concern.

Through a careful reading of Rabbi Perelmuter's essays both Jews and Christians will enhance their understanding of the depth of tradition in responding to contemporary challenges. Rabbi Perelmuter does not always have the full answer to these challenges, but his provocative reflections will truly help us as we search for an understanding of prayer, as we try to frame the relationship between the Church and the Jewish People, as we deal with possible meanings of transcendence for our time.

Part I
Approaches to American Judaism

CHAPTER ONE

Transcendence in Context

I

On the eve of Shavuot, the festival of the Revelation of the To-rah at Sinai, in Zaduska-Wola near Lodz in the year 1943, the Germans ordered all the ghetto inhabitants to assemble in the marketplace. The Jews knew what to expect, and they knew that their tormentors, with a special subtlety, would especially pick holy days on which to do their evil as though to underscore to their victims the absence of God.

On the preceding day ten Hasidim had been arrested on spu-rious charges of sabotage. They were to be hanged on the eve of the festival. The choice of ten was as deliberate as the choice of the day. It was as though the tormentors intended to take vengeance upon the People of the Covenant for perpetrating the Ten Commandments upon world society.

Shlomo Zlichovsky was among them. Little is known about him, although, according to one survivor, he was the son of a pious cantor, who on festivals would invite children from the schools to a party, teaching them Hasidic songs, marching

3

them through the town and letting the streets resound with their fervor.

The tormentors prepared for the hanging of the innocents as though it were a popular carnival. In prison the chosen ten prepared themselves for the end. Shlomo suggested that they treat it as a special, private Day of Atonement, the day of judgment, and despite the fact that the calendar said Shavuot, they used the Atonement Day liturgy under his guidance.

Before they could complete the all-day ritual with the special service of *Ne'ilah,* the Closing of the Gates, they were marched from prison. As they walked, Shlomo intoned the closing portions of the prayer. There was a quality of fervor and devotion that for the assembled Jews transformed what was meant to be a degradation of the spirit into a triumph of the soul.

Here is how an eyewitness reports it:

> Then, as the last preparations were being made for the hanging, I too looked into the face of Shlomo Zlichovsky. It was smiling with joy. I stood in the crowded place, in the midst of many humiliated Jews. But suddenly a spirit of encouragement passed over all of us. The gallows were standing in a row, under each of them a chair, in readiness. The Germans were in no hurry. A pity to waste a single moment of the "entertainment." But Shlomo Zlichovsky urged them on. "Nu (come on already)," he cried and jumped on the chair in order to put his head in the hanging loop. Some moments passed. We all held our breath. Deadly silence came over the marketplace, a silence that formed its redemption as Shlomo Zlichovsky's mighty voice was shattering it in his triumphant *Sh'ma Yisrael Adonay Elohenu Adonay Echad*—"Hear, O Israel, the Lord our God, the Lord is One!" We were all elevated. We were exalted. We shouted . . . without a sound; we cried . . . without tears; we straightened up . . . without a movement, and called, called together in the innermost recesses of our souls, "Sh'ma Yisrael . . ."[1]

At the moment when the Jewish people remembered their greatest collective experience, that transcendent breakthrough in the presence of the total community; at the moment they stood at the foot of Mount Sinai and renewed the covenant with the God of their ancestors; when God thundered forth His message to them and they responded; at such a moment, three millennia later, when it seemed that God was absent, silent, a son of that covenant witnessed his unyielding loyalty to that covenant, affirming at once his innate dignity and reality—and God's.

It is no wonder that Elie Wiesel has said that the Jewish experience of the transcendent rests upon two mysteries, the mystery of Sinai and the mystery of Auschwitz.

As we prepare to examine the question of transcendence in the context of contemporary Judaism, with all its varieties of approach, and with the widest spectrum of views, this central fact must be constantly borne in mind. To be sure, one can find a correspondence of forces at work within Judaism as within Christianity. After all, both were, in a sense, thrust at the same time upon the stage of history after the Roman destruction of Jerusalem. Rabbinic Judaism and Messianic Judaism both came out of the matrix of the pluralistic Jewish world that preceded it. Both confronted the breakup of the Roman Empire. Both achieved their classical form at approximately the same time, by the tenth and eleventh centuries.[2] Both confronted the rise of Islam. Both reacted to the Middle Ages and the Renaissance. Both confronted the scientific revolution and the Age of Reason. Both yielded to the enchantments of the rational and the secular.

In Christian theology the disillusion with our lofty scientific claims for ourselves set in with World War I and lay in ashes by the end of World War II. The same forces at work in Judaism express themselves with a characteristic difference, perhaps, at bottom, because what in the Christian world is symbolized by and through the Christ figure, as the personalized incarnation of the God-man covenant relationship inherent in Judaism, is symbolized in the Jewish world of thought as the Jewish-people-as-a-whole. It is almost as though the difference turned on who "the suffering servant of the Lord" is in the eyes of its special community in history.

II

The transcendent experience was there with Abraham when Judaism was born. It was there at Sinai when Israel confirmed its nationhood through its covenant with its ancestral God.

It has been wrestled with through the ages as Jacob wrestled with the angel. It has been tested in the fires of destruction and rebirth. It is at the core of Judaism, despite doubts and confusions. Without transcendence, Judaism would be an absurdity.

Transcendence is central to the Jewish experience, because the Jewish worldview, as recorded in its first spiritual biography, the Bible, and continued into history through the daring transformations within the continuing tradition of Rabbinic Judaism, centers around it.

The mythical world required no transcendence. Gods and men moved about in a universe of constant and ready contact with and communication between each other. Gods were glorified men, and men could be gods; and they shared the same dreams, passions, ambitions, and lusts.

Nor is transcendence crucial in the world of pagan religions. Here the gods were deifications of the animate and inanimate, noble and base; but in every case they were preceded by a realm prior to them. From the earliest beginnings in Babylonian, Egyptian, and Greek mythology, through their expressions in Greek philosophy, represented by Plato and Aristotle, this is clear.

All these "involve one idea which is the distinguishing mark of pagan thought: the idea that there exists a realm of being prior to the gods and above them, upon which the gods depend, and whose decrees they must obey."[3]

For Judaism, in its biblical record, the basic idea is affirmed that God is supreme over all, that there is no realm above or beside Him to set bounds to His sovereignty. God is utterly distinct from and other than the world, subject to no laws or powers that transcend Him. Yet He is involved with the human species in a special kind of relationship, a relationship symbolized by revelation and covenant.

This unique view of the One God is experienced, expressed, and reflected upon in the biblical account. It is a folk encounter reflected in the experience of its elect on the one hand, and at one crucial time by the entire people, on the other.

In the midst of a pagan universe, it is the progenitor Abraham who confronts this transcendence, and the encounter is sealed with a covenant which commits him and his progeny to it. The covenant is renewed with Isaac at the grim aftermath of the "binding," and with Jacob, in the vision of the ladder at Bethel and the wrestling match with the angel at Jabbok, thus becoming—Israel.

It is hidden yet implicit in the story and breaks out again through the burning bush and the Egyptianized Moses who returns to his people. It climaxes with the exodus, the crossing of the sea, and the stand at Sinai, where the entire people is witness to a breakthrough of transcendence that renews the covenant and sets the seal upon the direction into history of that special relationship.

The rest of the biblical record is an account of the continuing dialogue through especially chosen agents like Samuel, Elijah, and the rest of the prophets through whom God communicates as Voice and commanding force, across the chasm that separates the human from the transcendent.

Even in the biblical record there are set limits to that relationship. You can hear God, can know God, but cannot see Him face to face. Even Moses learns this in the cleft of the rock—"No one can see my face and live!" (Exod. 33:20). Isaiah is dazzled by a blinding vision; Ezekiel, by the chariot that blazes across his horizon.

Something of deep mystery has happened in this relationship across the chasm of transcendence, between a people and its transcendent God. It is recorded in its earliest records, and deeply graven upon the historical experience that shapes its future. Perhaps it can be summarized by the word *survival*.[4] It is as central today as it was then. Emil Fackenheim can write:

> The stake for modern Jewish thought is nothing less than survival. In premodern times Jewish thought showed a certain stubbornness to Greek philosophical universalism which it knew to be pagan, and to Christian and Muslim universalism, if only because they pushed Jewish existence into the limbo of "has been" or "never was."

Inherent in the covenant, a developing sense of mutual interdependence and awareness of the need to survive and to witness to the covenant surfaces. The biblical record of this relationship reflects the period of earliest beginnings, of relationship to the Promised Land, diaspora in Egypt, covenant at Sinai, and the period of the First Commonwealth. The traumatic end of this era, the destruction of the Temple and the state by the Babylonians, and the exile, made it appear almost as though the covenant had been shattered and the people destroyed.

"When the Temple was destroyed prophecy was taken from the prophets and given to the sages," we learn from the Talmud (Baba Batra 12a). A unique, direct bridge over the chasm of transcendence was severed. One form of being ended. A new form, continuing the old, was in the wings. "The Holy One, praised be He, prepares the cure before He strikes us with the disease" is an old folk maxim (Megillah 13b). How true this is when we consider Jeremiah's acts as the Temple in Jerusalem was going up in flames. He did two things: first he demonstratively purchased a plot of land in Jerusalem, proclaiming, "Houses and fields and vineyards shall yet be bought in this land" (Jer. 32:15, 29:1), and then he wrote a letter to the exiles in Babylon urging them to prepare for a long exile, and therefore to organize their communities for survival and ultimate return. The acceptance of this idea began the process, which took several centuries to develop, but which added a dimension to the Jewish people's capacity to survive for the covenant.

It prepared the ground for Rabbinic Judaism, which was the form Judaism assumed to make it capable of surviving what otherwise might have been the end. Through this mutation, the experience of transcendence took a new turn that profoundly influences how it is perceived and experienced in our contemporary context, as we shall presently see.

III

The destruction of the First Temple and the Judean state by the Babylonians was a watershed in the Jewish experience of transcendence. A curtain fell upon the biblical period of Jewish ex-

perience. To be sure much was left to be done: the Torah book
to be edited and put into its final form; the works of the last of
the prophets to be reduced to their final form; and some books
still to be written. But somehow it seemed that the covenant
had been ruptured and God's communication with the people
through elect prophetic spirits ended. Even God's indwelling
presence, it seemed, had gone into exile.

A process had quietly been born that made the transition possible. It moved slowly and surely into the developing of the Second Commonwealth, the rich variety of expressions of Jewish
being, and into the emergence of a capacity to rebuild and move
forward.

That process emerges as Rabbinic Judaism. It is quiet, imperceptible at first, but it has a power and a vision attuned to the
needs of the folk and growing out of it. With a strange and creative imagination, it achieves the remarkable metamorphosis of
the prophetic type into the bearers of tradition. It achieves a remarkable transformation. The former covenant relationship
with its fiery explosions of divine communication; the prophetic utterance, with its cutting edge of rebuke intertwined with
abiding love and hope, are transformed by the magic wand of
daring rabbinic innovation into a new relationship mediated by
the study and shaping of Torah at the hand of its skilled and dedicated devotees.

It is a revolutionary metamorphosis. Indeed, it goes a step further. It expands the very meaning of revelation and revealed
Torah. For side by side with the written Torah there emerges
the idea of an Oral Law, which is to make possible the extension
and deepening of the meaning of the Torah. Equal status with
the Written Law is achieved by the Oral Law, although not
without much struggle, and in effect this makes of revelation an
open-ended process.

But now it is to be achieved through study of the sacred texts, through expansion of their meaning by commentaries, and commentaries upon commentaries, which also, in the process, achieve a sacred status.

To be sure this process does not happen overnight. It germinates, grows, develops, ebbs and flows through the period of the Second Commonwealth. Through five centuries of creative development and growth the Jewish world confronts the Persian, Greek, and Roman worlds, and achieves a depth of purpose and of self-consciousness. From this the capacity of Judaism, not only to shape its own survival, but to sire Christianity and Islam, emerges.

The sages who are the architects of this transformation give themselves status by creating the concept of a chain of tradition that leads from Sinai to Moses, to Joshua, to the Judges, Elders, Prophets, and Men of the Great Assembly who are the bridge from the prophetic period to theirs. Gershom Scholem summarizes with brilliant insight Rabbinic Judaism's perception of the nature of truth with the words:

> Truth is given once and for all, and it is laid down with precision.
> . . . Not system but *commentary* is the legitimate form through which
> truth is approached. . . . Commentary thus became the characteristic expression of Jewish thinking about truth.

It is this touching of base with tradition through a link with sacred texts, immersing oneself in it, subordinating oneself to it and yet transforming it, that becomes the continuation of the covenant relationship and the shaping of the bridge to transcendence.

> In Judaism [Scholem continues], tradition becomes the reflective
> impulse that intervenes between the absoluteness of the Divine
> Word—revelation—and its receiver. Tradition thus raises a ques-

tion about the *possibility of immediacy* [emphasis added] in man's relationship to the Divine, though it has been incorporated in revelation.[5]

Raising the question about the possibility of the Divine Word confronting us without mediation, Rabbinic Judaism answers with a resounding negative. Every religious experience after that first revelation must be a mediated one.

When the Temple stood, the cult was a mediating process. Once the Temple is gone, Torah and its study and interpretation and its expansion through commentary must assume that role.

This is not to deny that the transcendent could be experienced by the reflective saint in mystical contemplation, and there are many examples of this in talmudic literature. One need only think of Yoḥanan ben Zakkai's disciple El'azar ben Arak, of whom it is written:

> Said [R. El'azar] to him [R. Yoḥanan]: Master, wherefore didst thou dismount from the ass? He answered: Is it proper that whilst thou art expanding the Work of the Chariot[6] and the Divine Presence is with us, and the ministering angels accompany us, I should ride on the ass! Forthwith R. El'azar b. Arak began his exposition of the Work of the Chariot, and fire came down from heaven and encompassed all the trees of the field; [thereupon] they all began to utter divine song.
>
> (B.T. Ḥagigah 14b; also Shabbat 80b)

Nor is it to say that the devout, simple soul, unsophisticated and intellectually untrained, could not, through devout practice of the divine commandments in everyday deed and prayer, make contact with the transcendent or reflect it in his life. The modalities are indeed reflected in the talmudic record by the *vita contemplativa* of the pious men of old—the virtuous and pious life led by ordinary folk who combined their daily toil with the ideal life of study of Torah as an "intellectual-spiritual form of the *vita activa*."[7]

But fundamentally a change *has* taken place. The pillar of cloud and the pillar of flame that had been evidence of the Divine Presence and its accessibility became the smoke and fire of destruction. The people had been wrenched from its land, God separated from His shrine. New forms needed to be fashioned to create the possibilities of a continuing (or renewed) encounter. This role was assumed by Rabbinic Judaism in its effort to link people with its divine source as it moved into history.

IV

We see, therefore, that Rabbinic Judaism was born out of the shock of the destruction of the First Jewish Commonwealth. Its period of gestation and growth came with the Second Commonwealth (ca. 500 B.C.E. to 113 C.E.), a period of extraordinary inward growth and development. With significant diasporas now in existence in Babylonia/Persia and the Greco-Roman world, the conserving and creative force of this form of Judaism deepened its influence and shaped the contours for survival.

In its confrontation with world powers, its experience of disasters actual and potential, the ideas of messianic redemption and restoration as a paradigm of national experience fermented. The upsurge of the messianic thrust, apparent in the Maccabean revolt and the final confrontations with Rome, left its mark in a tension between a messianism of instant result and a messianism of long-range expectation.

If Rabbi Akiba's support of the abortive Bar Kochba revolt

against Rome (135 C.E.) was expressive of the former, the careful compromise of Yoḥanan ben Zakkai with Rome (70 C.E.) was symptomatic of the latter. In a discussion on messianism in Tractate Sanhedrin of the Babylonian Talmud, a long and detailed discussion dealing with the short range and the long range, a sage could say: "Blasted be the bones of him who predicts the day of the coming of the Messiah!" (Sanhedrin 97b).

The Roman war against Judea left the Jewish people with three options—the struggle to the death (the strategy of the Zealots at Masada); the way of "instant" messianism, represented by the birth of Christianity and its ultimate conquest of Rome itself; and the way of Rabbinic Judaism, which represents a temporary retreat away from Rome to the Parthian world, to return later to the West in Judaism's unfolding history.

It is in this form that Judaism and the Jewish people confront the world of the powerful East and the world of the powerful West, represented by Islam and Christianity respectively, each surging in an attempt to dominate the other.

A sense of exile, of punishment for guilt, of hope for return, of awareness of the ultimate indestructibility of the Covenant and the stubborn uniqueness of the Sinaitic relationship, persists.

The way is fashioned, despite the triumphalism of the younger sibling faiths, each in their way combining religious with secular power. It is fashioned despite their might and their conviction that they had wrested the glorious crown of God's special choice from defeated and rejected Israel.

An inner and inward life, seemingly at the peripheries of the ruling cultures, yet deeply involved with them, sometimes in creative dialogue, but too often in a dialogue of pain and anguish, grows and develops. There is an awareness of a divine relationship, and the development of deed and study under a unifying law and social fabric linked to original sources.

This then is the structure through which Judaism survives and expresses itself throughout the Middle Ages and into and beyond the threshold of the modern era. It is a confrontation, for the most part, and a coexistence at some time with the ruling, dominant, triumphalist faiths of Christianity and Islam. It rises and falls, ebbs and flows, moves from center to center, but its inward life grows through layer upon layer of commentary and of expansion of the rabbinic way. The link with the transcendent continues in the mediated manner of Torah study and the performance of the deeds required by it.

There is always a sense of exile, of abandonment by God or of having been punished by Him, and yet always a conviction that their continued witness of Him was crucial, and that He would someday intervene in their behalf as in the days of yore. God was known in past rememberings, in immersion in the study of His Torah, and in the doing of His way.

Yet the drive to bridge the chasm of transcendence continued, despite the dropping of the curtain, despite the exile of the Shekhinah, despite the cessation of direct revelation to the prophets. The hunger to know and to experience continued in the hidden places, as though a subterranean secret river flowed within the mainstream of Jewish history.[8] This was the effort to continue the secret study of the mysteries of being, to achieve a capacity to "know God" face to face, to understand the forces that shaped creation and animated divine being.

This was the cultivation and study of Kabbalah, the mystic lore, the effort to understand the inner meaning and purpose of the universe, of Jewish being, of God Himself. Ancient gnostic roots combined with this hidden search whose goal was to give a new mythic base to the structure of Rabbinic Judaism as it moved into history.

The mystics produced a literature that took the devotee into the heavens and returned him to earth; produced secret works that described the realities of Creation; detailed the stature of God; described the Torah text as the mystical repository of the secrets of God's ultimate reality.

They developed elect and secret fellowships whose devotees immersed themselves in these studies, saw their visions, and on rare occasions experienced the ultimate revelation of the divine. And when the pain of exile grew increasingly acute with the horrors of the Crusades in the eleventh and twelfth centuries, the expulsion from Spain in the fifteenth century, the Chmielnicki pogroms in Poland in the seventeenth century, the emphasis of the mystic quest shifted from the effort to experience God, the effort to describe and understand the inner secret processes of His being, to the eager anticipation of His reentry into history as redeeming messianic force to bring an end to exile and suffering, and a restoration to the ancient homeland.

Thus it is that the Jewish people moves into the Christian and Moslem-dominated Middle Ages, witnessing to an ancestral covenant, living in counterpoint to these cultures with a realistic survival pattern that kept its link to divine roots through the expansion of the study of sacred texts, and living the sacred life in the face of the pragmatic struggle for survival. And just below the surface, the passion and the surge of the mystical quest flowed like a torrential, underground stream.[9]

V

It is never an easy thing to put the vital life force on the Procrustean bed of historical theory, nor is it easy to mark out sharp dividing lines in the historical process. Yet historians find it necessary to do so, and finite minds find it useful to function with neatly ordered categories.

Hence, when we speak of the end of the medieval era and the beginning of the modern age, can we place it precisely? The French Revolution and the beginning of the end of feudalism, perhaps? The discovery of America and the invention of printing, perhaps? The questing of the Greek philosophers in the Stoa, unseating the gods and making man the center of the universe, perhaps?

Who can know for sure? No exact and precise borderline can be drawn. Yet, imperceptibly perhaps, but nonetheless clearly, the process of placing the human person at the center of things, the capacity of the human mind to know and to understand, and the development of the inductive scientific method all combined to bring about the scientific revolution.

Man came to be seen as the measure of all things, an inexhaustible, glorious potential of creativity and achievement. He confronted the security that religion promised, and even when he made peace with it, he philosophized and interpreted it into a realm of irrelevancy. Science and philosophy alike threw down the gauntlet to religion. The transcendent was either defined as everything (and therefore nothing) or totally ignored.

The modern era could well be seen as the enthronement of the seeking, creating, discovering human mind, shaping a world's destiny. It delved, it groped, it analyzed, it defined, it discovered, it invented, it gloried in its potential and in its hopes. Nothing, it seemed, could be denied it, as nature yielded its mysteries and sired new and greater machines.

Industrial and intellectual growth marched forward, the Spinozas put God everywhere and therefore nowhere, the

Humes doubted, and the Voltaires denied God. Revolutions, the growth of individualism, the romanticizing of individualism, destructive wars and holocaust saw the growth, maturation, and decline of great secularisms.

The Jewish encounter with secularism oscillated between rejection and attraction. On the one hand, Judaism saw itself apart from a corrupt and corrupting world, holding steadfast to a unique covenant relationship with the one true God. On the other, it entered into a dialogue with the outside, making an attempt to interpret itself in their terms, and applying their techniques toward self-definition.

Medieval Jewish philosophy reflects this. Its great exponents, Saadia and Maimonides, to name but two, interpreted Judaism in terms of the dominant philosophical tendencies of their time, the Qalam[10] and Aristotelianism. Maimonides' interpretation of God and transcendence in such terms, though preserving the essential Jewish viewpoint, had enough of the God of the philosopher in it to incur the wrath and hostility of the mystics.

For the Jew, the medieval era represented repression and rejection. At best he was treated as a tolerated minority. At worst he was forced into ghettos, stripped of rights, expelled or massacred. It is in this light that secular modernism was looked upon with a sense of hope and promise. The Reformation, the French Revolution, and the Enlightenment began to open the doors. You could, if only you entered this new world of hope, become free and fulfilled.

Thus, while in the ghettos the old ways prevailed, Jews who moved westward tended to move into the mainstream. "To the Jews as individuals, everything; to the Jews as a nation, nothing!" rang out the promise of emancipation in France.[11] The promise was seized, and in many cases the best of the Jewish mind and the Jewish heart was given to it. Art, literature, commerce, philosophy, scholarship, journalism, the theater, politics, economics, and science received the full and enthusiastic gifts of the people that had so long dwelt apart. The ancient faith was interpreted, reformed or abandoned. The transcendent God came down to earth for Jews in the form of the unlimited possibilities of freedom in this world. The vision of unlimited progress "broadening down from precedent to precedent" became their vision. "Washington is my Zion, Cincinnati, my Jerusalem" was the triumphant proclamation of an American Reform Jew in the nineteenth century.[12]

Jewish scholars began to structure the corpus of Jewish learning in Western European forms. Steinschneider saw his task in gathering together the materials of Jewish bibliography and literature as preparing Judaism for a decent burial.[13] Jewish philosophers began to express Jewish theology in equally Western forms. Hermann Cohen, the great Kantian, could, for example, systematize his view of Judaism in Kantian terms, in his *Religion der Vernunft aus den Quellen des Judentums*.

But the germ of antisemitism moved out of the Middle Ages into the modern era. The dethroning of religion did not include eliminating the barnacles of irrational hate-fear, and they attached themselves to the vessels of the new age. It became clear that the price of total self-immolation to it was for many too big a price to pay. With the rise of modern nationalism, Jews took a look at Jewish national rebirth in modern terms. Jewish philosophers increasingly used the forms of Western philosophy to articulate a view of Judaism grounded in its roots, and resistant to the blandishments of the new secularism.

This is not to say that secularism did not strike deep roots in the Jewish psyche. It did in fact, and its influence is widely pervasive. Jewish secularism could turn its back on thoughts of transcendence. It could, so it appeared, exist without God. But if it remained Jewish, it could not exist without the Jewish people. And so long as the Jewish people continued to exist, you could not escape the problem of the covenant. And in dealing with the covenant, you could not escape the problem of the partner on the other side—God.

The traumas of World War I, the Holocaust, and Hiroshima, which had a devastating effect upon secularism and religion alike, had their impact on Judaism as well. They challenged and tested faith. They uprooted communities. They demanded self-examination and self-analysis. Whither was it all heading? What did it all mean? Where was God in all this?

VI

If World War I jolted the high hopes of the perfectibility of man in a man-centered world, World War II, with the Holocaust and Hiroshima, left it spiritually in shambles.

The presumptions of philosophy and science began to be questioned. Man's mind moved in the extreme to the hopelessness of existentialist aloneness, on the one hand, and to the need for a God that cared and had meaning on the other. God was either dead or had to be discovered in a new reality beyond the "defining-away" of earlier philosophical and theological systems.

The Jew had thrown himself with great hopes into the arms of humanism and the promise of emancipation. It was not, however, a total immersion. There were some who had their doubts and uttered them. And among those who saw the promise of freedom there were signs of dissent.

It was in Central and Western Europe, where the giants of

philosophy and theology held sway, that this was apparent. Martin Buber blazed new trails in the transcendent quest, and went back to Hasidic roots to find the embers of a vanishing faith. Gershom Scholem, rejecting the Europe of the optimistic advocates of emancipation, undertook the monumental task of plumbing the depths of meaning of the mystical stream of Jewish experience and the Kabbalah, returning to Israel to do his work. Franz Rosenzweig stepped back from the brink of apostasy into a deeper study of the *mysterium tremendum* of Judaism. Zionist theorists, political and cultural, did their work. It was all grist for the mill of the individual quest and the perception of a group-folk destiny that was seen as a possible clue for a transcendent insight.

One must recognize the fact that the secularist, humanist forces deeply affected the Jewish world. In a world that expanded realms where religion did not count, being a Jew was no longer a handicap. Jews pursued secularity, and gave up religious practice to fit into the new society. The power of humanity to create a just social order could take the place of a saving and redeeming God. Eugene Borowitz writes:

> Jewish spirituality now largely sublimated itself to the best of Western civilization. In my opinion that still remains the fundamental faith of contemporary Jewry as a whole. It lives out a vision engendered by Emancipation. All that follows should be understood as a qualification of that premise.[14]

It is against the background of this residual humanism that he describes a kind of return, a questing for values and transcendence, discernible in segments of seeking and searching young Jews as they confront the aftermath of the Holocaust. Some go back to the security of an Orthodoxy, in vibrant communities created by learned, pious, observant native-born Americans. A minority of liberals, who have moved beyond reliance on secular rationality, seek to live their personal freedom with tradition as their guide.

This devaluation of modernity has moved many Jews to a deeper, more direct spirituality. They faced up to the agnosticism which much of secular Jewish life had assumed, and found it wanting.

> When . . . these Jews hold on to their high sense of values with continuing devotion, despite the loss of their secularized rationale for them, their social and ethnic idealism is a response to something that lies beyond reason and self and society, and is at the core of the universe itself. Through some such experience as this, a sizeable minority in the Jewish community is discovering a transcendent dimension to existence. The Jewish spirit . . . is moving back to God. Astonishingly, we are seeing a direct spirituality being reborn among us. The covenant, our ancient partnership, is newly alive in our fresh perception of the Other, who meets and helps and commands and judges and forgives and saves and vindicates.[15]

The trauma of the Holocaust experience, long in sinking in, is the benchmark. The reaction to it sharply involves an approach to transcendence, whether in acceptance or in rejection. From this perspective we look at some examples of thinking about transcendence. No attempt is made at completeness. No effort is made to look at and describe those individuals who cling to an unaltered faith and know for certain that God is there beyond the veil, eternal and caring. An Abraham Isaac Kook and a Joseph Soloveitchik deserve a special study on their own.

There is, for example, Elie Wiesel, snatched as an adolescent from the warmth and security of the simple faith of his Hasidic surroundings into the hell of Auschwitz. He comes out of it dazed, silent at first, and then the torrent of his witness pours out, perceptive and feeling. His is a strange dialectic anger at the silence of God at this dreadful abyss that witnessed what he saw as the death of humanity; and at the same time a passionate urge to confront God, to speak to Him, to hear from Him, to engage Him in dialogue, to call Him to account. A little of Abraham, a little of Jeremiah, a little of Reb Levi Yitzhak of Berditchev speak through him.

It is such rebels within faith against God—Abraham in the matters of Sodom and Gomorrah, and, reading the midrashim carefully, after the trauma of the binding of Isaac; Jeremiah in his cry against the apparent success of the wicked; Elisha ben Abuya and the death of the martyrs; or Reb Levi Yitzhak of Berditchev, who summons God to judgment in his town marketplace—who are the natural antecedents.

As Wiesel reflects, he finds the yearning for dialogue with the transcendent a pressing fact. He sees a parallel in the writer's task, this drive to dialogue, this communication of solitudes:

> Between author and reader there must be a dialogue. The creative process is a strange one: it comes from solitude and it goes to solitude, and yet it is a meeting between two solitudes. It is just like man's solitude faced with God's solitude. Once you have this confrontation, you have art, and religion, and more. You have a certain communion in the best and purest sense of the word. . . . When both are sincere God is there.[16]

For Wiesel the transcendent veil is broken in the process. He likes to cite Franz Kafka, who observed that man has the power to speak to God but not about God.[17] Implicit, too, is a deeply felt need for worship. For Wiesel writing was such a need. A need to adore. But he is ambivalent when he raises the question: "To whom?" He can understand our purposes for God. He wonders about God's purposes for us.

Elie Wiesel has often stated that Auschwitz and Sinai are the two central Jewish mysteries of all time. At Sinai the covenant was made. At Auschwitz perhaps the covenant was broken. The Jewish people did its part to keep it, he avers. Did God do His? A people was taken, he tells us in his poetic language, and turned into flames, and the flames turned into clouds. Now they come back to him as clouds to haunt him, to make him remember. It was as though they were an echo of the cloud that hovered over the Ark of the Covenant. The covenant was broken, but

> Maybe it will be renewed, perhaps later; maybe it was renewed even then, on a different level. So many Jews kept their faith or even strengthened it. But it was broken because of the clouds and because of the fire.[18]

We shall encounter that theme of stubborn, unilateral renewal of the covenant again and again.

It is through his madmen that Wiesel's images of the transcendent concern come through with greatest clarity. A world that tolerated Auschwitz, that made it possible through its genteel unconcern, that represented itself as the acme of civilization and sanity, seemed to call for madness as the only way to protest against its sham. Wiesel crafts characters who are mad because "sanity" led to the ovens, and they have decided in favor of God and of man. Sanity and madness trade places. Moshe the Madman in "The Madness of God," and Michael in *The Town Beyond the Wall* assume madness the better to be witnesses to man and to God!

We know that God is a father. We know that God is a master. But is God a friend? The madman is asking the question and that is why he is mad. Who is mad? Someone who tries to see God. Because then, either he dies—according to the Bible he must die; he who sees God dies—or if he doesn't die he must go mad and maybe he goes mad in order not to die.[19]

For Wiesel, then, there is pain, anger, a need to speak, a need to confront God, a recognition of the urge to confront transcendence, and a recognition of the profound problem which we encounter in the process.

There is the young American theologian, Richard Rubenstein, who could not accept God as the omnipotent author of the historical drama in view of the reality of Auschwitz. This was driven home to him in his conversations on the Holocaust with German Evangelical Lutheran leaders, when Dean Heinrich Gruber, an active anti-Nazi, nevertheless affirmed God's omnipotent rule even over the events of Auschwitz.[20] "I could not possibly believe in such a God, nor could I believe in Israel as the chosen people of God after Auschwitz," writes Rubenstein in the wake of this encounter.

After Auschwitz he could speak only of "the death of God." He could see himself as a religious existentialist. He could see the thread uniting God and man, heaven and earth, as broken. He could aver: "We stand in a cold, silent, unfeeling cosmos, unaided by any purposeful power beyond our resources. After Auschwitz, what can a Jew say about God?"[21]

For him there is a void where once God's presence was experienced, but Judaism has not lost its power. If Bonhoeffer saw that the problem was to speak of God in an age of religion, Rubenstein saw it in terms of speaking of religion in an age of no God. He becomes a kind of Camus in clerical garb! What remains for him is the Torah as the link, the record of Israel's encounter with God in "His terrible holiness." There remains the excruciating experience of death and resurrection, Auschwitz and Israel reborn, for the Jewish people in the twentieth century. Losing all hope and faith, one has also lost the possibility of disappointment. Rubenstein puts it this way: "Expecting absolutely nothing from God or man, we rejoice in whatever we receive. We accept our nothingness—nay we even rejoice in it—for in finding our nothingness, we have found both ourselves and the God who alone is the true substance."[22]

It is to the hidden, darkly mythical God of Nothingness at the heart of mysticism to which he turns, to an end of estrangement implicit in the "return to Israel's earth and to the divinities at the source of that earth." It is a kind of return to a mythical paganism, a kind of Canaanism reminiscent of one of the secular revolts in the Jewish-Zionist response to the onset of modernism in nineteenth-century Russia and the first two decades of the twentieth century in Israel. Its goal—self-liberation and self-discovery; a return to the bosom of Mother Earth. In his view Torah remains, but not as a mediating force to transcendence and tradition as perceived by Scholem and later reemphasized by Neusner.[23]

And there is Emil Fackenheim, who asks whether after Auschwitz the messianic faith is not already falsified; whether a Messiah who could have come and yet did not come at Auschwitz has become a religious impossibility. The response is there in a great *nevertheless,* by the nature and fact of the people's survival out of Auschwitz. It may not have found its full articulation in thought, but it exists in the actual life-commitment of the people. It is not a mediating response, for this, in his view, is too much to expect of the Holocaust kingdom. It must be confronted by a radical opposition. In spite of the negation of all that the covenant relationship stood for, the Jewish survivor is the expression par excellence of this fact by the mere decision to remain a Jew. By this decision, the survivor has become the paradigm of the whole Jewish people. A strange intertwining of the secular and the religious occurs:

> The Holocaust Kingdom murdered religious and secularist Jews alike. The decision just referred to requires philosophical thought to restructure the categories of religiosity and secularity. Only by virtue of a radical "secular" self-reliance that acts as though the God who once saved could save no more, can even the most "religious" survivor hold fast to the Sinaitic past or the Messianic future. And only by virtue of a radical "religious" memory and hope, can even the "secularist" survivor rally either the courage or the motivation to remain a Jew when every natural impulse tempts him to seek forgetfulness.[24]

This Jewish testimony is, indeed, an extraordinary testimony. For despite the pain, despite the agony, despite the despair, it calls back into history, perhaps with anger, perhaps with defiance, perhaps even with love, the transcendent analogue to an eternal covenant relationship. After Auschwitz

> the religious Jew still submits to the Commanding Voice of Sinai, which bids him witness to the one true God. He is now joined, however, by the secular Jew, who by the act of remaining a Jew submits to a commanding voice heard from Auschwitz that bids him testify that some gods are false. No Jew can remain a Jew without ipso facto testifying that idolatry is real in the modern world.[25]

The decision to survive, to bring children into the world, to rebuild life in a reborn state and in communities throughout the world, becomes a ringing affirmation from one side of the cov-

enant, that clearly implies the other side. This commingling of
religiosity and secularity has found its embodiment, in his view,
in the Jewish state, for "it has always been impossible to understand the Zionist movement either in purely religious or purely
secularist categories. . . . After the Holocaust, the Israeli nation
has become collectively, what the survivor is individually."[26]

The perception of the *Jewish-people-as-a-whole* as God's suffering servant, as the eternal witness to a transcendent possibility,
is, in my view, a crucial perception. As Fackenheim sees it, Jewish death at Auschwitz and Jewish rebirth at Jerusalem might
make Hegel, who once affirmed that no nation appears more
than once on the world-historical scene, wonder whether at
least one people is not doing just that, and with consequences
yet unknown.

The merging of the secular with the religious seems to be a
significant fact in the process. It is a perception not foreign to
theological developments in contemporary Judaism. One need
only observe how Gershom Scholem used the secular tool of
scientific historiography to plumb the depths of Jewish historical
and mystical religious experience, to understand this.[27]

VII

The mystery and the power of the Jewish response to the transcendent fact, the linking of the eternity of the Jewish people to
the eternal reality of God, persists.

Never mind the doubts. Never mind the harsh and brutal historical events that make the entire episode, in the words of a beloved teacher of mine, Henry Slonimsky, "heartbreak house";
it persists. For the surviving Jew theophily made it possible to
cope with theodicy.

Looking at the body of a lifeless child dangling from the gallows at Auschwitz, Elie Wiesel responds to the question "Where is God?" with the answer: "Hanging there on the gallows."[28] But his writing and thinking are directed at a transcendent Other, who *must* give answers, and Who is affirmed by what the martyrs stood for.

If I began these reflections on transcendence in the Jewish context with the episode of Shlomo Zlichovsy, a Hasid who died on the gallows with a cry of faith on his lips, let us end with one who was not so sure, and who survived and returned.

Pavel Friedlander lived in Prague in the years when Hitler came to power. He grew up in an assimilated milieu, his father a successful businessman and lover of music. On his mother's side there were some vague Zionist memories. He remembers his mother visiting what was then Palestine, and an uncle going to settle there.

With Munich and the invasion, his family fled, always just a step ahead of the invaders. His father never quite understood the realities, and so could never act decisively enough or soon enough, as some few fortunates did. They found their way to France; France fell, and they fled to Vichy. By this time the options kept narrowing and narrowing.

Here, due to the collaboration of the Petain regime, the fugitives were turned over to the Nazis. Pavel's parents, in a last desperate decision, placed their child in the hands of Christian friends, to be secured against deportation as a Frenchman and Christian. Ironically, it was another wrong decision, for his parents were forbidden entry to Switzerland, to which they fled, because only refugees with little children were allowed to cross the border! All others were sent back to Vichy France, destined for Auschwitz via Drancy. Of this experience Friedlander writes:

As I entered the portals of Saint Beranger, the boarding school of
the sodality where I was to live from now on, I became someone
else: Paul-Henri Ferland, an unequivocally Catholic name, to
which Marie was added at my baptism, so as to make it even more
authentic, or perhaps it was an invocation of protection of the Vir-
gin, the heavenly mother safe from torment, less vulnerable than
the earthly mother, who at this very moment the whirlwind was already sweeping away.[29]

He was treated with love, compassion, and concern by people
who for the most part, in this entirely

new world [of] the strictest Catholicism . . . almost Royalist, fero-
ciously pro-Petain, anti-Semitic France, to the ladies of the Sodality, who were going to save a soul, but who were also taking serious
risks, because the soul they were saving was that of a Jewish child.[30]

There are spasmodic contacts with his parents, as their flight
to Switzerland fails, and they move from camp to camp with
Auschwitz as the final destination.

A few pictures, a few letters, a watch from his father, are all
that he had to remind him of his past reality. A vague, fuzzy
knowledge of what had happened was in his mind. He was
completely adjusted in the bosom of his protectors. He oscillated between hatred of Jews and a vague sense of pride when he
learned, one day, that Henri Bergson, almost a Catholic, was in
fact a Jew.

It was Father L., a Jesuit priest, who had taken a liking to him,
and to whom he was sent for a while for instruction and guidance, who turned him around. As they walked and talked
through the church in the tiny village, they paused at a side
chapel, and suddenly Father L., just why no one will ever know,
began telling him about Auschwitz, about the extermination of
the Jews, about himself. He recalls:

I knew nothing of the extermination, [it was all] enveloped in vague images . . . that bore no relation to the real course of events. And so, in front of this obscure Christ, I listened: Auschwitz, the trains, the gas chambers, the cemetery, the ovens, the millions of dead . . .[31]

Who can ever begin to understand the grace and the purpose that guided Father L., in the depths of his spiritual sensitivity, to give this child a clear image of whom he was, and who can begin to understand its purpose?

"For the first time I felt myself Jewish," Friedlander writes, "no longer despite myself or secretly, but through a sensation of absolute loyalty."

Father L. did not press him to choose one path or another. Perhaps he would have preferred to see him remain a Catholic. His sense of justice and charity had led him to recognize the youngster's right to judge for himself.

Friedlander resumed his former name, in its Hebrew version, Saul. Israel was then struggling for its existence in the first days of the War of Liberation, and he made his way there. Today he is a university professor and lives in Jerusalem. He has come home after a day of lectures. He waits for his daughter to come home from school.

School is out. Michal comes breezing in. . . . In the oldest of three photographs I have of my mother, she is a little girl: the same features, the same smile.[32]

He recalls his childhood days in Prague, receiving his first lessons about Judaism and puzzling over the story of Abraham and Isaac, and God's terrible command:

Why is this one of the first stories of our people? . . . I have read all sorts of interpretations and explanations of it, but this text does not leave me in peace! "Take now thy son, thine only son, . . . and offer him as a burnt offering . . ." Abraham's obedience explains our entire history. Today most Jews no longer obey God's injunctions, yet they still obey the call of some mysterious destiny. Why this fidelity? In the name of what?[33]

The certainty of Zlichovsky and the doubt of Friedlander are one in confronting the transcendent reality, for which "absolute loyalty" and "total fidelity" are evidence of its reality from this side of the covenant.

This essay was published in two installments in Spirituality Today.

CHAPTER TWO

American Judaism in Transition

==

I

To speak of American Judaism in transition here in Lublin is for me both a moving and an evocative experience.

Though I have never been here before, I know this place well, through David Darshan, who was the town preacher here in 1573 and 1574. Rabbi David was an itinerant preacher and scholar who was born in Cracow, wandered all over Central Europe and Northern Italy, and was last here in Lublin before all trace of him was lost and he disappeared into limbo on the way to the Land of Israel.

My first visit to Lublin was a visit of the imagination. This took place when I first came upon his little book *In Defense of Preachers,* which was published here in 1574.[1] Thus I explored Lublin through contemporary sources and varied accounts of the city.

And now I am here at the invitation of Professor Szymon, who served with distinction as a visiting professor at the Catholic Theological Union last year.

II

When David Darshan was town preacher, writer, and editor in Lublin, Poland was rapidly becoming the largest Jewish community in Europe. In 1490, less than a century previously, there had been almost half a million Jews in Spain and Portugal, representing half of world Jewry, while in Poland there were only thirty thousand, a mere five percent. And America was two years away from being discovered.[2]

By 1574, the Polish Jewish community, with mass immigration from Central and Western Europe and Spain, was in the midst of immense economic expansion, for the country was on the way to becoming the largest single center. In America, a small number of crypto-Jews (Marranos) could be found in areas of Spanish and Portuguese settlement, and none in what was to become the United States.

In the world of 1574, the largest settlement of Jews was to be found in the Ottoman Empire, which extended from Central Asia westward through Egypt and North Africa. Jewish refugees from Spain had even settled in large numbers in Safed and Tiberias, in Galilee. The next important center was in Italy, where perhaps a hundred thousand Jews lived, and soon there would be stirrings of Jewish settlement in Holland and England.

Today, half of world Jewry lives in the Americas, with almost six million in the United States, and approximately a million in Canada and Latin America.

Almost four thousand years of continuing history make for dazzling shifts and changes. They include independent statehood for six hundred years, diaspora, another six hundred years of statehood with a growing diaspora, so that in the first century some six million Jews are estimated to have lived in the Roman

Empire with almost a million in the Land of Israel. Then almost two thousand years of diaspora with shifting centers, and now in our own time the rebirth of the state following the dreadful Holocaust experience.

Above all, the changes include the emergence of Rabbinic Judaism during the Second Jewish Commonwealth (400 B.C.E.–135 C.E.). It was the crucial mutation in the development of Judaism that made possible its continuation after the Temple and state were destroyed and the people exiled. It was a method of at once of keeping old memories alive and striking out into the future with new vigor.

Its technique was the development of the concept of an Oral Law to supplement the Written Law, by making it possible, through the use of hermeneutic methods (Midrash), to reinterpret the Torah and make it meaningful for new conditions. Its method was communication by teaching, both to the elite and to the masses, in which it succeeded in reaching the people. Not just the elect priesthood, but the people as a whole, was to be the collective instrument of God's work in history.

Through the extension of Torah into Mishnah and Talmud, through the use of the house of study and preaching as the means of communication, every Jew had his "portable native land," and the capacity to bring the sacred community of Israel into being wherever a minimum quorum of ten existed. The direct study of Torah by every competent individual made the divine transcendence available through study and commentary.

Rabbinic Judaism cultivated the messianic ideal implicit in the exodus. Through its capacity to reach all people, and the openness of all to learning, the messianic impulse gave rise at the very beginning of the emergence of Rabbinic Judaism to a long-range messianic role for the Jewish people as a whole, and of a short-range messianic Judaism which became Christianity.[3]

The theme of this conference, "Non-Christian Religions in Transition," is interesting in this sense: Judaism is here ranked with non-Christian religions, which is technically correct. And yet, looking at it the other way, Christianity can certainly be seen as Jewish in origin, and the interest in recovering awareness of those origins is an important aspect of current religious thought. The Judaism we shall be examining, in transition in the United States, is Rabbinic Judaism as it evolved in its existence both under Christianity and Islam in the last two millennia, with all the changes and adaptations brought on by the vicissitudes of history, including the Holocaust and the birth of a third Jewish state.

III

Reflecting on the course of Jewish experience in history, a talmudic sage once remarked: "God provides His people with the cure before He strikes them with the disease."[4] How true this is of the discovery of America!

Christopher Columbus set sail on his voyage of discovery on the ninth day of the Jewish month of Ab in the year 1492. That was the anniversary of the destruction of the Temple, and the very day that the edict of the expulsion of the Jews from Spain went into effect. It was a cataclysmic day in Jewish history, the end of a thousand years of glorious history and achievement. Nothing like it had occurred since the destruction of the Temple, and it was to be surpassed only four and a half centuries later with the Nazi horror.

Certainly the despairing Jewish boat people leaving their ports, and perhaps passing the *Santa Maria, Niña,* and *Pinta,* could scarcely have dreamed that these three small vessels were on a journey to discover a land of redemption. Nor did Columbus' Jewish ship's doctor, Maestre Bernal, or his Marrano crew member, Luis de Torres, who were the first to set foot on the soil of the New World, dream that they were discovering the land where the largest Jewish community of the twentieth century would be living.[5]

In the Spanish and Portuguese colonies at the southern end of North America, Mexico, Central and South America, Jews were not allowed to settle. But we do know that Jews reached there as Marranos. And that their numbers were not inconsiderable we find from Inquisition records dealing with "relapsed Jews."[6]

The beginnings of Jewish settlement in what was to become the United States had to do with the imperial rivalry between the Dutch and English, on the one hand, and the Spanish and Portuguese, on the other. At one point, in the middle of the seventeenth century, the Dutch wrested Pernambuco and Recife on the western tip of Brazil from the Portuguese. In Holland, which had broken away from Spain, Jews could now live freely, and were active in helping the development of the country.

When the Dutch came, many Brazilian Marranos, descended from Jews forcibly converted to Christianity, identified themselves as Jews. Unfortunately for them, when the Portuguese retook these towns in 1654, they could not stay. One day that year a French ship landed twenty-three of these Jewish refugees in New Amsterdam (later New York) and a reluctant Governor Peter Stuyvesant was ordered by the Dutch West India Company to allow them to stay.[7]

That was the beginning of the American Jewish community.

The colonial period saw a small trickle of settlers, principally Spanish and Portuguese Jews, settling in the coastal cities of a chain of British colonies (the Dutch period came to an end in 1664) principally as merchants and entrepreneurs. They established synagogues in Rhode Island, New York, Philadelphia, Charleston, South Carolina, and Savannah, Georgia. Although not all of the early Jewish settlers were of Spanish and Portuguese origin, some coming from Germany and Poland, the character of American Judaism as expressed in the earliest synagogues could be described as Sephardic, that is to say, following the liturgical style of the Jews of Spain and Portugal.

Although in the thirteen colonies the situation of Jews varied from colony to colony, and in some they had to struggle vigorously for their rights, the restrictions which Jews had to face everywhere in medieval and early modern Europe existed nowhere in the new land.

Indeed, when George Washington was installed as the first President of the United States in 1790, he received letters of congratulation from all five synagogues, and wrote them in return that the United States "gave to bigotry no sanction."[8]

At the time of the American Revolution there were approximately thirty-five hundred Jews out of a population of three and one-half million. This was just about the time that the French Revolution brought a new spirit to Europe and the beginnings of Jewish political and social emancipation.

The next major wave of Jewish migration came from German lands. The repression of Jews in German lands, and the effects of the French Revolution and the Napoleonic wars, started a trickle of German Jewish migration. First very slowly, and after the abortive revolutions of 1848 in greater numbers. This migration differed from the first in two major respects. In the first place, these were not immigrants with experience in international trade. They came to the cities as peddlers who became merchants, and they settled not only in the coastal cities, but inland after America began its rapid move westward with the Louisiana Purchase.[9]

This wave of immigration included a cultured group who had already been involved in the movements for religious reform stirring in Western Europe. Between 1830 and 1880 a quarter of a million German Jews settled in the United States. The German Jewish settlement established Jewish communities in all the cities of the United States, and they made a great impact on the development of Judaism in America, as we shall presently see.

The third wave of migration came between 1880 and 1925, when millions of immigrants swarmed to the United States from Italy, and from Central and Eastern Europe. They came in droves until they had reached some eight million. Among them were a million and a half Jews from Russia, Poland, Rumania, and the eastern part of the Austro-Hungarian Empire. By this time the Jews in these regions numbered eight million, and suffered as persecuted minorities in Russia and other parts of Eastern Europe.

They were principally Yiddish-speaking, and the religious traditions they brought with them were Eastern European Orthodox. They settled principally in the eastern seaboard cities, and at the turn of the century there were more than three hundred thousand Jews in the Lower East Side of New York. By time the spigot of immigration was shut off in 1925, there were already three and a half million Jews in the United States, with almost two million in New York City.

The fourth major wave of immigration came after the rise of the Nazis to power. In the years when escape from Europe was still possible, up to the outbreak of the war, and despite the fact that the immigration laws were exclusionary, several hundred thousand German and Austrian Jews were able to enter the United States. This was a migration of great talent and ability, including such immigrants as Albert Einstein, Arnold Schoenberg, Henry Kissinger, and Billy Wilder.[10]

There is now a fifth—not to be termed a wave. This migration consists of Jews from the Soviet Union, and in the last ten years perhaps forty thousand Jews from the Soviet Union have entered.

The churning movements of the Jewish people in history became a tributary of the enormous mass movements of populations that came to the United states and shaped its culture and its destiny. It was part of that culture and that destiny, and at the same time it was shaped by and itself shaped the fabric of the ongoing thrust of Jewish history.

IV

As has already been indicated, at the time of the American Revolution and the birth of the United States, there were little more than three thousand Jews and perhaps five synagogues in the coastal cities. These were Orthodox in form and Sephardic in liturgical mode.

In Europe, just a few years later, the French Revolution exploded, rapidly changing the face of Western Europe and its religious structure. Secularism, which had its seeds in the Renaissance, and which flourished in the seventeenth century, came to its fruition as America was born and Europe was transformed.

This could not fail to have its impact on the Jews of Europe, the vast majority of whom lived in the area that had once been

Poland but which was now partitioned between Russia, the Austrian Empire, and Prussia. The Judaism of Europe at this period was Orthodox, and relatively unchanged in form and structure since its fashioning by Rabbinic Judaism.

The differences in the religious Jewish world were territorial rather than doctrinal. The traditional forms were expressed as Sephardic (the Hebrew for "Spanish") Judaism in the lands under Spanish and Arab rule; and Ashkenazic (the Hebrew for "German") in Germany, Central and Eastern Europe.

Jews lived apart from their non-Jewish neighbors, either in special zones of settlement or in ghettos within the cities, under their own laws, and with corporate rights from the rulers. To be a Jew was to be a member of community with special status in the eyes of the government.

But now came civil rights for individuals and the opportunity to integrate into the surrounding society. This opportunity was enthusiastically accepted, and while some Jews even converted to Christianity, most felt that the continuation of Judaism was not inconsistent with their integration into the majority society. Thus the scientific study of Judaism through western university methods came into being. The intent was to present Judaism and its culture as part of the evolving western civilization. This led to a trend toward modernizing Judaism which was the beginning of the Reform Movement.

This involved the beginnings of reform in worship forms, beginning with Israel Jacobson's congregation in Seesen (Westphalia) in 1810 and the introduction of the sermon in the vernacular using western homiletical forms to interpret Judaism.[11]

In Europe, the problem for reformers was the fact that the community, which had governmental sanction, was more con-

servative, and though the movement spread, it spread slowly
and tentatively. This was not the case in the United States, because, in the first place, there was separation of church and state,
and every religious group was on its own. Furthermore, American society was voluntaristic; that is to say, whether to belong
or not to belong to a religious group was a matter of choice, and
there was no special political or economic handicap in not belonging. Hence, if there was to be a community, it had to be
fashioned from within.

Already in the early nineteenth century, probably influenced
by the confederation of the thirteen colonies, and with the
number of synagogues increasing, there were efforts to bring
them together in some kind of federation that would create a
broader community. Isaac Leeser, a modern Orthodox rabbi in
Philadelphia, made the first attempt.

But the urge for reform, as a means of integrating the synagogue into the broader American scene, was already afoot. By
1819 reforms were instituted in the synagogue in Charleston,
South Carolina, along the lines of the early German Jewish ex-
periment.

The growing migration of German Jews, bringing the early
experiences of emancipation to the new land of freedom, acted
as a spur. This wave of immigration now included rabbis who
had already been influenced by reformist ideas, and who saw the
United States as fertile soil for such a movement. Rabbis like
David Einhorn, Samuel Adler, and Isaac Mayer Wise were in
the van of the movement. Wise, who moved from Albany,
New York, to Cincinnati, Ohio, in the middle of the nineteenth century, had great organizing genius; he founded the
Hebrew Union college as a seminary for the training of rabbis
in 1875, brought the Reform synagogues together in the Union

of American Hebrew Congregations in 1876, and formed the Central Conference of American Rabbis several years later.[12]

This was the beginning of the structuring of the American Jewish community in a voluntary union of congregations. The Reform movement was swept along in a spirit of excitement and a sense of creativity, seeing itself as adapting Judaism to a new environment in tune with the broader movements in the land. It shaped a liturgy largely in the vernacular, introduced the organ and decorous services, added to it an emphasis upon prophetic social order and an optimistic view of a messianic age in the not-too-distant future. It discarded much of the structure of traditional religious practices, and shaped Jewish theology in terms of Western romantic idealism.

The changes were seen as too much too soon by the more tradition-minded segment of the Jewish community, and as a result the movement of Conservative Judaism was born. It founded a seminary for the training of rabbis (the Jewish Theological Seminary) in 1887, which, for its first few years, made little progress, but a number of circumstances soon altered this. The large influx of Jews from Eastern Europe, whose religious background was either Orthodox or secularist/socialist, and who brought their synagogal organization with them, were to be attracted to this middle-of-the-road movement as they became integrated into the American scene.

Solomon Schechter, reader in rabbinics at Cambridge, liberal and inclusive in his view of traditional Judaism, came to the seminary as its president in 1901. He had the support of the prominent German Jewish leaders of New York, themselves Reform Jews, and he had a vision, by virtue of his English-speaking background, of training rabbis who could be Americanizers without too great a break with tradition. Schechter differed both from Orthodoxy and Reform in his perception of a broad unity in diversity within Judaism expressed by his view of "Catholic Israel" (his translation of the Hebrew term *Knesset Yisrael*).[13]

Before too long, a Conservative movement was in place, with its own rabbinical seminary, with the United Synagogue, its own congregational union, and with the Rabbinic Assembly, in which its rabbis were organized; and it too entered a period of rapid growth.

The organization of Reform and Conservative Judaism was a stimulus to American Orthodoxy, which at first was small and unorganized, to do likewise, and before too long there were theological seminaries like the Isaac Elchanan Seminary in New York (now Yeshiva University) and the Hebrew Theological Seminary in Chicago, to name but two; unions of congregations, organizations of rabbinic bodies to monitor kashrut (the provision of meats according to the traditional manner); and the establishment of day schools.

During this period, the American Jewish community was influenced by the Zionist movement, which had as its goal the rebirth of the Jewish people in its ancient land, and a view of Jewish peoplehood. Rabbis and lay people in the Reform and Conservative wings began to be influenced. A young Reform rabbi, Stephen S. Wise, and a famous American jurist, Louis Brandeis, himself a secularist Jew, became part of this movement.

This had an impact on the Reform movement, very slowly at first, and made for some inevitable changes. Thus, in 1922, because he could not agree with the anti-nationalism and extreme anti-traditionalism of the Reform movement, Rabbi Wise founded the Jewish Institute of Religion in New York, whose goal it was to cross denominational lines and to have a faculty and student body that would represent the three wings of Judaism.

This acted as a catalyst to the interdenominationalism and feelings for religious and cultural unity that were in the air. At this time, a gifted young professor of education at the Jewish Theological Seminary, Mordecai Kaplan,[14] developed his view of Judaism as a civilization and community, with a liberal neo-humanist theology influenced by John Dewey and William James, and the view that Jewish religious practices had sociological and cultural worth, and that Zionism was a proper force within Judaism and the Jewish community. This gave rise to a fourth religious movement within American Judaism, known as Reconstructionism, which, though considerably smaller than the other three, has influenced both rabbis and laity, and currently has a training school for rabbis in Philadelphia, and a handful of congregations throughout the country.

The growth of Zionist sentiment, the emergence of Nazism, and its seizure of power in Germany did much to arrest the splintering of the American Jewish community. The suburbanization of the American Jewish community, hastened by the process of suburbanization generally after World War II, created a self-confident and integrated Jewish community centered around the institution of the synagogue.

In the Reform movement the shift was back to the center. By 1936 it had declared that Zionism and Reform Judaism were no longer incompatible. The turn within Reform back to traditional values and practices was influenced by the entry into the movement of suburban Jews whose background had been Eastern European. By 1947, it was no longer necessary to have two separate Reform-oriented training schools for rabbis; the Hebrew Union College and Jewish Institute of Religion merged, and now have schools in Cincinnati, New York, Los Angeles, and Jerusalem.[15]

If Reform moved toward the center, Conservatism tended to move a little to the left, with its eye always on its right. As for Orthodoxy, a great segment tended to become Americanized, certainly in organizational structure.

The Holocaust and World War II had the effect of bringing to the United States remnants of the Hasidic movement, fleeing from Poland to the United States, and establishing themselves largely in New York, where, for example, the Lubavitch and Satmar wings of Hasidism gave new impetus to American Orthodoxy.

Although in Israel and in Europe the tension between Orthodoxy and religious liberalism is very sharp, on the American scene, though there are tensions, there is dialogue. Nationally, the Synagogue Council of America brings the major wings of religious Judaism together for consultation. In the major centers there are boards of rabbis where the four major groups meet and take counsel together.

American Judaism is not monolithic. It exists in a pluralistic society where the widest approaches to Judaism can find expression, but there is a creativity and a variety that somehow, nevertheless, seems to express an awareness of an historic collectivity.

V

This energy expresses itself not only through the medium of the synagogue and the organized religious institutions. It expresses itself in a secular manner that on the surface seems to reflect America's "secular religion." In reality this is a reflection of the inseparability of the secular and the religious in the equation of American Judaism because of the close link between community and faith, between peoplehood and belief. The American scene, with its variety and its pluralism, makes this possible. On the surface one sees a kaleidoscopic variety that seems to be going off in all directions, and yet on a closer look one sees that it all hangs together.[16]

We can see this, for example, when we examine the history of the labor movement in the United States and note the role of Jewish immigrants from Eastern Europe in founding the unions in the apparel industries. Although by and large the members of these unions were alienated from religious institutions and saw themselves as secularists, their unions were permeated with the Jewish values of social justice, and their lives were shaped by Jewish culture.

The children of these earlier generations of labor unionists, as they moved upwards in the scale of American society, open to all, found the synagogue as their means of identification with Judaism and the Jewish people. And though the Amalgamated Clothing Workers Union and the International Ladies Garment Workers Union are now made up of other minorities, the values of the founders seem to endure. Thus the teachings of the Hebrew prophets found their way into contemporary union ideology.[17]

So too with the Zionist movement, which won the loyalty and adherence of many Jews for whom religious Judaism seemed to have lost its attraction. Their goal was to advance the national aims of the Jewish people, and in so doing, they had to know everything about the Jewish people, and that involved its history, culture, and religion.

The same can be said for the development of the Jewish

community centers. This movement developed in the secular atmosphere of America, to provide a place for Jews to go to meet together for social, athletic, and recreational purposes. Jewish centers and Young Men's (and Women's) Hebrew Associations proliferated. One could belong to a center and not set foot in a synagogue. Rivalries between the two institutions was intense.

And yet, since the centers involved Jews, they were involved with Jewish culture and the widest variety of Jewish activities. Indeed, as centers of culture, it was not possible to separate out the religious and the cultural. The reality was that both center and synagogue were reciprocal in expressing the widest spectrum of Jewish values. In fact center and synagogue vied with each other to express the widest range of Jewish thought.

One should remember that in its origins the synagogue was a house of prayer, a house of assembly, and a house of study. And it was also the center for philanthropic activity, feeding the hungry, healing the sick, and burying the dead.

On the American scene, with its extreme voluntarism, there was a specialization, which on the surface looked competitive but in reality was an expression of the whole.

What holds true for community centers in this sense also holds true for philanthropy. The smaller, decentralized philanthropic activities, especially because of the great crises resulting from World War I and World War II, with a mass of Jewish refugees, the need to build a homeland, and the wide range of local social needs, hospitals, home for the aged, and community centers, called into being federations to support local institutions and overseas needs.

Thus, Jewish fund-raising became a huge, centralized activity centered in federations and welfare funds, and this attracted a large body of Jewish leadership, for the most part from the synagogues. Here too, the idea of *zedakah,* or philanthropy, central to Judaism, had moved out of the synagogue. Yet the awareness of interaction constantly grew. There had to be Jews to support Jewish institutions, and the synagogues were where Jews were shaped. The dialogue across the divide of the secular and the religious in Judaism is constant and patient.

On the American scene, American Judaism is influenced by the centripetal and centrifugal forces that surround it. On the one hand, American pluralism and voluntarism have their mirror image in the Jewish world. On the other hand, also at work is the centrifugal force allows for wide varieties within Judaism but is attracted by the gravitational pull of the Sinaitic Covenant and the sense of having endured through history that is characteristic of the Jewish people. The Holocaust experience and the reemergence of the State of Israel have had an enormous gravitational, centrifugal effect on American Judaism.

VII

The American motto, "E pluribus unum," is appropriate to the experience of American Judaism. This is not to say that the openness of American society, in its own way, cannot be as threatening to the survival of Judaism and the Jewish people as were the repressions of the past. The price of freedom is assimilation. Certainly there are signs of this on the American Jewish scene. An open society can ease the way to the loss of a minority identity in a majority society.

There are those who view the high rate of intermarriage and the sharp drop in the Jewish birthrate as threatening to the Jewish future. There are pessimistic demographers who predict that the American Jewish population will be less than half a million in the twenty-second century. They look with alarm at the large number of Jewish children who receive minimal or no Jewish education.[18]

But the optimists take another view. They note that in perhaps more than half of the intermarriages, the non-Jewish partner encourages the family to associate with the Jewish community, that many convert to Judaism, and that there is a net gain.

They also point to an extraordinary explosion of interest in Judaism in the Jewish community. The phenomenal growth of Jewish camps in all denominations, religious and secular, plays a significant role in shaping adolescent attitudes. There has been a significant growth of Jewish day schools in Orthodox and Conservative Judaism, and now in Reform.

There has been an explosive growth of departments of Jewish studies in universities all over the United States. This is a phenomenon that hardly existed forty years ago. Not only rabbis, but Jewish academicians are being trained in greater numbers, and this is reflected in a large body of writing on theological, religious, and cultural matters.

American Jewish writers and artists are increasingly unselfconscious about expressing their Jewish identity and Jewish values, and there is a growing understanding and appreciation of the Jewish ethic and ethos on the American scene. This is not to deny that antisemitism persists and can be worrisome, in view of past experience, but it does not diminish the sense of forward growth.

VIII

We can perhaps sum our analysis up with a look at the state of contemporary Jewish thought and Jewish–Christian dialogue.

It will be helpful to bear in mind that while I have made some allusions to antisemitism and have also discussed the loss of a sense of religious and cultural identity through the process of assimilation in the United States, I have emphasized the positive forces that have been at work in the American Jewish experience.

Regrettably, despite the revulsion against the ultimate in antisemitism as expressed by the Nazi policy of a Final Solution to the Jewish Question, the problem of antisemitism remains to be confronted. It is not absent in the United States. In addition, modern secularism, the openness of American society, and the sense of freedom have taken their toll.

If World War I jolted the high hopes for the perfectibility of the human species, World War II and Hiroshima left it in shambles. The presumptions of philosophy and science began to be questioned. The thinking mind moved in the one extreme to hopelessness and existentialist aloneness, and in the other, to a God that cared and had meaning beyond transcendence. God was either dead or had to be discovered in a new reality beyond the "defining away" of earlier systems.

The Jew had thrown himself with great hopes into the arms of humanism and the promise of emancipation. But there were those who had reservations, and the theology of contemporary American Judaism has been deeply shaped by them.

I refer to Martin Buber, who blazed new trails in the transcendent quest, and went back to Hasidic roots to find the embers of a vanishing faith. Also to Gershom Scholem, who rejected the optimistic view of Europe held by the advocates of emancipation, and undertook the monumental task of plumbing the depths of meaning of the mystical streams of Jewish experience. And, as well, to Franz Rosenzweig, who stepped back from the brink of apostasy in a deeper study of the *mysterium tremendum*.

It is against this background of humanism that a contemporary American Jewish thinker like Eugene Borowitz describes the return to core religious values in contemporary Judaism.[19] Elie Wiesel comes out of the trauma of silence after his Auschwitz experience, to teach, guide, and inspire American and world Jewry.[20]

The recent appearance of the two-volume encyclopedic study of Jewish spirituality is evidence of the creative and spiritual forces at work.[21] To this writer it appears that this perception of the Jewish people-as-a-whole as God's suffering servant, as the eternal witness to a transcendent possibility, is crucial. Gershom Scholem has shown how the conscious and subconscious minds march hand in hand, uneasily but inevitably and creatively, in the ongoing course of Jewish history.[22]

As to the Christian-Jewish dialogue, this writer dares to suggest that out of the unique openness and pluralism of the American scene, American Judaism is in a position to carry forward the millennial Christian-Jewish dialogue in a new direction of positive mutual understanding.

In early-twentieth-century America, friendships between a rabbi and a minister or priest here and there marked the beginning of a new direction. The friendship between Rabbi Stephen Wise and Reverend John Haynes Holmes was a case in point.[23] Exponents of interfaith amity began to tour the country, putting all faiths in awe because they were on the platform together, but the dialogue on the whole was inclined to be superficial.

As in so many other areas, Hitlerism and the Holocaust marked a watershed. Sensitive and thoughtful Christians began to examine themselves in a new light. They saw that the Jew, marked for destruction by the Nazi, really included Jesus the

Jew, with Christianity as a form of crypto-Judaism, to be ultimately destroyed because it was corruptive of the true, pagan,
Germanic spirit it had deified.[24]

Vatican II was symptomatic of this. Pope John XXIII, as papal
nuncio in Istanbul during the war, saw the catastrophe close at
hand and understood. There was a monumental shift in collective attitudes toward the Jew and Judaism. The same process
went on in the Western world, and especially in America. A
new awareness of antisemitism and its Christian roots and of the
need to rediscover the Jewish roots of Christianity moved the
process from a dialogue of the deaf to a process of genuinely lis-
tening to each other and hearing.

What has emerged has been a dialogue of consequence. At
the academic-theological level, Jewish and Christian theologians talked with each other. They faced their painful differences with candor and a recognition that the one side did not
have to convert the other. They saw that what they possessed in
common outweighed their differences. They saw that the problems of bigotry and nuclear holocaust called for common efforts. They had no illusions about instant transformations, but
they discovered that they could talk to each other and learn
from each other.[25]

A Samuel Sandmel could write a book entitled *We Jews and
Jesus,* and a Eugene Borowitz could give us a Jewish view of
Christology. A Clemens Thoma could write a *Christian Theology of Judaism,* and a Franklin Sherman, as a Lutheran, could face
up to and confront Martin Luther's antisemitism. In dialogue it
became possible to consider the theory of two mutually valid
covenants, and to consider the view that the Jewish rejection of
Jesus made possible the movement of that message out to the
gentile world.

At the Graduate Theological Union in Berkeley, California,

where all the Christian denominations meet with Jewish scholars to consider these questions, a course could be taught on "Paul the Jew" by a Christian New Testament scholar and a Jewish professor of rabbinics, in which a seminar consisting of Catholic, Protestant, and Jewish graduate students could face the central questions in an atmosphere of candor and openness.[26]

Of course there are still problems and questions. Christians still find it difficult to understand that the qualities Christians see incarnate in the personhood of Christ can be expressed in Judaism as applying to the Jewish-people-as-a-whole as God's suffering servant. Which explains the Jewish concern for peoplehood and the restoration to Zion.

But never in the history of the two faiths has there been an open dialogue of this kind, made possible by the openness and pluralism of the American scene. The ecumenical dialogue grows. Jews and Christians communicate more openly and in relaxed fashion at the theological, clerical, and lay level. The understanding grows. The messianic goal of total understanding still lies in the distance. But the realization of the need for a better understanding of self through understanding the other, and the onward march of dialogue, beckons the future with its promise.

IX

In transition? American Judaism is indeed in transition. But then, is it not true to suggest that the story of Judaism and the story of the Jewish people is a study in transitions, Abraham from Ur of the Chaldees to Canaan; Moses from Egypt via Sinai to the Promised Land; or Maestre Bernal sailing with Columbus into the unknown.

Transitions involve space, and they involve time. But they always orbit around a center that acts as a unifying factor. That center has always been the Covenant between the one eternal God and an eternal people, witnessing to the world yet always cognizant of the Passover Haggadah's "Next year in Jerusalem" call.

The American scene, whose climate has been so nurturing to freedom, has made it possible for American Judaism to express this dazzling sense of variety without losing that basic unity of purpose.

The great Jewish centers of Babylonia, Spain, and Poland are glorious tales already told. The American Jewish tale is still in the telling, with its sparks of pluralism exploding, and its achievements yet to be realized.

This paper was originally delivered at a symposium on Non-Christian Religions in Transition, marking the thirtieth anniversary of the reactivation of the chair for History of Religion and Ethnology of Religion at the Catholic University of Lublin, November 18–19, 1988.

Part II
Prayer and Preaching

CHAPTER THREE

When Sacrifice Became Prayer

When David Darshan, the Polish-Jewish itinerant preacher, returned to Cracow in 1569 and tried to open a study house, un-
successfully as it turned out, he wrote in his prospectus, among
other things:

> I shall bring to it more than four hundred choice books . . . collect-
> ed with much effort for twenty-five years, from the time that I was
> a young man of nineteen. I collected them from the four corners of
> the world, and spent many a hundred zloty on them. And foremost
> among them I prepared a new Torah Scroll with large script in or-
> der to be able *to pray where we study*.[1]

"To pray where we study." What a quantum leap from biblical days, when you were obligated to pray at the Temple in
Jerusalem. Private prayer was a personal matter. It is about that
change, from Temple worship to synagogue-centered liturgy, as
it emerged after the destruction of Jerusalem in the year 70 C.E.,
that we are here concerned. The moment of transition is captured by the following passage from the Talmud:

It happened that Rabban Yoḥanan ben Zakkai was coming out of Jerusalem followed by Rabbi Joshua, and he beheld the Temple in ruins. "Woe to us," cried Rabbi Joshua, "for this house that lies in ruins, the place where atonement was made for the sins of the children of Israel." Rabban Yoḥanan said to him, "My son, be not grieved, for we have another means of atonement which is as effective, and that is the practice of lovingkindness."[2]

And lovingkindness is defined in this text as "providing for the bride, attending the dead to the grave, giving alms to the poor, and *praying three times daily*"!

More than a thousand years before David Darshan, in the fourth century, we learn from the Talmud that Rav Ashi, head of the academy at Sura in Babylonia, would stop in the middle of his lecture to say his prayers.[3] At Ashi's academy the congregation remained seated when the Shema, the watchword of Israel's faith, was uttered three times a day in prayer. Commenting on this statement in the Talmud, Rashi, a commentator who lived in France in the eleventh century, could write: "Rav Ashi did not say his morning prayers before he lectured. In the middle of the lecture he would instruct his aide to continue, while he silently recited his prayers [including the Shema]."

Underscoring the importance of prayer as viewed in the traditions of Rabbinic Judaism is an extraordinary image wherein God alone is the One who teaches Moses how to pray. This occurs in an interpretation of the theophany in Exodus 34:6, after Moses has succeeded in averting the destruction of Israel because of the sin of the golden calf, and receives a new revelation of the divine from the perspective of the cleft of the rock.

Moses has put his life on the line for his people, succeeds in bending God's will, and senses the precious moment when he might experience what no other human being had ever experienced in knowing God. What Moses hears are the words:

> The Lord! the Lord! a God compassionate and gracious, slow to anger, abounding in kindness and faithfulness, extending kindness to the thousandth generation, forgiving iniquity, transgression, and sin; yet He does not remit all punishment, but visits the iniquity of parents upon children and children's children, upon the third and fourth generation.
>
> (Exod. 34:6–7)

This is the passage that finds its final resting place in the synagogue liturgy for the Days of Awe and the three Pilgrim Festivals, as the ark is opened and the Torah is taken out for reading. It is a high moment in the liturgical experience.

This is what the Talmud has to say about it:

And the Lord passed before him and proclaimed, etc.

> R. Yoḥanan said: Were it not written in the text, it would be impossible for us to say such a thing. This verse teaches us that the Holy One, blessed be He, drew his prayer shawl round him like a cantor of the congregation and showed Moses the order of prayer. He said to him: Whenever Israel sin[s], let them carry out this service before Me, and I will forgive them.[4]

In this fanciful passage, God is represented as teaching Moses how to be a cantor and leader of prayer!

When we stop to remember that for the phase of the development of Judaism in the period up to the destruction of the Temple by the Romans (70 C.E.) Jewish worship was centered on the Temple and oriented to sacrifice, this represents change of quantum proportions. To be sure, individual Jews prayed individual prayers. Solomon prayed when the Temple was dedi-

cated (1 Kings 8:12–23, 2 Chron. 6:1–2). Hannah prayed on the
Tabernacle premises in Shilo while her husband was offering
sacrifices on behalf of fruitful Penina and childless Hannah (1
Sam. 2:1–10). Jonah prayed in the belly of the fish (Jon. 2:3–10).
Samson prayed for revenge (Judg. 16:28), and Hezekiah prayed
for salvation (2 Kings. 29:3).

And then there are the psalms. They have become central in
both Jewish and Christian liturgy as later developed, but in their
time, I am disposed to suggest that they were poetry of the re-
ligiously questing, and often suffering individual; or texts for the
musical adornment of the Temple liturgy. But they were not
prayer qua structured liturgy.

In order to understand this, one has to look at the evolution
of Rabbinic Judaism and its development during the five centuries of the Second Jewish Commonwealth. This creative
movement in the history of Judaism developed structured
prayer and the liturgy of the synagogue as a successor to the
Temple form of worship. For the Temple had been destroyed,
the monarchy ended, and the priesthood had become a memory.

Most simply put, what we know as Rabbinic, or Pharisaic,
Judaism was the movement that developed within Judaism,
probably beginning with Jeremiah's letter to the Babylonian exiles (Jer. 29:1–28), to prepare the techniques for Jewish survival
in the face of the destruction of state, Temple, monarchy, and
priesthood. It was carefully nurtured during the period of the
Second Commonwealth, that period of dazzling variety and
pluralism in the development of Judaism. It developed a conception of the messianic dream which in its long-range version
shaped the Judaism of these last twenty centuries, while its
short-range version emerged as Christianity.

Its survival technique was to complete the process of canonization of the existing sacred writings to form the Hebrew Bible; to develop the revolutionary concept of Oral Law as coequal in authority with the Written Law so that there could be change within the framework of continuity (when eventually codified, it became the Mishnah, Talmud, and Midrash); and finally to develop the Siddur, the prayerbook, for public worship in the synagogue. The synagogue, perhaps first developed during the period of the Babylonian exile, after 586 B.C.E. was to become a central institution in Judaism with a threefold function as house of prayer, house of study, and house of assembly. It was the institution that made possible Jewish survival into the difficult years of dispersion that were to follow.

The man who can be credited with giving authority to this dramatic shift, Yoḥanan ben Zakkai, was the man who was spirited out of Jerusalem in the year 70 as the Temple was going up in flames, who made a nonaggression agreement with the Emperor Vespasian, and made the little coastal town of Yavneh the center for the organization of the quieter form of resistance that finally gave us Judaism as we know it. As we have already seen, he was the man who made the decision that prayer was to replace sacrifice as the central form of Jewish worship. Here Scripture was canonized. Here the Mishnah began to be fashioned. Here the ordering of prayers for the synagogue worship was begun.

Thus the elaborate structure of Temple worship, with its sacrifices, its centrality of location in Jerusalem, and the exclusive mediation of the priesthood, gives way to the prayer book and the possibility that any Jewish man qualified by his education could lead the people in group prayer wherever they were, and that the individual could pray alone, if necessary, wherever he might be.

Central were two elements of core prayer, the Shema and its

blessings, and the Tefillah, a prayer with nineteen benedictions. To these were added preliminaries at the beginning; a ritual for the reading of the Torah; and a series of concluding prayers.[5] Here psalms found their place principally as part of the preliminaries. But they also found their place within the rubric of the worship, in a very interesting way.

By way of example: the opening prayer of the liturgy for morning worship is the Ma Tovu prayer. Ma Tovu begins with Balaam's "How goodly are thy tents, O Jacob" and reads as follows:

> How goodly are thy tents, O Jacob, thy dwelling places, O Israel! As for me, in the abundance of thy lovingkindness will I come into thy house: I will worship toward thy holy temple in the fear of thee. Lord I love the habitation of thy house, and the place where thy glory dwelleth. I will worship and bow down: I will bend the knee before Thee Lord, my Maker. May my prayer unto thee, O Lord, be in an acceptable time: O God, in the abundance of thy loving-kindness, answer me with thy sure salvation.[6]

This prayer, let it be noted, is a weaving of biblical verses from Numbers 24:5 and three verses from Psalms, 5:8, 26:8, 69:14. So carefully culled disparate verses come together to fashion new prayer, the prayer uttered by any Jew anywhere when first entering the synagogue.

Not only do the rabbinic architects of the new liturgy show unusual skill in stringing various verses into the necklace of an exquisite prayer, but there is a subtlety of purpose in the selection. On the surface one might well ask, Why use a quotation from Balaam to begin prayer? Was not Balaam an enemy of the Jewish people? Was he not eager to curse them, if God had only permitted it? His last words before he left appeared to be a blessing, but in reality it was the reverse. For immediately after his words of blessing come the terrible events of the orgy at Baal Pe'or, and we learn a few chapters later in Numbers that Moses sent Pinchas the priest to lead a battle expedition against the Midianites and Balaam because of Balaam's counsel that they tempt the Israelite youth with Midianite prostitutes. His "How goodly are your tents" was really a cover for that destructive strategy.

Thus to begin the Ma Tovu prayer with words of Balaam was to say in effect, "Your counsel to destroy this people was in vain. Every time they enter a synagogue, they begin with the words that you craftily intended to presage their doom, and turn them into the beginning of their prayer, which demonstrates that they still endure!"

Similarly, the prayer that was used to end the preliminary period of prayers and prepare the way for the Shema and its blessings is compounded of Psalms 84:5, 144:15, and all of 145. What we get is not three psalms, but a new prayer, the Ashrei, which begins:

> Happy are they that dwell in thy house: they will forever be praising Thee, Selah [Ps. 84:5].

> Happy is the people that is thus favored, happy the people whose God is the Lord [Ps. 144:15].

Then follows the alphabetical Psalm 145 in its entirety. Thus the psalm becomes something else: the psalms pass into the prayer book, shaped for transition by the sages. This technique of shaping new prayer forms out of material that had been part of the Temple service was characteristic of Rabbinic Judaism.

The Lord's Prayer as we find it in Matthew is clearly in this genre. Jesus took the "Our Father in Heaven" formula, which occurs frequently in the Talmud, added several sentences from the opening of the Kaddish prayer, several sentences from the Tefillah, and ended with 1 Chronicles 29:11. This was the way prayers were shaped in Jesus' day. At least, it was one of the ways.

Another method of creating liturgy was the inclusion in the fixed liturgical structure of individual, spontaneous prayers of individual sages. Many of these prayers must have struck home, and the people kept them; finally they were included in the Siddur. It should be noted that the prayer book was not a closed book. Every generation made its additions, and thus it has come to be the repository of the collective religious experience of the people.

The core prayers are structured out of material from the Bible, formed from rabbinic sources of many generations. Anguished experiences from the Crusades find their way into it; the deep pain of the Spanish expulsion; the profound religious spirit of medieval poets; the rebirth of Zion, the Holocaust— they are all there.

So now that we have seen how new prayers could he fashioned by selecting biblical phrases, let us examine how prayers of sages and scholars became the possession of the people.

The talmudic tractate Berakhot, which deals with the details of the structure and timing of public worship, records these prayers in a fascinating section. For suddenly we come across a passage that begins: "Rabbi Eliezer, on concluding his prayer [i.e., the regular worship service], used to say the following . . ." Then his closing prayer is quoted. And so it is for Rabbi Yohanan, Rabbi Zeira, Rabbi Hiyya, Rab, Rabbi Safra, Rabbi Alexandri, Raba, and Mar the son of Ravina.

You might wonder about the necessity of adding something after the fixed prayer had been completed. For the requirement for prayer was the Shema and its blessings, a brief sequence that came directly out of the Pentateuch; and the Amidah, an extra-biblical series of benedictions whose origins go back at least to the fourth pre-Christian century.

But already it seems to have been established that spontaneous prayer was not to be excluded by fixed prayer. It is in this way that the prayer book grew with accretions over the ages, added, however, with great care.

Let us begin with the last sage named, Mar the son of Ravina, glance at his prayer, and see what happened to it:

> My God, keep my tongue from evil and my lips from speaking guile. May my soul be silent to them that curse me, and may my soul be as the dust to all. Open Thou my heart in Thy law, and may my soul pursue Thy commandments, and deliver me from evil hap, from the evil impulse, and from an evil woman, and from all evils that threaten to come upon the world. As for all that design evil against me, speedily annul their counsel and frustrate their designs. May the words of my mouth and the meditation of my heart be acceptable before Thee, O Lord, my rock and my redeemer!
>
> (Berakhot 17a)

Mar's prayer found its place into the core Tefillah prayer as a closing meditation, with the exception of the phrase "and deliver me from evil hap, from the evil impulse, and from an evil woman, and from all evils that threaten to come upon the world."

The compilers of the liturgy were apparently turned off by this phrase and seemed to prefer the formulation along these lines attributed to Rabbi. This, of course, was Judah the Prince, and his prayer was found more suitable as an inclusion for preliminary prayer. We can see why:

> May it be Thy will to deliver us from the impudent and from impudence, from an evil man, from evil hap, from evil impulse, from an evil companion, from an evil neighbor, and from the destructive Accuser, from a hard lawsuit and from a hard opponent, whether he is a son of the covenant, or not a son of the covenant.
>
> (Berakhot 16b)

Judah the Prince, under whose jurisdiction the Mishnah was completed, and who was recognized by the Romans as the highest Jewish public official, probably uttered this prayer feeling fully aware of his responsibilities. This is clearly evident from the closing phrase of this account, "Thus did he pray, although guards were appointed to protect Rabbi."

Rabbi Ḥiyya and Rabbi Alexandri concluded their prayer with a petition for a healthy psyche, clear vision, and an existence focused on the study of Torah. The former would say, "May it be Thy will, O Lord our God, that our Torah may be our occupation, and that our heart may not be sick nor our eyes darkened" (Berakhot 17a). And the latter would conclude with: "May it be Thy will, O Lord our God, to station us in an illumined corner, and do not station us in a darkened corner, and let not our heart be sick nor our eyes darkened!" (ibid.).

Rabbi Yoḥanan and Rabbi Zeira were concerned with our human frailties and prayed for help in this direction. Yoḥanan called on God "to look upon our shame, and behold our evil plight," urging that in judging us the quality of mercy outweigh the quality of strict justice. Similarly Zeira prayed that "we sin not nor bring upon ourselves shame or disgrace before our fathers" (ibid. 16b). Rab, who was a son-in-law of Judah the

Prince and the founder of one of the major academies in Babylonia, would conclude his prayer with words which became a central opening prayer in the liturgy of the blessing of the New Moon in the Sabbath services. When he ended his fixed prayer he would add:

> May it be Thy will, O Lord our God, to grant us a long life, a life of peace, a life of good, a life of blessing, a life of sustenance, a life of bodily vigor, a life in which there is fear of sin, a life free from shame and confusion, a life of riches and honor, a life in which we may be filled with the love of Torah and fear of heaven, a life in which Thou shalt fulfill all the desires of our heart for good.
>
> (ibid.)

And these words too found their place of permanence in the prayer book.

Even though the reality of the end of animal sacrifices as a form of worship was recognized, nostalgia remained. Into the preliminary section of the morning service, a compilation from Bible and Mishnah describing how sacrifices were offered, came the reflection, "As I have read about it may it be as though I had performed it." That is to say, it cannot be anymore, but once it was. And poignantly, when he ended his prayers on a fast-day, likely the Day of Atonement, Rabbi Sheshet would say:

> Sovereign of the Universe, Thou knowest full well that in the time that the Temple was standing, if a man sinned, he used to bring a sacrifice, and though all that was offered of it was its fat and blood, atonement was made for him therewith. Now I have kept a fast and my fat and blood have diminished. May it be Thy will to account my fat and blood which have been diminished as if I had offered them before Thee on the altar, and do thou favor me.
>
> (ibid. 17a)

The nostalgia is clear, and clear also it is that the old practice has been left behind and something new has taken its place. Sheshet's prayer has a contemporary ring, in our time when we are told that leanness means good health, and cholesterol is a curse! And Rabbi Eleazer prayed for peace, brotherhood, friendship, many disciples, and good friends. For at the end of his fixed prayers he would pray thus:

> May it be Thy will, O Lord our God, to cause to dwell in our lot love and brotherhood and peace and friendship, and mayest Thou make our borders rich in disciples and prosper our latter end with good prospects and hope, and set our portion in Paradise, and confirm us with a good companion and a good impulse in Thy world, and may we rise early and obtain the yearning of our heart to fear Thy name, and mayest Thou be pleased to grant the satisfaction of our desires.
>
> (ibid. 16b)

What is common about all the personal rabbinic prayers that we encounter is a spontaneity and a direct simplicity of utterance that spoke directly to the heart of the people. To biblical sources, psalms, fixed prayer forms, and prayer formulae, a new dimension is added. It comes from the kind of people among whom Jesus lived and studied and taught. The "Lead us not into temptation and deliver us from evil" in the prayer the disciples remembered has a very familiar ring in this context.

With respect to postbiblical prayer forms in Judaism, one additional word may perhaps be said here. Following the period of the canonization of the Talmud, and the beginning of what we know as the geonic period, which comes after the sixth century, we get another prayer form known as the *piyyut*. This came in response to the forbidding of preaching in the synagogue toward the end of the Byzantine period.

To get around the prohibition, liturgists developed the technique of concealing sermons in prayers. Thus we get a whole series of prayers introduced into the liturgy that were really homilies. The liturgical poets of this period, among them Yose ben Yose, Yannai, and Eliezer Kalir, gave midrashic sermons in short, cryptic sermon replacements. So their liturgical poetry too found its place in the prayer hook. This process was widespread in Judea and Galilee during the late Byzantine and Islamic periods.

It was, however, resisted in Babylonia, where there was more freedom. But one of the great religious leaders, Natronai Gaon (850 C.E.), ruled that "Those who add *piyyutim* to the . . . [liturgy] . . . on the festivals, and thus provide words of comfort, have permission to do so."[7]

Here, for example is a *piyyut* which has been included in the cantor's repetition of the Tefillah on the Day of Atonement:

> The nation likened to the lily of the valley keepeth the Sabbath of solemn rest; root and branch, parents and children with one accord observe the fast. Ever since the foundations of her sanctuary were removed, hath she trusted in Thy favor found in Thy sight by the pillars of her stock; to them she fasteneth the pins of her tent; unto them that rest in Machpelah [i.e., the patriarchs and matriarchs] she joineth her tenons. She supporteth herself by the work of the rocks, upon the piety of the founders of her race. O bring healing to the oppressed and darken the world to the oppressor. Children of the four noble mothers, Israel unnumbered in their fourfold camp, cry aloud unto Thee in a fourfold strain of prayer; regard and justify them . . .[8]

It is at once clear that something new is going on here. It takes little imagination to see how this could easily have been a sermon of encouragement and consolation. What may not be so clear to the reader is the Hebrew style from which this has been translated. The Hebrew is compressed, crisp, and allusive. It has a compact poetic form and poetic cadence. It sings, it has a special kind of rhythm, and it prays. It made the prayer book an open experience to the people.

For some five centuries, deep into the Middle Ages, the *piyyut* form of prayer writing came into the liturgy and made a deep impact upon it. It reflects the experiences of the late Byzantine era, Islam, and the persecutions of the Crusades and the expulsions in the West. Though they lengthened the liturgy—some thought too much—they enriched it.

Thus as we look back at the transition from the end of the biblical and Temple period we see the following process: The basic prayer forms and structures are in place before the end. What is new is the transformation of psalm prayer forms into new prayers for the liturgy; the addition of postbiblical personal prayers; and finally the period of the medieval writers of poetic sermon-prayers. These latter contributed, one might add, not only to the liturgy, but to the development of medieval Hebrew poetry, which underwent a great renaissance.

Perhaps the bottom line is this: The Christian world, especially post-Holocaust and post-Vatican II, has tended to return to its Jewish roots in a reevaluation of the relationship between Christianity and Rabbinic Judaism. This has involved a Christian-Jewish dialogue on a new and creative level. It has involved the rediscovery of Rabbinic Judaism and its cultural heritage in a way that has radically changed not only the relationship of Christian and Jew, but also the way that Christianity looks at itself.

Christianity has been recovering the Jewish world of Jesus in a new and meaningful way. Much attention is being given to rabbinic literature, especially sources in Talmud and Midrash. Much is being written, and much is being taught. Perhaps another forward step can be taken in a similar examination of rabbinic and postrabbinic prayer. That way, perhaps, lies the path not only to deeper mutual understanding, but to self-understanding. Prayer has its own way of reconciliation, not merely between humankind and God, but between person and person.

This essay originally appeared in Scripture and Prayer: A Celebration for Carroll Stuhlmueller, C.P., *edited by Carolyn Osiek, R.S.O.V., and Donald Senior, C.P. (Wilmington, Del.: Michael Glazier, 1988).*

CHAPTER FOUR

Once a Pun a Preacher

When Rabbi David Darshan of Cracow published a little sample of his writings in 1571 he projected it with a pun, and it was a very natural thing for him to have done. He adorns the top of the introductory page with a short quotation from Genesis 29:7, to suggest that his book should be read "to water the flock, come and see." Now the text reads *re'u,* spelled with an *ayin* ("pasture"), but he changes it to read *re'u,* spelled with an *aleph* ("see"), to make his visual pun. The English translation "browse" would capture the force of both meanings. He makes his point and is not one whit concerned about tampering with the spelling of the sacred text. He feels comfortable in making a pun, knowing quite well that this practice goes back to the very origins of our people and its literature.

Wordplay has intrigued mankind in all generations, and we find it everywhere in the literature of the world. One need only think of James Joyce and *Ulysses,* for example, to be aware of this. For Shakespeare, puns were a game, a way in which to demonstrate his literary virtuosity, much as a performing violinist might take off on a cadenza. And the verbal cadenzas paid off in laughs. But as often as not Shakespeare would use the pun not only as a jest or a game but as a technique to express some deeper insight.

In *Twelfth Night* (Act III, scene i), for example, there is an exchange between Viola and a clown which goes like this:

VIOLA: Save thee, friend, and thy music! Dost thou live by the tabor?

CLOWN: No, sir, I live by the church.

VIOLA: Art thou a churchman?

CLOWN: No such matter, sir. I do live by the church; for I do live at my house, and my house doth stand by the church.

VIOLA: So thou mayest say, the king lies by a beggar, if a beggar dwell near him; or, the church stands by the tabor, if the tabor stand by the church.

CLOWN: You have said, sir. To see this age! *A sentence is but a chev'ril glove to a good wit. How quickly the wrong side may be turn'd outward!*

So with pun, that turns meaning on its end, that turns the glove the "wrong way." The pun, with the pleasure it gives, can be made for its own sake or to turn meaning around. Whether the turn takes you into a deeper truth or a deeper error becomes, of course, something that must concern us.

Wordplay comes with the word spoken and written. It can be either auditory or visual, or both. Somehow it seems inherent in words as communication, and from the very beginning, men have been aware of it to a great degree.

Immanuel Casanowitz, in his brilliant study, *Paranomasia in the Old Testament,* makes the point that this phenomenon, early noted in Hebrew Scripture, can be found in all other literatures, in Latin and Greek, Old German, Anglo-Saxon, Old Scandinavian, in the Semitic languages as well. The possibilities in Hebrew for extended wordplay are greater, for there are a longer number of differing letters with the same sound, such as *aleph/ ayin, khaph/ḥet, kuph/kaph, ẓadi/samekh* just to mention a few. Casanowitz lists some five hundred examples of wordplay in its various forms in the Old Testament.

Paranomasia as a conscious technique in rhetoric, as an adornment or deepening form in literary style, was recognized and discussed by the Greeks as early as the time of Plato, who refers to it as *isa* (*Symposium* 180). Aristotle, in his *Rhetoric,* refers to it as *parisosis,* while Hermogenes is the first to refer to it as *paranomasia.*[1]

We do not get such self-conscious analysis of Jewish literary style until much later. The tendency of the Greek was to structure and analyze its philosophy and theory; for the Jew it was implicit in Jewish literature and needed to be extracted like precious metal from veins in the ore of the fascinating material.

Although wordplay abounds in Scripture, the first time we encounter a reference to it as a technique is in the twelfth century, in Kimḥi's comment to heavily punned Micah 1:10 (*b'gath al tagidu*), on which he observes: "This is an example of wordplay for grace in literary style" (*lashon nofel al lashon derekh ẓahut*).

Despite the fact that we do not find it as a defined technique, the use of wordplay grows as a midrashic technique, and we find its use widespread in the Midrash and the Talmud. It is also a very popular technique in medieval Hebrew poetry and popular preaching. The appropriate *"vertel"* (*bon mot*), ever the joy of Jewish preaching or teaching tour de force, testifies to this.

I well remember my father's amused description of a learned but hard-headed landlord in his synagogue when he evicted a tenant who failed to pay his rent. "He lives by the principle of Kohelet 5:4," he said with a wry smile: "better that he not *live* there (*tov asher lo tidor*), than he live there and not pay (*mishetidor v'lo tishalem*)!" The wordplay on the Hebrew *tidor* ("vow") and the Yiddish *dira* ("flat") tickled his fancy and is an example of how the pun bridges differences in language while acting as a unifying cultural source.

In more recent times writers like Good see in wordplay a superb example of biblical irony, a conscious effort to deepen and sharpen insights.[2] Sandmel notes its probable beginnings in the J narrators with their enormous sense of fun.[3] Perhaps the East European Jewish joy in the *vertel* and the *vort* (*ah, taki a gut vort!*) stems from there. Pfeiffer is not quite as enthusiastic, although he acknowledges the technique. "Numerous puns and verbal repetitions, *usually* far-fetched and in questionable taste, occur in [Isa.] 24–27,"[4] and "Isaiah 5:7b consists of a rather prosaic pun,"[5] indicate the extent to which he is underwhelmed by the whole process.

Let us first examine a random sampling of puns and wordplay. There is no pretension here to completeness, but rather an effort to note its variety and extent. In the "temptation story in Genesis, the serpent is *arum* ("wily, cunning"), and Adam and Eve discover themselves to be *erum* ("naked"). In Isaiah 5:7 we find: "He looked for justice (*mishpat*), but lo! bloodshed (*mispaḥ*), for righteousness (*zedakah*), but lo! a cry (*ze'akah*)." "For Gaza (*Azah*) shall be deserted (*azuvah*)," cries Zephaniah (2:4), "and Ekron (*Ekron*) shall be uprooted (*te'aker*)."

We have seen how wordplay on names is a popular ploy. There are, for example, Jacob and "heel" or "supplanter" (*ekev*); Abraham and "father of many nations" (*av hamon goyim*). And in the eloquent rhetoric of Isaiah (17:1–6), we have a literal cascade of puns, describing a decline in the fortunes of Israel with catastrophic harvests: "So the bulwark will be stripped from Ephraim . . . it will be as when the reaper gathers the standing grain (*kazir kamah*) and his arm reaps the ears (*shibalim yikzor*), or as when the olive tree is beaten and gleanings are left on it . . . four or five on the boughs (*bis'ifeha poriyah*)."

Or Job, punning on his own name (13:24) "Why dost thou hide thy face and reckon me as a foe? (*vetahsheveni oyev*)"; and playing on earth (*adamah*) and man (*adam*) in 5:5–6, "Surely misfortune does not come forth from the dust . . . but man is born for trouble."

Guillaume affirms the Old Testament writer's love of paranomasia, finding it used more than fifty times in the Book of Genesis alone, to "explain" the meaning of names, especially proper names.[6] He points to the obvious, *adam, ishah, Reuven,* and to the not so obvious Moab, which he suggests is a pun on *me'av*, "from the father," i.e., begotten by his grandfather out of his sister; and the more remote relationship of *hevel* to the Arabic *habilat*. "she was bereft of her son. " For him paranomasia is of great value for exegesis and lexicography.[7]

Casanowitz and Good have both structured the various types of paranomasia. They include:

a. The juxtaposition of two uses of the same word with ironic implications.

b. The juxtaposition of two forms of the same verb or root with different meanings.

c. The use of double meanings.

d. The use of words that mean the opposite.

e. Play on sounds.[8]

For Glicksberg, in his classic history of Jewish preaching, wordplay is represented in three of the fifteen categories by which the midrashic preacher communicated meaning to his audience.[9] The preacher might take a text, unvarnished and unchanged, as a model for conduct; he might introduce a new idea into a given text; he might develop an idea suggested by the proximity of two texts; he might use the numerical value of words; he might draw his lesson from nature or from fables; he might deal with actual events; he might indulge in dialectic; and he could use wordplay in several ways.

He might, for example, change the meaning of a word by pun to get a new meaning. He might play upon the difference between *keri* and *ketib*; he might introduce a bold change by arbitrarily developing a different meaning by introducing the idea with "do not read it this way, but rather in that way" (*al tikre . . . ela*); or he might play on words with *gematria* (numerical values) or *notarikon* (stringing together the first letters of successive words).

This was considered justifiable, nay desirable, if the idea developed was ennobling or theologically sound. Maimonides, for example, saw it as a poetic convention, and threw in a note of caution: "For these (namely, the Midrashim) have in their opinion the status of poetical conceits; they are not meant to bring out the meaning of the text in question."[10] Then speaking reprovingly of the tendency of the unlettered to take these poetic ideas literally, he adds, "I do not think that anyone of sound intellect will be of this opinion. But this is a most witty poetical conceit by means of which he instills a noble moral quality."

Obviously, the converse would have to be carefully watched. You could be tempted to say, for example, that the words "messiah" (*mashiah*) and "serpent" (*nahash*) were really the same thing because both had the same numerical value (358). Or you could interpret the phrase "loose the bound" (*mattir assurim*) in the Amidah to be read as "permits the forbidden" (*mattir issurim*)—as Shabbetai Zevi ultimately did.[11]

This informal look at paranomasia is prompted by the widespread use of puns in the sermons of popular preachers, whose function was to entertain, to instruct, and to uplift. "God gave me an eloquent tongue," writes David Darshan of Cracow, "to speak entertaining words to the crowd, to show them the right way, in accordance with Halacha and Torah."[12] This use of wordplay, carried perhaps to extremes, is clearly in a continuing scriptural tradition that is expanded in talmudic and midrashic literature and comes to full bloom in the popular preaching of the sixteenth century.

The crowds loved it, but sometimes the leadership demurred, as did the author of *Zera Berakh,* when, in the introduction to the second edition of his sermons published in Amsterdam in 1666 (the first edition having appeared in Cracow in 1648), he saw the practice of *wenden* by preachers as one of the causes of the Chmielnicki pogroms![13] *Wenden* was punning carried to extremes, where the meanings of words and ideas were twisted out of any recognized congruence with original meanings, just for the sake of effect, carrying pilpulism and hillukism to an ultimate absurdity.

With such ample evidence of wordplay for sheer fun, for the testing of the intellectual sharpness of the listener, for the driving home of the ethical or moral lesson with sledgehammer force, it is not surprising to find wordplays widely used in talmudic and midrashic literature for much the same purpose and in much the same way.

Rabbinic Judaism took upon itself the task of continuing the covenant relationship with Torah. By confronting the challenge of shaping Jewish survival into history through the fire and sword of catastrophe, it took the central route of midrash, or exegesis, to interpret the meaning of Scripture and to shape the institutions of surviving Jewish life in its spirit.

The whole of talmudic literature is an enormous process of such midrash, and its crucial function was a process of communication by word—I might even say, of "mouth-to-mouth resuscitation." It was teacher to student, and *darshan* through *meturgeman,* to the people.

Wordplays and puns play their role in the process. It is manifestly impossible to be complete, but a flavor of the process can be given by a few examples.

Rabbi Jonathan, speaking on resisting temptation (Baba Batra 78b), quoted Numbers 21:27, *al ken yomru hamoshlim ba'u ḥeshbon* ("This is how the bards came to say: 'Come to Heshbon, let it be built . . . '"). He sets aside the surface meaning, takes advantage of the fact that the root *mashal* can mean "accounting." So out of it comes a personal moral lesson in self-control: "Therefore they who rule [over their evil impulse] say, 'Come and take an accounting [of the consequences of your deeds].'"

Rabbi Il'a, interested in making the point that restraint during a violent quarrel is a praiseworthy thing, finds support for this idea in Job, and declares: "The world endures by virtue of him who keeps his mouth shut during a quarrel, as it is written, 'He hangs the world on nothing' (*blimah*)." In addition to the obvious "without anything," the root *blm* can mean "to restrain, curb, or muzzle." In modern Hebrew *b'lom pikha* means "shut up!"

Or, let us take a few random samples of well-known rabbinic insights. There are many aphorisms to describe how we humans unconsciously reveal ourselves. The Latin *in vino veritas* quickly comes to mind. The sages, in suggesting that man reveals his true character in his cups, in his anger, and in his charity, make the point with a forceful play of words: *b'sheloshah derakhim ha-adam nikar, b'kisso, b'kosso, b'ka'asso* (Erubin 65b). The man who recognizes the problems within himself from his passions, and outside himself in the problem of theodicy, cries out: *oy li mey-izri v'oy li miyozri* ("I have problems with my impulse and my Creator alike") (Berakhot 61a). A perfect brief summary of the "Catch-22" aspect of the human condition! Then there is that great passage in Baba Batra where several pages of discussion are devoted to the Book of Job: "Rabba said: Job blasphemed with [mention of] a tempest, and with a tempest he was answered. He blasphemed with [mention of] a tempest, as it is written, 'For He breaketh me as with a tempest.' Job said to God: 'Perhaps a tempest passed before Thee and caused Thee to confuse Job (*Iyov*) with enemy (*oyev*)'" (Baba Batra 16a).

We have, as well, a whole series of transformations of meaning by changes in the vowels of the Masoretic text, always with the intention of yielding a deeper meaning.

Item: In Genesis 12, Abraham is commanded: "Be thou a blessing." To which the Midrash comments, do not read it *be-rakhah* ("blessing"); but rather *b'rekhah* ("well of water"). Abraham is bidden to be like a well of water in the desert, and thus the word "blessing" achieves a deeper meaning.

Item: In the case of the Ten Commandments, the narrative

tells us that the words were engraved (*harut*) by the finger of God. "Do not read the word to mean 'engraved,'" cautions the Midrash, "read it rather as *herut* ('freedom')!" The word becomes more than a divine creation, it liberates the human potential.

The Talmud picks up the biblical predilection for puns on names In rabbinic thought the first Jeroboam was one of the archvillains. The force of anger which in medieval Christianity went to the name Judas is found in the name Jeroboam ben Nebat, symbolizing the ultimate in apostasy. It is not surprising that he received rough treatment in puns. In Sanhedrin (101b) they have a field day with his name: Jeroboam, who encourages the people to sexual immorality (*sherivah am*); who created discord among the people (*she'asah merivah ba'am*); who drove a wedge between Israel and God (*she'asah merivah bein Yisrael v'avihem shebashamayim*).

It is also by a pun that Ahasuerus is shown to be the brother of Nebuchadnezzar (Megillah 11a). How is this achieved? Quite easily, for after all, the word Ahasuerus suggests (by assonance) *ahiv shel rosh* ("brother of the head") and is not Nebuchadnezzar thus referred to in Daniel 2:38—"thou art the head of gold"! It was their whimsical way of saying that the bibulous Persian king was in the same class as the destroyer of Jerusalem, because he gave Haman the green light to "do in" the Jewish people.

And if you were concerned about affirming the primacy of expertise in Torah, and wished to make the point with sledge-hammer force that a bastard who is a scholar takes precedence over an ignorant high priest, what better way than to make the tour de force with a pun? And what better way than to build the pun on the *keri* and *ketib* of Proverbs 3:15, where the *keri* is *p'ni-im* and the *ketib* is *p'ninim,* and the usual reading is: "She [wisdom or Torah] is more precious than pearls." By pulling *p'niim* and *p'ninim* together you achieve the full force of the pun with the meaning: "She is more precious than [he who enters] the Holy of Holies!" (*lifnei u'lifnim*).

Or, when Exodus Rabbah comments on Pharaoh working the slaves brutally hard, the term *baparekh* yields an insight into the psychology of persuading slaves to go unresisting to their work. First Pharaoh approached them *b'peh rakh,* with soft and persuasive words, and then with the hammer stroke of *baparekh.* Shades of *Arbeit macht frei* at the gates of Auschwitz.

The rabbinic penchant for puns finds its way into the *piyyutim,* which flourished in areas under Byzantine control where Torah instruction through the talmudic *darshan* was prohibited.[14] And it surfaces widely in medieval Hebrew poetry, where the stringing together of fragments of biblical allusion spiced with wordplay is a common phenomenon. Let one example in this category suffice. In Yehudah Halevi's classic poem of longing for Zion, "My Heart Is in the East," the poignant description of a Jewish diaspora under Christian and Arab control is expressed in a pun of assonance between *khevel* ("chains") and *hevel* ("rope"): "Zion is in the chains of Edom, and I in the bonds of Islam" (*Ziyon b'khevel Edom v'ani b'hevel Arav*).

In Kabbalah the pun was used to move words and meaning into deeper levels. This technique was not simply an entertainment device for the popular preacher. It would be used as an important interpretive tool by the "philosopher of Kabbalism." Joseph ibn Gikatila is a case in point. A contemporary of Moses de Leon, he was one of the shapers of Spanish Kabbalah, and his *Sha'arei Orah* became a classic in the analysis of the spherotic structure in Jewish mysticism.

When discussing in detail the meaning and implication of the second sphere, he deals with the significance of an oath (*shevuah*) which a man makes, as exemplified by Abraham and Abimelech at Be'er-Sheba.[15] He dwells on the many-sided meaning of the word *shevuah,* "oath," "seven," and the name of a city. As he puts it: "The reason for this is that the word *shevuah* is derived from the root *shev'a,* and the real meaning is to be found in what our father Abraham said to Abimelech, 'You will accept the *seven* ewe lambs from my hand to serve as witness that I dug this well. Therefore they called the place Be'er-*Sheba* because there the two of them *took an oath.*'" You will note that the three uses of the word are a play on words (*milah nofel al milah*). And here he uses precisely the words that Kimḥi used in his commentary less than a century before.[16] Clearly, the use of paranomasia as a technique was noted by Jewish scholars, noted and used.

So the *derashah,* the oral process of interpretation, moves into the later Middle Ages, carrying the pun, a survivor of early biblical days, as a source of amusement, tour de force, and key to deeper insights. Not even Don Isaac Abarbanel, statesman and scholar, is immune. He was a scholar and teacher when he was a courtier in Spain. He remained a scholar and teacher in exile. His books of commentary on the Bible and the Haggadah were probably, as most such works, spoken as public sermons. He describes Deborah as a woman fiery with zeal, and demonstrates this from the fact that her husband's name, Lapidot, means "torch."[17] The scriptural verse "You must never ascend My altar with steps" (Exod. 20:23) leads to a pun on *ma'alot,* which means both "steps" and "excellences." So the meaning becomes "You shall not decorate (*ta'aleh*) My altar with [artificial] excellences,"[18] a slap at ostentation, of which presumably he had his fill.

David Darshan of Cracow made the same pun when he published the first sampler of his writings in Cracow in 1571. When he picked the title *Shir HaMa'alot l'David,* he was using a pun to take advantage of the wide acceptance of a much-better-selling book than his—the Psalms; but he had another purpose, for he was interested in more than self-advertisement. He intended the reader to think in terms of excellence and virtues when he picked up the book.

It is my interest in David Darshan that has prompted this brief survey of paranomasia. As the first *darshan* to be published in Poland after the reintroduction of a Hebrew printing press to Cracow in 1569,[19] his work and style have a special interest. His two published works, surviving in one or two rare copies of each, include a handbook of several sermons, responsa, poems, and occasional writings (*Sefer Shir HaMa'alot l'David,* Cracow, 1571) and a handbook for preachers and defense of preaching (*K'tav Hitnaẓẓelut l'Darshanim,* Lublin, 1574). Here paranomasia proliferates and puns reign supreme. One sees clearly the continuing of the talmudic penchant, expanded and sharpened, used both to delight and to deepen, but used widely, sometimes prodigally.

In his handbook for preachers, Rabbi David undertakes to categorize types of sermons and techniques of preaching. And when he does, perhaps to underscore his analysis, perhaps to show his skill and wit, or perhaps to provide a mnemonic device, he relates it to a scriptural verse through a pun.

"Unlimited are the ways of preaching on the Torah, but they all have one goal," he writes, "to draw the good close, and drive the ugly away."[20] The first approach, he suggests, is to begin with humor to attract attention. It is important "to cheer up the exhausted and the overburdened [with life's daily struggle]."[21] For did not the great sage Rava, when he arose to give his exposition of Torah, begin with something humorous (Pesaḥim

117a)? So start with a joke to get the audience involved. Indeed, this technique was suggested by Amos (5:4) when he said: *dirshuni viḥyu.* What it means for the preacher is: "Interpret me, [that the hearers] may live!"

Another attention-getting formula is the hyperbole or startling opener. For example, when R. Yoḥanan saw some people dozing, he began: "There was one woman in Egypt who bore six hundred thousand at one time!" And when they awoke with a start, he continued that this was Jochebed, the mother of Moses, who led six hundred thousand Israelites to freedom and made them a nation (Song of Songs Rabbah). And the text that suggests this and by which it can be remembered, naturally, is Ezekiel 33:6, "But his blood will I require (*edrash*) at the watchman's (*haẓofeh*) hand!" And by what method could you transform this into a mnemonic for waking up the sleeping parishioner with an outrageous hyperbole? With a pun, of course: the audience is *haẓofeh,* and the verb *edrosh* combines the idea of demand and the word for preacher. "Seize the attention of the listener with hyperbole, O preacher!"

There is also a special technique in gauging the intellectual level of the audience. Don't go over the head of your audience, he warns.[22] "Give your homily without precise reasons because of the limited scientific capacity of the audience. Explain [natural phenomena] in simpler terms." And for the scriptural text from which this method can be deduced he turns to II Chronicles 16:12: "In his disease (*b'ḥolyo*) he sought not (*lo darash*) the Lord." From poor King Asa in his misery to the admonition not to get involved in too much technical detail for the "feebleminded" masses! The pun may sound absurd, but the admonition to the preacher not to go over the head of his audience is certainly sound.

In David Darshan's sermons, talmudic wordplay abounds. A

fertile mind such as his learns quickly and amplifies the learning
with its own wit and insight. But all the while he is very careful
to remain within the tradition and not to tip-toe along the dangerous borders of heresy.

His concerns in his sermons and his exegesis of any given text
included three aspects of the four-part division known as *PaR-
DeS* (*P'shat,* plain meaning; *Remez,* allegorical meaning; *D'rash,*
homiletical meaning; and *Sod,* mystical or esoteric meaning).[23]
In his printed sermons he always omits the fourth category, because it was deemed inappropriate, nay, dangerous, to employ
it. In addition, he did not preach exclusively on scriptural texts.
He would be more apt to preach on parallel texts, one from the
Torah portion of the week and one from the Talmud which he
linked to the former by exegesis. This was an expression of defiance against the Christian exegetes who surrounded him, for
they had taken Scripture as their domain, and the Talmud was
left to the Jew as the last line of defense for the truth she es-
poused.[24]

In Rabbi David's case the dual texts are mined, in accordance
with this division, to examine the condition of exile, the individual's struggle against the evil impulse, and the hopes for the
Messiah's advent. In all this process, it is through puns that he
advances his thought. This essay can point to only a few by way
of example.

A sermon on the text "He tethers his ass to the vine, and his
ass's colt to the choicest vine; he washes his garments in wine,
and his robes in the blood of grapes" (Gen. 49:11) is coupled
with the passage on the law of the covering of the blood from
Mishnah Ḥullin 6:1. This is not the place to go into this fascinating sermon in detail, but the example of pun use is instructive.

That this verse had messianic overtones for the Jewish reader was long accepted as fact. The Targum to this passage already identified Shiloh as a name for the Messiah, and David, of course, accepts this. Now, in the personal interpretation, with regard to battling the evil impulse, he puns on Scripture's use of the term *ayir* ("donkey's foal") and the interpretation in Nedarim (32b) of the passage about the little city under attack, where the "little city" under attack is interpreted to be the fallible human, subject to temptation. So "tethering the foal to the vine" in Rabbi David's sermon really means binding your "city," i.e., your struggling, temptation-ridden person, to the vine that represents the righteous one. In a word, the good man controls his impulse.

Then he tackles the Mishnah phrase "covering the blood" (*kissui hadam*). Here comes a chain of puns. The second part of the scriptural verse, "and his garments (*suto*) in the blood of grapes," gives him the occasion to derive the pun *k'suto* ("that which covers him") and *hasatah* ("the process of inciting"), so *kissui hadam* really means covering or restraining the evil impulse. Now with respect to the Mishnah passage he takes the punned exegesis a step further. The law of "covering the blood" is based, he observes, on Leviticus 17:3: "And whatever man there be of the children of Israel, or the stranger that sojourneth among them (*ha-ger ha-gar*), that taketh in hunting beast or fowl that may be eaten, he shall pour out the blood thereof and cover it with dust." It is on the words *ha-ger ha-gar* that he makes the pun *hamegareh* ("inciter"), and so he gets the idea of temptation out of a word in the scriptural base text, and from a word in the Mishnah that expands this text for quite another purpose! Binding a donkey foal, covering the blood, and a stranger that sojourneth are all transformed to mean inciter or tempter to sin that must be controlled!

Thus the pun process makes a transit from the fun-intoxicated J narrator, through the prophets, through the Mishnah and Talmud to a sixteenth-century Cracow synagogue on some Saturday afternoon, where the people are warned to mind their personal morals and are told that how they shape their ethical existence can make its contribution to bringing on the messianic age!

For me the most interesting of all is the pun David Darshan uses to describe his vocation as deriving in a special sense from the prophet.[25] The prophet is inspired to speak God's word, which comes to him in direct revelation. The *darshan* is inspired to interpret God's word and bring it to the people. Thus, describing his vocation as *darshan,* he refers to Jeremiah's call to prophecy from the very moment he was conceived. The cadence of Jeremiah is in his very words as he writes:

> That being the case, it is for me to give praise and thanks to the Lord of all, who declares the end of all from the beginning, who knew me before He formed me in the womb, who consecrated me before I was born, to be a gadfly to the arrogant (*novev lag'e'im*).[26]

The play on *navi lagoyim* and the relationship to Jeremiah's mission is clear.

David took himself seriously as a *darshan,* was deeply aware of his role in assuring the continuity of Israel's historic tradition, based himself firmly in the scriptural text, carrying into his time and beyond with the techniques shaped by the genius of Rabbinic Judaism.

So paranomasia comes full circle, from early Scripture to *darshan's* art. It may be a literary conceit and poetic fancy. In the hands of those who shaped Jewish survival and played their role in implanting its values in the bloodstream of the people, it was an important tool of the process. It merits further and deeper study.

This essay originally appeared in the Journal of Reform Judaism, *Spring 1980.*

CHAPTER FIVE

Introduction to the Writings of David Darshan

I

This volume is a labor of love and an act of recovery. It is designed to bring two obscure little books to life, and to make them accessible to two categories of readers.

For the Hebrew reader, to whom the world of medieval literature is a constant reservoir of discovery and rediscovery, the republication of the original texts of David Darshan's *Shir Ha-Ma'alot l'David* and *K'tav Hitnazzelut l'Darshanim* provides reproductions of texts that were popular in their time. They are now in the category of endangered species, with perhaps three copies of the former (none in perfect condition) and one of the latter extant.[1]

For general readers and scholars, to whom the complex, pilpulistic, constantly allusive type of late medieval Hebrew represents a barrier, their translation as *Song of the Steps* and *In De-*

fense of Preachers unlocks a door, not often opened, to an understanding of the inner life of Polish Jewry in the late Renaissance period of its emergence as a luminous and creative center of Jewish life. It is a period that can be compared to the Golden Age of Spain or to the flowering of Babylonian Jewry and the final redaction of the Talmud.

The corpus of popular Jewish homiletical literature has received too little attention from modern scholars. Yet it is literally a gold mine of information and insight into the processes whereby Rabbinic Judaism and Jewish values were transmitted to the folk, and sheds light on their needs and aspirations. It is to be hoped that more such works will find their way to translation and scholarly analysis, so that this field might be opened to a wider body of general scholarship.

We are talking about a first—the first of the itinerant Jewish scholar-preachers in Poland to emerge into the light of day with the reintroduction of the Hebrew printing press in Cracow in 1569. For *Shir HaMa'alot l'David* was the first book of printed sermons for popular consumption to be published in Poland, and *K'tav Hitnazzelut l'Darshanim* (Lublin, 1574) was the first handbook for preachers,[2] providing clear evidence that the popular preacher needed a defense.

It is worth noting that the former was the second book to come off the reestablished press, while the first volume, a commentary to the Midrash Rabbah to the Five Scrolls,[3] bore a dedicatory poem by this *darshan* who was associated with the printer as proofreader and editor. In Italy, where the first printed Hebrew books came off the Soncino Press in 1483, fifty-nine books appeared in the next twenty-four years, including Talmud folios, Bible commentaries, and prayer books. Not before 1507 did the collection of the works of a popular preacher ap-

pear. This was the *Bi'ur* of Baḥya ben Asher (d. 1360), a homiletical classic constantly used by subsequent *darshanim* as a source
book. In the years that followed (1514, 1517, 1526), the fre-
quency of new editions indicates a growing interest in this genre
of literature.[4]

In his history of Jewish preaching, Leopold Zunz listed nine
books which were written as handbooks for preachers. The earliest of these is listed as *Hitnazzelut l'Darshanim,* Lublin, 1548.
This is clearly David Darshan's work, although Zunz errs in the
publication year, as did Shabbetai Bass in his *Sifte Yeshenim* (Amsterdam, 1680).[5] That David was a first in this type of literature
is clear.

II

The sermon as a means of communication and the *darshan* as
communicator are a unique development of Rabbinic Judaism.
Midrash, the process of extracting deeper meaning from the
Torah text and communicating it to the covenant people, was
the technique through which biblical, prophetic, and priestly
Judaism was transformed so that it could survive beyond the destruction of the First and Second Jewish Commonwealths into
the two millennia that followed.

The beginnings of the process from which the preacher as a
type began to appear are shrouded in mystery, but it seems rather clear that it began with the establishment of the Babylonian
Jewish community, perhaps already adumbrated by Jeremiah's
famous letter.[6] In any event, the process was at work in the beginning of the Second Commonwealth with Ezra, the Men of
the Great Synagogue, and the quiet development of Rabbinic
Judaism and its "two laws" (oral and written). It was as though
"the cure was being developed prior to the disease,"[7] so that

when the Jewish state collapsed under the hammer blows of Rome, the survival mechanism was at hand: canonized Bible, Mishnah, Talmud, and prayer book, and a structure for community survival within a unique legal, religious, and national framework, in a diaspora setting.

As early as the time of Ezra, the *meturgeman* was there to interpret the Torah to the people as it was read to them in public.[8] The Targum, the earliest Aramaic translation of the Talmud, already had elements of the homiletical interpretation within it.

The spoken homily of the *darshan,* communicating Torah and its meaning to the people, seems to have developed in mishnaic and talmudic times. It became one of the chief means of instructing all the people—common folk, women, and children. It was a means of guiding them and strengthening their faith. It was the method, too, of reinterpreting the Bible in such a way as to give expression, often in a bold manner, to burning issues of the time.

For example, when, in times of extreme persecution in the Roman era, it became hard to believe in the premise that the righteous were rewarded in this life, the *darshanim* made bold changes. The meaning of the text "He has given food unto them that fear him, He will ever be mindful of His covenant"[9] was transformed by a play on words. Since the word *teref* ("food") could be read as *teruf* ("confusion"), they offered this reading: "He has given confusion to those who fear him in this world; He will ever be mindful of His covenant in the next!"[10] It comes out all right in the end.

The vast body of homilies preached by the *darshanim* in mishnaic and talmudic times have come down to us in rich collections of midrashim. In this medium the sermons have survived in the barest of outlines. Only very occasionally do we find a complete sermon preserved, as, for example, in Talmud Bavli, Shabbat 30b and Ḥagigah 3a.

The message was all-important, but the medium was not to be lightly dismissed. In fact, as time passed, it tended to become as important, and therein lurked a problem. For the sermon not only edified, it entertained. *Darshanim* who were dramatic and effective in their presentations attracted throngs.[11] They used every imaginable technique to seize and to hold the attention of the audience.[12] The people flocked to hear them, and even went so far, through the use of the *eruv,* as to extend the distance they could properly travel on the Sabbath to hear a good *darshan.*[13]

The vast body of midrashic literature, to say nothing of the aggadic material in the Talmud, preserves the traces of this rich and creative process. The classical midrashim probably drew the bulk of their material from the texts of countless sermons that had actually been preached in the synagogues of Palestine.

Some of the outstanding sages known as *darshanim* in the talmudic period included Shemaiah and Abtalion, Hillel's teachers, Ben Azzai and Ben Zoma, Eliezer the son of Yose the Galilean, Levi ben Sisi,[14] Joshua ben Levi, Abbahu, Elazar ben Arakh, and Judah ben Pedayah.[15]

Clearly the same process that was at work when the Talmud was evolving continued into the medieval period. The Jewish communities, developing in Italy, Spain, France, and Germany's Rhineland, turned first to Babylonia for guidance, but before very long were developing their own communal structures and authority. The religious, philosophic, and mystical developments went hand in hand, and the *darshanim* continued their work of communication.

The institutionalization of the *darshan* in this role is evidenced by Moses ben Maimon's ruling that "each Jewish congregation must arrange to have a respected and wise elder who has been known for his piety from his youth and is beloved by the people, who will publicly admonish the community and cause them to repent."[16] He is, however, careful to point out that great care must be exercised to share the insights of Judaism with the masses in a way that is appropriate to their understanding. It is not wise to transmit profound ideas to those who are incapable of understanding them; as he puts it: "Instruction to the masses must be by allegory and parables, so that even women, youths, and children might comprehend, and as their understanding grows, they come to understand deeper truths."[17]

He is also very concerned about abuses. In his detailed discussion on the many levels of understanding the meaning of the idea of the world to come as it occurs in the last chapter of Sanhedrin, he has this to say in his commentary to the Mishnah of that section:

> Too frequently *darshanim* are wont to communicate to the crowd what they do not really understand, and one wishes that they would remain silent . . . or that they would say: "We do not understand what the sages meant by this passage" instead of: "This is how it is to be interpreted." They believe that they understand it, and they try to submit their feeble understanding of the last chapter of Sanhedrin [concerning the world to come] and other such matters, interpreting them literally.

And three and a half centuries later in Cracow, David Darshan's teacher, Moses Isserles, concerned with the fact that too many unqualified people were reading the recently printed kabbalistic books, could write:

. . . and so many of the crowd jump into study of Kabbalah, for it is tempting to the eye . . . and ordinary householders who do not know their right hand from their left hasten to its study . . . and everyone who has little knowledge of it inflates himself with it and preaches to the masses, and will someday be brought before the bar of divine justice.[18]

As the post-talmudic age merged into the medieval period, we find the darshanic process expressed in a variety of ways. The authors of the *piyyutim* (liturgical poems written between the eighth and twelfth centuries) that found their way into the prayer books had a homiletic function and expressed the folk experience. Alongside this process the *darshanim,* carrying on their work of communication, emerge. Rashi's frequent references to Rabbi Moses haDarshan make us aware of their continuing role. The homily was already an accepted part of Jewish life in Germany in the eleventh and twelfth centuries. A good many of the stories and ethical teachings in the *Sefer haHasidim* seem to be passages from sermons. Eleazer ben Judah ben Kalonymos of Worms wrote: "One must preach in words more precious than gold on the Sabbath . . . one must assemble the people at that time and preach to them,"[19] while Moses of Coucy describes a journey he made through Spain giving sermons of admonition.[20] This wandering halakhist was one of the earliest itinerant preachers of the Middle Ages to emerge as an ethical teacher of the masses. From the thirteenth to the fifteenth century in Provence and Spain, *darshanim* developed, some with a philosophic bent, like Yedaiah Penini of Béziers (d. 1340) and Jacob Anatoli (b. 1194); some with a mystical bent, like Bahya ben Asher (d. 1340); and some, like Isaac Arama (b. 1420), who combined speculative analysis with the popular faith of the believers in times of stress.

Joel ibn Shuaib (ca. 1490), a *darshan* of the time of the expulsion from Spain, sums up the form and aesthetic tradition of the sermon in Spain in the introduction to his *Olat Shabbat*,[21] counseling concern with the integrity of the subject matter and the perfection of the manner of expression.

In Italy, the sermon developed in the sixteenth and seventeenth centuries among the exiles from Spain, who at the same time were nourished by Renaissance culture. Preachers like Judah Moscato (d. 1594) and Leone Modena (d. 1648) combined the forms of Jewish interpretation with the graces of the cultural rebirth inspired by a return to classical forms.

It was the Italy of the sixteenth century, the Italy of the time of David Darshan, that became a creative center. To it came the exiles from Spain and Portugal. To it came scholars from Germany, Bohemia, and Poland, to study in its universities and yeshivot.

The Italian communities of the late Renaissance period were indeed a gathering center of the major Jewries from all directions, and the developing printing presses, and the stream of Hebrew books published, acted as a great catalyst. Here communities of Jews from the lands of Sefarad and Ashkenaz, as well as the indigenous Italian Jewish community, were in a creative interaction with each other and with their environment.

It was here that our Cracow *darshan* spent some of his crucial years of development at least between 1556 and perhaps 1558, as we shall see in greater detail in the subsequent sections.

The Polish *darshanim* were influenced by their predecessors but took a different tack. The growth of Poland as a new economic frontier, between the Christian West of the Renaissance period and the Turkish-governed Islamic East, the explosive growth and expansion of its Jewish community, principally Ashkenazic, opened new economic, cultural, and social vistas.[22]

The first group of Polish *darshanim,* beginning with David

ben Manasseh, *darshan* of Cracow, and including such figures as Ephraim of Lunschitz (d. 1619)[23] and Yedidiah Gottlieb (d. 1645) among others, reflects a differing emphasis. The social criticism of an Ephraim of Lunschitz was particularly sharp. He violently attacked hypocrisy, insincerity, ostentation, and the intrusion of materialism into the worship service.[24] One finds preachers like David Darshan attacking the rich and greedy on the one hand,[25] and on the other attempting to justify the use of rather startling *pilpul* (dialetical tricks in hermeneutics) as a means of edifying and entertaining, as well as admonishing.[26] One finds a greater emphasis of preaching on talmudic texts and relating them to biblical texts, because the Talmud had come under fire in Church circles and talmudic exegesis was seen as a last refuge of Judaism from Christian intervention.

Rabbi Ḥayim ben Beẓalel, a contemporary of David Darshan's, represented this view vigorously. He took sharp exception to Naḥmanides' (1195–1270) description of aggadic material as "sermons," intending to downgrade passages that were hostile to Christianity in his disputations with the Church. For him, the very innermost secrets of Judaism were protected within such passages as difficult of access, to shield them from intrusion by Christian scholars and theologians who had already made the Bible their own![27] In short, the role of the *darshan* is an important factor in Jewish development that deserves deeper study. The books of printed sermons, the *hakdamot* (introductions), indeed, the data on the title pages and the printers' comments at the end of books, all become useful grist for the mill of scholarship and cry out for continuing study.[28]

David Darshan and his works are a useful mirror of his time and his craft. Human and fallible as he turns out to be, enigmatic and fascinating, he refracts the personality and psyche of Polish Jewry at the crest of its development.

The Shoah of our century left Polish Jewry a shambles, and its grandeur a memory. But its influence on contemporary Jewish life, in Israel and the Western diaspora, defies measurement. Whatever can be done to bring alive its incandescent spirit is something more than a sentimental journey. It is a pilgrimage in reverence where every name is named, and achieves, in a real sense, enduring life.

III

Wanderer, scholar, preacher, scribe, artist, healer by charms, bibliophile and reference librarian, rabbi, poet, proofreader-editor, and father of unmarried daughters—all these, and perhaps more, was David b. Manasseh, *darshan* of Cracow.

He was a sad and troubled man by his own admission. He saw himself as "a man weighed down by troubles and burdened with daughters . . . the most troubled of men."[29] While traveling in Italy (1556–58), he averred that "all this I have written under pressure"[30] at the end of a responsum which he wrote at the request of Rabbi Jacob Reiner of Ferrara; and while writing an essay on amulets at the request of Joseph Minz to demonstrate his competence, he ended with the words: "all this I have written under pressure."[31] Troubles seemed to follow him wherever he went. He complained about being buffeted from his earliest years by one setback after another.[32]

What a striking contrast is the case of Rabbi Moses Isserles, his distinguished teacher. The latter was born into a wealthy and influential family. His father, Israel, was a *parnas* of the community and a man of substance. His father-in-law, Rabbi Solomon Shakhna, had been appointed chief rabbi of Poland by the Polish king (Sigismund I).[33] When, in 1556, Moses fled Cracow for temporary refuge in Szydlow, he wrote a commentary on the Purim Megillah as a gift for his father. He found the town to which he had fled dull and uncultured, "without fig tree and vine," and the book was the result of his leisure. No mention of pressure and troubles here. As he put it: "I sent it during Purim as a gift to my father, Israel, head of an incomparable community. . . . he is the mightiest of the mighty." So a rich man's son sent his rich and powerful father a beautiful book crafted by Vincenzo Conti in Cremona in 1559.[34]

Yes, troubles and anonymity were David's sad lot. For a long time simply a name in bibliographic catalogues and occasionally a short paragraph in an encyclopedia and in a few histories of the Jews in Poland, he emerges on reexamination with increased stature, a heightened interest. He becomes something of a person rather than a mere cipher on a list. And he forms a wedge for the entry into a deeper insight into the life of sixteenth-century Polish Jewry, precisely because in an unselfconscious way he mirrors the forces and foibles at work among the more undistinguished masses of the people. And not through the eyes of the famous, the well-known, and the privileged, but rather from sources which thus far have been unexamined and little known.

When Leopold Zunz was writing his classic history of Jewish preaching, he mentioned David's book, as we noted earlier, but not his name. But in the last four decades, with efforts to delve into the social and cultural history of vanished Polish Jewry growing, an important work in this field by Hayim Hillel Ben-Sasson gave significant place to this *darshan* in an analysis of his work.[35] And not too long ago, when Asher Ziv brought out his updated scholarly edition of the responsa of Moses Isserles,[36] significant attention was focused on David in connection with his mention on one responsum and his authorship of another.

His lifespan covered a period of rich growth in Polish Jewry. A generation before his birth, there were fewer than 50,000 Jews in all of Poland. A generation after his death there were perhaps 500,000.[37] He was born a generation removed from the expulsion of the Jews from Spain, a calamity that filled his world with wandering refugees, and gave great impetus to the development and spread of mysticism. The principal direction of the movement of refugees was North Africa, Italy, Holland, and the Turkish Empire, but some made their way to Poland as an area of enormously developing economic opportunities. So it is not surprising to find, immediately after 1492, Isaac Hispanus as court physician to Kings John, Alexander, and Sigismund and to the archbishop of Gnesen,[38] or Solomon Calahora as physician to Stephen Batory and a leading farmer of salt mines, hardly a century later.

In the land of his birth, Talmud study was on the rise, having been given its first impetus by Jacob Pollack (1460–1541), who is credited with the development of Polish pilpulism. Pollack was succeeded by Solomon Shakhna, the great rabbi of Lublin and famous as teacher (and father-in-law) of Moses Isserles and Solomon Luria. It was early in his lifetime that the great institution of Jewish autonomy, the Council of the Four Lands, probably came into being.[39]

David Darshan was the son of the martyred scholar and rabbi Manasseh.[40] He was born, probably in Cracow, in (or around) the year 1527. In the introduction to *Shir haMa'alot l'David*, written in 1571, he refers to the fact that he collected his library of four hundred books over a period of twenty-five years from the time he was nineteen, in the *baḥur* stage of his studies.[41]

The Cracow of David's childhood and youth, under the enlightened rule of the two Sigismunds of the Jagiellon dynasty, was deeply influenced by the humanism of the West and by Renaissance culture.[42] Sigismund's wife, Bona, was a member of the Sforza family. Fully one-third of the Polish nobility was Lutheran or Calvinist. It was a varied dialogue of the faiths, with the Greek Orthodox Church to the east, the Roman Church struggling to regain power, and Judaism flourishing through the burgeoning yeshivot. The death of Sigismund II in 1574 and the accession of Stephen Batory, a staunch Catholic, following hard on the heels of the intense work of the Jesuits and the Counter-Reformation, changed the atmosphere—especially for Jews.

The Jew, in the midst of these contemporary forces, religious, social, and ethnic, lived at a constant edge of danger, but in an expanding economy that gave him a significant role and saw his economic and spiritual life grow in strength and influence. David indicates that he studied with Rabbis Moses Isserles, Solomon Luria, Joseph Cohen, and Isaac ben Bezalel (brother of the MaHaRaL of Prague). The yeshiva of that period centered around the distinguished and respected teacher. This was especially so in the case of the sages Isserles, Luria, and Cohen, who were eminent scholars, came from families of wealth and position, and could support the scholars who came to study with them. It represented a kind of inner circle of special privilege, which expressed itself in the emergence of community-authorized yeshivot,[43] and probably accounts for David's difficulties in getting his to endure.

David describes his difficulties in this context vividly. He writes that he was barred, against his will, from academies of Torah. There "many of the privileged in learning and in wealth" turned against him. "They prevented me from studying

Torah in the proper time, and I was considered a pariah among them. . . . They also made it difficult for me to make a living by preventing students from studying with me."[44] His anger and resentment break out in one of his sermon models on the problem of how the wicked, living under a lucky star and prospering, finally get their comeuppance. In this vein he writes: "Now . . . these men of Israel who oppress their fellows are treated like the oppressing nations and have no portion in the God of Israel. . . . for the moment fate smiles on them, but when the influence of their stars wanes they will stand in judgment for the enormity of their sins. *And we have seen how many individuals and families, who rule and oppress their fellows have been destroyed, they, their power and their wealth*" (emphasis added).[45] There is a bitterness and bite here, in a time of expansion and growth, that appears to prefigure the massive reaction almost two centuries later in the breakout of the Hasidic movement.

Among his fellow students at the academy of Moses Isserles were David Gans and Abraham Halevi Horowitz.[46] The former was the author of *Ẓemaḥ David,* a secular historical work, and a student of astronomy and mathematics; the latter was, in his youth, a keen student of philosophy and the author of a commentary on Maimonides. Both received their prime impulse to such secular studies in Isserles' academy.

Isserles was in fact sharply criticized by his brother-in-law Solomon Luria for permitting secular studies. The latter complained that he had found the "prayer of Aristotle" written in a prayer book of one of the former's students. To this Isserles responded by denying the charges and asserting that if it had happened without his knowledge it was "an evil root inherited from their fathers, who studied [Greek] philosophers and followed their ways,"[47] but he defended his study of Greek philosophy through Maimonides. The humanist and rationalist tendencies, eventually to be suppressed, show their traces here.[48]

At times David was a spokesman for the *ḥaverim,* rabbinical students who had passed the second phase of their studies and were ready for ordination. We find a question put to the ReMa with respect to a problem concerning the placing of Hanukkah candles that is submitted by David, who ends with the words: "Your humble servant David submits this question with the consent of the *ḥaverim,*" whereupon, in a clear indication of the intimacy of relationship, the Master responds: "My beloved friend, after you have read this please return it to me so that I may give it to a copyist that I may have it in my records."[49] It is clear that at the time of the writing of the question he had not yet received ordination, for Isserles refers to him in the responsum without an honorific: "these are the words of David."

This responsum, which is not dated, must have been written well before 1556. For in that year Isserles left Cracow because of the plague,[50] and David was already in Italy, for in that year he copied the manuscript of the *Perush haYeri'ah haG'dolah,*[51] a commentary on the Ten Spheres, in Modena. It is a beautiful piece of scribal art, written in a fine Ashkenazic style, and magnificently illustrated with a sketch of Rabbi Akiva entering and leaving the Pardes unscathed, surrounded by the four creatures of Ezekiel's Chariot Vision.

We may reasonably conclude that David received his ordination sometime before this, because in the period between 1556 and 1558 there is ample evidence that it had occurred. He certified one Uri ben Shlomo haCohen as *shoḥet* (ritual slaughterer) in 1558, in Mori near Rovere;[52] he wrote a recommendation for a student named Avigdor who was related by marriage to his

Italian patrons, the Bordolani. Avigdor moved from Venice to Cremona to study with him, and referred to him by his rabbinic title.[53] Furthermore, he wrote a responsum and an essay on amulets for Rabbis Joseph Minz and Jacob Reiner to establish his credentials in Italy, where he acted as rabbi and tutored in the household of the aforementioned Bordolanis.[54]

By his own admission, he followed the practice of yeshiva students, moving in groups or individually from city to city, as was the general custom of university students in the Middle Ages.[55] He was sustained, he writes, "by a bounteous spirit . . . which I drew from many yeshiva heads, namely the sages of Russia, Poland, Moravia, and Italy."[56]

At any rate, no later than 1556, and at least until 1558, we find him in Italy, where, in the flourishing late Renaissance cities of the north, there were thriving Jewish communities, a creative confluence of Italian, Spanish, and Ashkenazic communities. For example, Venice and its surrounding towns had a population of 3,000 Jews, Mantua and Ferrara had 2,000 each, Padua almost 1,000, the Papal States almost 12,500; and in all there were perhaps 25,000 in all of Italy.[57]

He served as rabbi and tutor for the wealthy banking family of Moses Bordolano, to whom the privilege of lending money at interest was restored in 1557.[58] Mirroring the prevailing custom of noble households as centers of learning and culture, they frequently maintained their own rabbi and yeshiva. David spent time in Ferrara and its environs with them, developing a relationship that was long sustained.

It was not uncommon for Polish Jews to visit Italy, and similarly for Italian Jews to visit Poland. In this period Poland had become an important trade link between Northern Europe and the Turkish Empire and maintained links with Italy. There was, in fact, a great deal of intercourse between the Jewish communities of Poland and Italy. The restored printing presses in Poland were set up by Jews who had come from Italy.[59] Polish rabbis were frequently in communication with Italian rabbis.[60] Many young Polish Jews went to Italy to study medicine, especially at the University of Padua.[61] In 1590, a Pentateuch appeared in Lemberg with commentaries in both Yiddish and Italian.[62] Many Polish Jews came to Poland via Italy, as physicians or apothecaries.[63] The famous court physician and statesman to the Turkish court, Solomon Ashkenazi, followed a route that led to Turkey via Cracow. And we have already noted that a Sforza princess was queen of Poland.

David came to Italy during a critical time for Italian Jewry. A quarrel over printing rights for an edition of Maimonides' *Mishneh Torah* had exploded with recriminations between the non-Jewish publishers in Venice. Two editions had been brought out, both with a commentary by Rabbi Meir Katzenellenbogen of Padua, a kinsman of David's teacher, the ReMa. Katzenellenbogen favored one over the other, and got Isserles to proclaim a ban on the pirated edition. This controversy, brought to the Vatican with nasty testimony by apostates supporting each publisher, resulted in the confiscation and burning of the Talmud in 1553.[64] Shortly before David came to Ferarra, a rabbinic synod had met there to decree that no Hebrew book was to be published unless approved by three rabbis and the community closest to the site of the printing press. This form of self-censorship was designed to prevent further attacks on Jewish books.[65]

This was the time also of the controversy over the printing of the *Zohar*.[66] The *Zohar*, the *Tikkunei haZohar*, and the commentary to the *Ma'arekhet haElohut* all appeared in 1558, and their appearance was enthusiastically noted by R. David. He referred especially to the latter as "a work which is adorned sevenfold as is known to whomever reads it." And speaking of its author he added, "He is as his name—there is no limit to his praise!"[67] The printing of the *Zohar* was opposed by the abovementioned MaHaRam of Padua, and as we have already noted, Moses Isserles expressed strong reservations about the too-easy availability of kabbalistic material.[68]

It was probably at this time that David added the kabbalistic books to his library, as he informs us in speaking of it that "among them will be found some new kinds of books which have been hidden away for some years."[69] In his essay on amulets he quotes from the *Sefer Yezirah* and adds: "The effectiveness of amulets becomes much better understood by anyone who has had the privilege of perusing the book *Shi'ur Koma* or the *Prayer of Nehuniah ben haKaneh,* or the *Prayer of Rav Hammuna Sava* or the book of the *Seventy-Two Names of Metatron* which are currently to be found in my library."[70]

That his possession and dissemination of such books caused him problems in Cracow later may certainly be deemed a possibility. Clearly he may well have acquired the bulk of his library in this period. He indicates that he used money earned from writing amulets to buy books, and wrote hundreds in Posen and Ferrara, and other places. He collected them, he tells us, "from the four corners of the world" and spent a good deal of money on them.[71]

His must be considered an unusually large library for its time. We can judge this by an inventory of the libraries of the Jews of Mantua made by the Inquisition in 1595.[72] Some 20,000 books, belonging to approximately 500 owners (individuals and synagogues), were examined by the Inquisition, and among them we find only six libraries of 400 books or more, and only one with more than 1,000 volumes. Some twenty-five individuals possessed between 100 and 200 books. In one library, that of Abraham Provinziali, we find that six of the almost 600 volumes had been printed in Cracow.

In Ferrara David's credentials as a rabbi were tested by the resident rabbi of the community, Jacob Reiner, in 1557. Responding to this request, David wrote a responsum on a question concerning the validity of a marriage between two Marranos, who had married in the presence of two Jewish witnesses and affirmed their intention to return to Judaism.[73] It is interesting to note that this effort, described in *Shir HaMa'alot l'David* (1571), appeared in the responsa of Moses Isserles without identification.[74] David must have sent it to his mentor, and it was among the sage's responsa when they were published for the first time sixty-eight years after his death.

Rabbi Jacob Reiner was involved in the setting up of a "studium" in Ferrara. He was an Ashkenazic rabbi who came to Italy, served as rabbi of the Ashkenazic yeshiva in Mantua, spent some time in Verona, and came to Ferrara, where he was appointed head of the yeshiva. This yeshiva was established with the blessing of Duke Ercole II, who exempted those enrolled in it from all tolls, observing: "This can only prove to be the honor and advantage to be derived from it by many Jewish and non-Jewish students, both natives and foreigners."[75] This he did at the request of Solomon Rivo, and David must have been one of the scholars who benefited from it. Indeed, it likely provided him with the idea of setting up a similar "studium" when he returned to Cracow.[76]

Just how long he remained in Italy, and precisely when he returned to Cracow, where he became the town *darshan,* is unclear. He was certainly in Cracow by 1567, for in that year he wrote a responsum for one Elijah Galatz, who wished to know whether his wife could be compelled to testify personally in a litigation, or whether he might testify on her behalf.[77]

The following year David was in a position to return a favor extended him by his friends, the Bordolani. They had been involved in a bitter controversy with the D'Ato family, in which the Sephardic rabbis of the area supported the latter, and the Ashkenazic rabbis, the former. The whole case caused quite a stir, and it is recorded in detail in two responsa by Rabbi Isaac di Lattes[78] and in a Bet Din transcript of the case.[79] Mutual bans were traded, the D'Atos took the Bordolani to a secular court, and Moses Bordolano came to Cracow to seek support from the rabbis of that community.

Bordolano brought with him bans of excommunication directed against Rabbi Moses di Rossi (father of the historian Azariah di Rossi), who had permitted the D'Atos to take the case to a gentile court. David wrote: "I am exceedingly amazed at you, Moses di Rossi, for pursuing, assaulting like a wild beast, and spreading venom in the midst of God's holy people, leading them to ignore the injunctions of the great scholars of the world,"[80] and added his ban to the list of excommunications.

The years of his return coincided with the struggle successfully concluded to reintroduce the printing of Hebrew books to Cracow. David was clearly involved in the process, perhaps even from the time of his Italian sojourn. The first Hebrew printing press had been introduced as early as 1534 by the brothers Helitz, who began publishing Hebrew books for the burgeoning academies and general population.[81] Three years later they converted to Christianity, but they continued to print and import Hebrew books. Perhaps as an outcome of the spread of the Reformation and the vigorous counterattack of the Catholic Church, Jews were held responsible for the backsliding and defections, and leading Jews were held responsible, arrested, and put under extreme pressure. It may be that under such pressure the Ḥelitz brothers submitted to baptism. For whatever reason, they came under the protection of the Church and Bishop Gamrat in their subsequent publishing problems.[82]

As could well be expected, Jews refused to buy the Ḥelitz books. Could prayer books, Bibles, and Talmud folios be purchased from such a source? To protect their interests, the Ḥelitz brothers turned their stock over to a Christian bookseller, who offered them a very low price, but his offer was rejected. Facing bankruptcy, the publishers begged the king (Sigismund Augustus II) to force the community to pay. A commission was set up to inventory the books—they totaled 3,350, and the further importation of Hebrew books was prohibited until the bill was paid.[83] Cracow turned to the neighboring community of Posen for help, and together the money was raised, the books purchased and hidden away, and the importation of Hebrew books from Italy and Bohemia proceeded.

Cracow's academies continued to grow; books had to be imported, and they were expensive. We have already noted the existence of the relationship between Italy and Poland. Licenses to import Hebrew books were given and renewed by the king. In 1566, King Sigismund Augustus II gave permission to Baruch Halevi to import Hebrew books for a period of four years.[84] But clearly it would be more feasible economically if a printing press were in place in Cracow.

Isaac of Prosstitz, with whom David became associated, set out to fill this need. He had worked in the printing house of Giovanni Grypho in Venice, and had purchased his type fonts and equipment when he went out of business.[85] This done, he moved to Cracow. It is quite possible that David had contact with him in Venice, for he wrote a letter of recommendation in Venice for a kinsman of the Bordolano family on his way to study in Cremona.[86]

In any event, Isaac began his work in Cracow, when David was already there, with the printing of an edition of the *Ḥamesh Megillot Rabbah* with a commentary by Naftali Herẓ ben Menaḥem. The Church intervened to stop the publication, the king ordered the books seized and examined, and it appeared for a little while as if the Prosstitz effort would be aborted. Isaac vigorously carried on the battle for his rights, supported by the community leaders, and the book finally saw the light of day in the summer of that year. It was a red-letter day in the life of the community, and R. David was called upon to write a dedicatory poem. He appears to have filled the role of Cracow's poet laureate as well as *darshan*. Thus it transpires that on the last page of the very first Hebrew book to come off the presses in Cracow after the Ḥelitz debacle some thirty years earlier, we read the following: "When the poet David Darshan of Cracow beheld the beauty of the piety of the sage Rabbi Herẓ, interpreting the difficult words of the *Five Megillot Rabbah,* and when he beheld the flawless beauty of the printed edition, he spontaneously burst into song with a simple quatrain."[87] In a way it was a reaction, Cracow-style, reminiscent of the enthusiasm of John Keats's "On Looking into Chapman's Homer." David did not allow modesty to get in his way, and in the laudatory poem, well-written in the medieval style, with Bible quotations and puns, he inserted his own name in acrostic:

Discover a book with beautiful sayings,[88] no shame in it,[89] fruit providing[90]

Verily showing, word by word, wondrous wonders, hidden phrases,

Direction giving, who can price it—breaking shells, line by line

Dared words utter, future, past, carefully crafting myriad insights

Read words lightly in Five Megillot, saw vast depths beneath their surface

Seeking surely reputation,[91] that sage Herẓ, the best of scholars, expands horizons

Now its done, day twenty-nine, of sad month Av, creating joy, in the short count.[92]

The next book to appear from his press was Moses Isserles' *Torat haHatat* in 1570, and in the following year, in quick succession, two books in Yiddish, a folk book and a translation of a prayer book, and then David's own sampler of his works, his *Shir haMa'alot l'David,* with its rich variety of content—sermons, responsa, sample letters and poems, and biographical material.

David announced that he had brought a substantial library to the community, and hoped to establish a *midrash* (studium), where ordinary folk could come to consult books, where scholars could study, where teachers could receive instruction in educational techniques for children, and children and young people could be taught. He would be a link to yeshiva heads, transmitting questions which he himself could not handle. And he would be very careful not to become involved in community affairs in such a way as to interfere with existing authority:

"And all of this with the clear understanding that I will not have any interest in any aspect of office or honor whatsoever, either in community affairs or in rabbinical function, except those given on the occasion of a mitzvah at the time of the sermon as it will be required."[93]

Finally he appealed for financial help for his project: "And the end and core of it all is something that cannot be measured, for whoever supports this project assures himself of a secure footing in both worlds and will be granted long life and good fortune. . . . For while he goes about his business and commerce, others will be occupied in the *midrash* [study hall] with the holiness of the Torah. And because of this, everything he does will prosper and it will be granted him to see the coming of the Messiah."[94] Unfortunately no help was forthcoming, and despite the fact that he had preached and taught, written amulets, served as a healer, acted as intermediary for the yeshiva head, he had to depart for a while "until some money will turn up and I can collect enough . . . for dowry and ornament," to marry off his many daughters.[95] A much more literate but equally hapless Tevye the Dairyman indeed!

One of the projected books announced in his sampler, its introduction completed in Cracow in 1571,[96] was to be called *Maskil l'David.* This was intended as an introduction to a book which David completed a few years later in Lublin, where he went after leaving Cracow. Here he worked as editor and proofreader for a competitor of his Prosstitz employer, Kalonymos ben Mordecai Jaffe,[97] and was involved in the publishing of Isaac Duran's *Sha'arei Dura,* a popular handbook on the mitzvot before the appearance of the *Shulḥan Arukh.* This book appeared in 1574, and its title page informs us that "it was proofread with great care by that eminent sage Rabbi David Darshan." In that year he published his *K'tav Hitnaẓẓelut l'Darshanim* ("In Defense of Preachers"), which contains his introduction *Maskil l'David,* a defense of the preaching interpreter's art, and samples of interpretations of the Torah text for each Sabbath in tandem with an appropriate talmudic text, as we are informed by the title page: "He demonstrates to the student the basic principle whereby the Torah portion may be linked with the talmudic saying and the Midrash;"[98] and to serve as an especially useful tool for preachers, he informs the reader: "I have prepared four different interpretations for each Torah portion. . . . With this resource the preacher will be able to preach in the Temple Court every Sabbath for four consecutive years, something new interpreted in several ways, without being upbraided for repenting himself."[99]

David indicated on the title page that he intended to leave for the Holy Land,[100] where, presumably, it was his intention to complete the many writings which he had projected in his two printed books. From this source we learn that he did not succeed in setting up his study hall, and because there were those who derided and attacked the *darshan,*[101] he was publishing his defense now, but would expand it later. He apparently left that year, breaking off his work of editing *Sha'arei Dura.* Indeed we read at the end of the latter book: "Proofread by Rabbi David, son of the martyr Manasseh, mentioned at the beginning of the book, up to the Fifth Gate."[102]

David was headed for the Land of Israel, probably Safed, which was at this time a vital center of kabbalistic creativity, where Isaac Luria, Joseph Caro, Ḥayim Vital, and Moses Cordovero were the center of an enormously influential coterie. Whether he ever reached his destination we may never know, for there is no tangible evidence of this.

One final trace of our David that long went unnoticed crops up, embedded in a short commentary to an edition of the Talmud Yerushalmi which was printed in Cracow by the Prosstitz press in 1609. The author of the commentary, who is not identified, wrote a brief introduction in which he indicates the importance of the appearance of this version of the Talmud, which was not getting the same attention as the more widely studied Babylonian version. The second edition of this Yerushalmi appeared in Krotoschin in 1866, and here the title page reads: ". . . containing a short commentary by an unknown writer who concealed his name." A notation in the margin of the title page in the Hebrew University Library by an anonymous scholar who used the book reads: "Nevertheless he revealed his name in Nazir 54c." And here, buried in the commentary there appears the phrase: "Thus it seems to me, David Darshan."[103] On the basis of this, Professor Lieberman concluded that R. David was likely the author of the commentary. A careful comparison of R. David's style in his printed books with the style of the commentary and the short introduction seems to confirm this.

Was he then in Cracow when the book was printed? Was it a work he left behind to be published later? Or did he send it to Cracow from Safed (if he ever got there) to emphasize that the Talmud of the Land of Israel, the Yerushalmi, needed new emphasis in days of great messianic anticipation? There is as yet no answer to these questions. They continue to haunt and to intrigue us.

What we can say with certainty is that the two printed books he published, the manuscript he copied, the books he edited, the commentary he authored, and the library he owned, all reflect a man of talent and promise, who mirrored the deep range of Jewish culture and learning in his age, a crucial period in Jewish history, and a seminal age in the history of the world. He was among the significant building blocks of the rich and many-hued stream of the developing Jewish learning and Jewish society, whose mark was deeply etched in the character of Polish Jewry in a critical period of transition.

A deeper and more carefully analytical study of his works will, it is to be hoped, yield a deeper insight into this fascinating and significant period of Jewish history, and it is to be hoped that the publication of the translation of his two little books, together with their rare texts, will contribute to this process.

For they reflect a man of his time, a Jewish scholar to whom books and learning meant more than anything else. They reflect a man whose dreams were not matched by the realities he confronted, and yet who reflected an unconquerable persistence, an irrepressible curiosity, always, it seems, on the wrong side of the success syndrome.

When he completed his first printed book he wrote: "I give praise and thanks to the Most High as I come to the completion of the *Song of the Steps* and to the preeminent community of Cracow, which is outstanding in scholarship and achievement. Who can adequately describe her virtues? She is indeed entitled to the complete blessings of the patriarchs, and is truly the keystone of the Jewish world."[104] Was this an effusive darshanic exaggeration, or did he perhaps touch the nerve of truth? Not the "big guns," but the "silent souls" so well described by the poet Bialik, have been a shaping force that deserves to be studied and affirmed.

This chapter appeared as the introduction to the David Darshan book, published by Hebrew Union College Press (Cincinnati, 1985).

CHAPTER SIX

Gershom Scholem: Jewish Revolutionary of Our Time

I

Gershom Scholem, in my view, is one of the most important Jews of the twentieth century. His work on Jewish mysticism, messianism, and sectarianism constitutes one of the major achievements of the historical imagination of our time. As a scholar, he created a new discipline. As a thinker, he took an obscure, parochial subject and gave it a universal thrust. As a Jew and a Zionist, he linked scholarship with survival and historiography with historical experience. He brought Jewish mysticism out of the closet and made it part of the academic mainstream. He taught us to see how even the most exotic and bizarre, though sometimes touched with madness, could be seen as a prism through which the realities of the historic Jewish experience would be better understood.

Scholem has been a quiet revolutionary in the field of Jewish scholarship. For almost seventy years, up to his death in 1981 at

119

the age of eighty-five, he worked diligently, using the tools of German scholarship and Jewish enlightenment, to refute some of its most cherished conclusions. He touched off an entire process of reevaluating Jewish history, bringing to it a new and profound series of insights.

This was brought home to me vividly some time ago, at Northwestern University, where he had been scheduled to lecture to a small group in the religion department. I went to greet him as an old friend and to hear him. The lecture had been scheduled for a small classroom, but people kept streaming in, and the group moved from one larger room to the next, until finally more than two thousand people crammed the Alice Miller Chapel to listen to a highly technical lecture most of them really did not understand. The fact was that a predominantly non-Jewish audience, academic and lay, had attended just to be in the presence of a great spirit of our time. It was a great tribute to a scholar who used philosophy to unlock the mysteries of Jewish (and, for that matter, human) existence.

II

I met Scholem for the first time in 1938 while I was a third-year rabbinical student in New York. Few people in this hemisphere had, at that time, an inkling of what Scholem was about. He had been invited to give a series of lectures on major trends in Jewish mysticism, which was a distillation of his work since the early 1920s and represented his first entry into the English-speaking world.

How well I remember the day my professor, who had invited him, stopped me in the hall and asked if I could give a few evenings of my time to help a great scholar who was to lecture in English publicly for the first time in his life, and who was very nervous about it. Would I help him with his English pronunciation? So there I was, a callow student in the presence of this tall, awkward-looking scholar, who read to me what was to become *Major Trends in Jewish Mysticism,* and my function was to say: "No, Dr. Scholem, not 'thruff' but 'through'; no, Dr. Scholem, it's not 'roo,' it's 'rough.'" "Ach, this English," this master of philology would growl.

No more than seventy-five people heard the lectures, and only a few paid much attention to *Major Trends* when it appeared in 1941. I was hooked on the spot and remained hooked. It gave me a new insight into the dynamics of Jewish history and experience, informed the research in which I was engaged, and gave me a model and mentor to watch. A closer look at the man, his life, his work, his method, and his impact will illustrate my estimation of him.

III

Scholem was born in Berlin in 1897 into a bourgeois fourth-generation Berlin Jewish family. His father was an assimilationist, a product of almost a century of intense Jewish efforts to acculturate into German society. The four sons in this family were a paradigm of Jewish experience: two became arch-conservative German nationalists (one brother, now living in Australia, would have become a Nazi if he could, Scholem once told me), one became a Communist, and Gershom became a Zionist. These latter two must have driven their father up the wall, rejecting everything he cherished, standing for everything he abhorred. Both opposed World War I vehemently. In fact, in 1917, Gershom was thrown out of his home (and out of school, too) and put on his own.

Deep down in Scholem's consciousness was an awareness of

the optimists of previous generations, who had believed that all one needed to do was to express Judaism in Western terms, show how compatible Judaism was with Western civilization, and all would be well. The shapers of this view were Leopold Zunz and Moritz Steinschneider, among others. They and their colleagues developed *Jüdische Wissenschaft* as a technique to define and describe Jewish historical experience of the past to show that its essence was rationalistic and quite acceptable. As Steinschneider once put it, their work was designed to give Judaism a decent burial, for its life force had come to an end.

Through the work of the historian Graetz (though he was a rationalist and contemptuous of the kabbalistic mania), Scholem acquired a sense of the continuing peoplehood of Israel. On his mother's side, there was an eccentric uncle who was a Zionist. The family never celebrated Jewish holidays, but one winter he received a Christmas present from his mother—a portrait of Theodor Herzl!

In 1917 Scholem was kicked out of his home for being a Zionist and an opponent of the war. He took the latter position not so much because he was a pacifist, but because he did not think it would in any way advance the cause of Jewish interests. That was the year of the Balfour Declaration and the year he met the grandson of Moritz Steinschneider, Gustav, who was torn between Zionism and Communism. He was much like his grandfather, Scholem reflected, whose task had been to give Judaism a decent burial! Jews were still alive and struggling.

That, too, was the year Scholem moved to the kosher pension in Berlin, where young Russian Jewish students, fleeing tsarist persecution, gathered. He lived as neighbor with Zalman Rubashov (later Zalman Shazar, president of Israel), a leader of the Zionist coterie. Here, for a glorious moment in contempo-

rary Jewish history, were gathered shapers of the Zionist movement and Hebrew literature—writers and poets such as Agnon
and Bialik, and thinkers such as Shai Hurwitz. Here Scholem
made close contact with the Jews of Eastern Europe, touching
their rich vitality and depth. He gave up the idea of becoming
a mathematician and decided to come to know himself as a Jew
and discover his own culture and background. He realized that
to do this he must master Hebrew. This he did with vigor and
ferocity, and, in the process, he came to see a link between rational philosophy, Jewish apologetics, and assimilationism. It
was at that time that he became deeply aware of the substratum
of mysticism and Kabbalah in Jewish history, and understood
that perhaps it was the key to Jewish being.

Unlike other cultural leaders in Germany (for example, Buber
and Rosenzweig), Scholem, by this time, decided that he must
go to Palestine, to work at the task of restructuring Jewish life
for survival through his scholarship and historiography. This, in
fact, he did in 1923, when he became involved with the Hebrew University at the time of its founding. His first job was as
bibliographer for the library; and a year or so later, when they
were looking for a professor of kabbalistic studies, they found
they had the candidate in their own midst.

In a letter to Zalman Schocken, the great German-Jewish de-
partment-store tycoon, Scholem himself describes how he came
to Kabbalah. The letter was written in the 1950s as a birthday
tribute to that latter-day Maecenas. He wrote that he had developed a healthy skepticism about his fields of study, which were
then mathematics and epistemology, because, as he put it, he
had developed "an intuitive affirmation of mystical theses which
walked the fine line between religion and nihilism." He went
on to say that he had found in Franz Kafka the perfect expres-

sion of this fine line, which he termed "a secular statement of the Kabbalistic world feeling in a modern spirit." It was a Christian named Molitor, writing (not very scientifically) about Kabbalah, who had defined Kabbalah as the underground reality of Jewish history, and this gave Scholem the address where the secret life of Judaism seemed once to have dwelt.

This seventeenth-century writer, whom he encountered in his teens when he was already steeped in kabbalistic documents, gave him his sense of direction. He was persuaded that the greats of Jewish philosophy—Saadia, Maimonides, and Hermann Cohen (rationalists all)—were determined to demythologize Judaism. Thus, he developed systems that argued against their constructive role in the philosophy of Judaism, for, as he put it, "Here in the first books of the kabbalists, which I read with ardent ignorance, I found to my surprise a way of thinking which clearly had not yet found a home."

Now the key was at hand. What was lacking was the courage to turn that key, to "venture out into an abyss, which one day could end up in us ourselves, to break through the wall of history and penetrate the symbolic pain." As he saw it, total truth could be visible in the purest way only through the discipline of commentary, and, as he himself so poetically put it, "in the singular mirror of philological criticism." Indeed, his work has lived in this paradox, "in the hope of a true communication from the mountain.

IV

Let us see how this rationalistic, pragmatic, systematic, encyclopedic mind, this relentless scholarship machine, proceeded with the seemingly impossible task of finding a present-day, once-in-a-lifetime communication from Mount Sinai.

In 1924, when it looked as though he might be called to head the newly established chair of kabbalistic studies at the Hebrew University, Scholem set forth his program in a letter to the great national poet and chairman of the search committee, Hayim Naḥman Bialik. It was five years after he had received his Ph.D. at Munich, for having edited the kabbalistic *Book of Bahir,* a task he performed totally unaided. He had examined all available kabbalistic manuscripts, having discovered them there and in the library of Rabbi Bloch (a great Enlightenment scholar, who had the best collection of kabbalistic books and manuscripts in Germany). "How marvelous, sir," cried the ardent young scholar Scholem, "that you have been able to read and study these sources!" To which the old man replied: "*Was? Den quatsch soll ich auch nun lesen?*" ("Am I expected to read this nonsense, too?). Here he clearly saw, so far as he was concerned, what the *Jüdische Wissenschaft* was all about.

Here was the essence of his proposal:

It would be necessary to examine the vast body of kabbalistic manuscripts in the libraries of Oxford, the British Museum, Paris, Parma, Rome, Florence, New York, and Cincinnati (in addition to Munich, which he had already worked through). This material must be catalogued, dated, and made available to scholars.

He further listed a group of key books that he felt must be quickly published and made available. It was vitally necessary to date, analyze, and organize them. "At the conclusion of all this work I hope that I may accomplish what I set out to do, to find an answer to the question, What is the real importance of Kabbalah?"

For the next dozen years he did just that, quietly, unspectacularly. He was like the builder of a great edifice who had to start from scratch, with one exception: The builder who had his plans ready would then simply order the steel, bricks, plumbing, and lumber, and go to work; Scholem first had to manufacture the building materials himself—dig the ore, roll the steel, and then fabricate it. He had to organize the materials, master them, get to know their properties, and then analyze them and put them together.

V

Thus, by the time Scholem came to New York with his nine lectures in the lucid English he pronounced so badly, he had accomplished the tasks he had set forth in his letter to Bialik. The plans had been made, the diagrams perfected, and the edifice reared. What a majestic edifice it was! Now the works poured out: *Major Trends in Jewish Mysticism* in 1941, *Sabbetai Sevi* (in Hebrew, in 1957, and in English, in 1971), and a host of others.

In *Major Trends* Scholem defines and outlines the mystical process in Jewish history. There he shows that Jewish mysticism was not just a seamless, inchoate whole with neither beginning nor end, but rather a process of identifiable development.

For him, there was no such thing as mysticism in the abstract. There were mysticisms—Greek, Christian, Islamic, and Jewish. You could not, for example, call Moses or the prophets mystics because of their religious experiences. Mysticism, for him, was a definite stage in the history of religion that made its appearance under certain well-defined conditions. There are three stages in the process.

First, there is the mythical epoch. During this period the world is filled with gods encountered by man at every step. There is no room for mysticism here, for there is no abyss between man and God. Adam could not be a mystic, neither could Ulysses. One saw and dealt with the gods face to face.

The *second stage* is the creative epoch, the breakthrough of what we know as religion. The function of this breakthrough is to destroy the dream harmony, to isolate man from the dream stage of mythical and primitive consciousness. It is the beginning of man's growing up. There is now an abyss between man and God, an abyss bridged only by voice—the voice of a commanding God and the voice of man in prayer. This is the essence of biblical religion, which is consciously anti-mythological, which insists on the abyss, which sees the crossing of the abyss as heresy.

It is in this second stage that classical religion develops. Mythic forces are repressed—gnostic and mystical forces in early Rabbinic Judaism, gnostic and Greek mysticism in Christianity.

All this time, the mystical impulse runs through the developing process of classical religion like a subterranean river, always there but rarely recognized. The stage is no longer nature but the moral and religious action of man.

The religious form has reached its classical stage. It has caged the mystical impulse that is at the heart of the national existence. Now, in the *third phase,* this impulse breaks out, not to destroy the religious organism, but to give it new life by reinterpreting it in terms of the suppressed myth. The goal is not to destroy the faith but to give it new meaning and new vitality.

It is no accident that the resurgence of mysticism comes at the end of this period (in the twelfth century) in Provence and Spain, the birthplace of the renewed force of both Christian and Jewish mysticism. Stage three marks the romantic period of religion, when mysticism enters. This period does not deny the abyss; it recognizes it, but tries to bridge it. As Scholem writes: "It strives to bring back the old unity which religion has destroyed, but on a new plane, where the world of mythology and that of revelation meet in the soul of man." In stage three, the process of the previous stage is still at work and the interaction can be either deepening or explosive. The central difference between Jewish mysticism and its Christian and Islamic counterparts is that it draws a line. The mystic must not identify himself with the other side of the abyss; he may only experience it. For the Christian mystic there is oneness in Christ, and for the Sufi mystic identification with Allah. To the extent that this happened in the history of Jewish mysticism, there lay the path to heresy.

Having mastered, analyzed, and dated the materials; having developed a scientific understanding of their complicated language and symbolism; having developed a broad theory against which this understanding could be tested and understood, Scholem could now take the phenomenon (which was known but not fully understood) and give it coherence and meaning.

We always knew there were mystics and mysticism. The Talmud gingerly lifts the curtain to show us sages involved in the esoteric search: Yoḥanan ben Zakkai, studying the secrets of Creation with his disciple Elazar ben Arakh; Shimon bar Yoḥai, hiding in the cave; Akiba and three colleagues entering Paradise for the ultimate glimpse, and he alone emerging unscathed. In geonic times we knew of the *Book of Creation,* with its theories of the mystical creative powers of the Hebrew letters and the spheres. The *Midrash Bahir* seemed to contain new and revolutionary insights. In the sixteenth century, Shabbetai Ẓevi was proclaiming the coming of the Messiah. The popular preachers occasionally alluded to mystics; the intellectual leaders cautioned against them. Maimonides could write disapprovingly in his commentary to the Mishnah: "Too frequently *darshanim* are wont to communicate to the crowd what they do not really understand, and one wishes they would remain silent." And the great Polish sage of the sixteenth century, Moses Isserles, could lament: "Many of the crowd jump into the study of the Kabbalah . . . and ordinary householders who do not know their right hand from the left hasten to its study." Mysticism was there—suspected, kept at arm's length—and when it had to be dealt with in rational circles, was shoved under the rug or described as meaningless drivel.

Scholem's hybridization of the phases of mysticism has given coherence and intelligibility to the movement. He draws a historical line from the early gnostics, who tried to understand the mysteries of the divine, to the systematic entry of these mysteries into Judaism in the late biblical period and early talmudic period (from perhaps the first pre-Christian century to the ninth or tenth century). This period he calls *heikhalot* mysticism, the mysticism of the palaces. The mystics during this time were involved with a personal quest of experience, with the desire to attain the supreme experience of the divine. This process entailed preparing oneself for that ultimate experience through the repetition of sacred texts, through personal discipline, and through a kind of self-induced trance.

With the Spanish mystics (twelfth century) the line took a turn. This was a period of flowering philosophic thought, and the mystics, though opposing the philosophers, developed a philosophical method of dealing with mysticism—a theosophic quest, if you will. The culmination of this quest was that great mystical commentary called the *Zohar* and the development of the theories of the *sefirot* as a way of apprehending God.

The destruction of Spanish Jewry with the expulsion in 1492 sent shock waves through the Jewish world. The mystics regrouped in Safed and gave their kabbalistic thinking a new turn.

With Lurianic Kabbalah, sired by Isaac Luria and a group of his brilliant disciples in the sixteenth century, the theosophic approach, whose goal was to shape the geography of the inner workings of the godhead, took a crucial turn. Mysticism no longer dealt just with the individual's relation to God; the whole Jewish people and its destiny were involved, and exile and redemption became the key.

The inner biography of the divine was seen in terms of exile and redemption: first was the original wholeness, next the cataclysmic breaking of the vessels whose fragments imprisoned the divine in the shell of the shattered debris, then the yearning for repair (*tikkun*), and finally the ultimate achievement of a renewed unity within God. The analogue of this was the experience of the Jewish people, for it captured the yearnings for redemption and return. The goal, of course, was messianism!

The idea that each Jew had a role in this repair (*tikkun*) caught fire. The *Shulḥan Arukh*—the code of Jewish laws and mitzvot—appeared at this time. This code gave the Jew the tools for his redemption through mitzvot. From it emerged the messianic movement of Shabbetai Ẓevi, with its explosive impact, which Scholem describes and analyzes in his second masterpiece, *Sabbetai Sevi: The Mystical Messiah*.

The messianic movements cross the horizons of Jewish history like comets, but end in disaster. Hasidism enters in the eighteenth century to pick up the pieces—to defuse the messianic impact and turn the fervor inward.

The Lurianic Kabbalah, with its messianic dream and its pressure to break out of the restraints of Rabbinic Judaism, which so taught the people to make peace with diaspora and exile, had within it an irrational thrust, which, at its deepest intensity, developed an anarchic force that tended to break out from previous restraints.

It is appropriate, at this point, to say a word about Scholem's second masterpiece, *Sabbetai Sevi: The Mystical Messiah*.

VI

We have already touched on Scholem's early conclusion that the major Jewish historians of the nineteenth century, worshiping at the altar of rationalism alone and uncomfortable with the hidden forces behind this process, refused to face the fact that the forces of mysticism and messianism play a significant role in Jewish history.

This is the main thrust of his monumental work on Shabbetai Zevi. It illuminates, perhaps, the grandest of all themes of Jewish history: the survival and redemption of the Jewish people. It is a book written not to apologize or condemn but to elucidate all aspects of this complex phenomenon. For here was a movement "that shook the House of Israel to its very foundations" and revealed not only the vitality of the Jewish people but also the dangerous shoals of the messianic idea. Scholem's perceptive statement that "Jewish historiography has generally chosen to ignore the fact that the Jewish people have paid a very high price for the messianic idea" is worth pondering. It is echoed by Israel Kolat's sober analysis of the Yom Kippur War in 1974 (in the Israeli quarterly *Molad*). He wrote that the whole concept of the Zionist movement, with its goal of a secure home for the Jewish people in a hostile world, becomes a terrifying reality when the state that came into being as a haven for future generations is devouring its present generation in constant wars.

Sabbetai Sevi is a portrait of an age. Like an instant replay, the action of several years in the mid-seventeenth century is frozen, and an entire panorama of events, revealing the throbbing heart of Jewish history, lies exposed before us for a minute examination.

The genius of Scholem is both macrocosmic and microscopic. He grasps vast expanses with an amazing mastery of the widest variety of sources, yet he has the capacity of squeezing the last drop from the dried-up lemon of some recondite source. He can perceive psychological nuances, read between the lines opaque evasiveness, pursue his quarry with relentless determination, and leave the reader with a sense of illumination and insight.

Shabbetai Zevi, that strange, charismatic sweet singer of Jewish liturgy and Spanish love songs, part manic-depressive, part paranoid, who comes to the kabbalist Nathan of Gaza seeking the "root of his soul" (as a modern does to his psychiatrist), is confirmed by this so-called prophet in his messianic claims. As a result of this meeting of a would-be messiah and his diagnostician apostle, a movement sweeps the Jewish world, encompassing rich and poor, Western and Oriental, sophisticate and *naïf,* in its irresistible appeal.

In the late Middle Ages, it swept beyond the bounds of the Jewish world, catching the attention of the vast number millennium-minded Christians waiting for a Second Coming. (We see an echo of this in the enthusiastic fundamentalist support for Israel today.) Diplomatic observers in Constantinople, Christian clergymen, a Yiddish-writing bookkeeper in Poland, and even the English diarist Samuel Pepys reacted to the event. Pepys's diary records this entry for February 19, 1666:

> I am told for certain, what I have heard once or twice already, of a Jew in town, that in the name of the rest do offer to give any man £10 to be paid £100 [i.e., *ten to one odds!*] if a certain person now at Smyrna be within these two years owned by all the princes of the East, particularly the Grand Signor, as the King of the world, in the

same manner we do the King of England here, and that this man is the true Messiah. . . . certainly this year of 1666 will be a year of great action; but what the consequences will be, God knows.

For a moment in history it seemed that the messianic impulse was poised to overthrow the existing powers, restoring hegemony to the House of Israel after sixteen hundred years. Scholem captures the flavor of the moment, helps us savor it, introduces us to the characters in the drama, and helps us to understand them and penetrate deeply into the forces that shaped them. Here, perhaps as nowhere else, we come to see how the development of mystical thought through Lurianic Kabbalah and the aftermath of the trauma of the expulsion from Spain come together in a messianic explosion. One cannot help but reflect, as one examines this fact, on the traumatic impact of the Holocaust and on the messianic quality of the eruption into history of the State of Israel.

At the peak of his messianic euphoria, Shabbetai Zevi abrogated halakhah. After all, the Messiah had come and the Torah was fulfilled. He turned Tisha be-Av, a day of mourning, into a day of rejoicing. Even when his movement collapsed, the messianic and antinomian impulse continued. Scholem sees the roots of modern Enlightenment, Zionism, and Reform Judaism emerging from this force!

VII

Gershom Scholem viewed the history of Judaism and the Jewish people, not as a monolithic, rationalistic expression of its monotheistic destiny expressed in halakhah, but as essentially pluralistic, with the rational surface and the subterranean mystical stream in a constant dialectic. He saw this halakhic, rabbinic system, followed by *Jüdische Wissenschaft* and rationalistic reform, as "a well-ordered house." For him a well-ordered house was a dangerous thing, for it needed an occasional airing. Jewish mysticism was for him an "anarchic breeze" blowing through the household of Israel, shaking it up and giving it a renewed vitality. In Freudian terms, we might say that Rabbinic Judaism and rationalism were the ego of Judaism, and mysticism was its id! Scholem persisted in expressing the dialectical character of Judaism: the perennial tension and conflict between the forces of conservation and the forces of change, between reason and instinct, between Orthodoxy and mythology.

Through his revision of Jewish history he developed a new and intense view of the vitality of Jewish existence, its varieties of expression, and above all its exciting open-endedness. Very early in his career, while yet in the Zionist youth movement, he could say, "We need men who have the courage to think Jewish thoughts as their final thoughts, who have the courage of radicalism in thought or deed, to be near their people." The Jewish people, he always felt, must address the non-Jewish world with confidence in their own identity and tradition, and without cutting themselves off from the non-Jewish cultures within which they had lived for so many generations. He could say, speaking to a group of Reform rabbis in Israel in 1974, "I speak as a Jew who believes that Judaism is a living phenomenon that has not exhausted its possibilities," adding that our ears should be attuned to the new voice that seeks to be heard, a voice that "he who believes in God as I do, will find it to be an echo from Sinai."

His friend Walter Benjamin said that Scholem "brushed Jewish history against the grain." That he did, indeed, and the grating of his acerbic mind opened our eyes and ears, and brought his audience to an awareness the extent of which has rarely before been experienced.

There was, indeed, an acerbic quality to Scholem. In his seminars, when Israeli students struggled over the proper pronunciation of *Zohar* Aramaic, his withering scorn left them literally in shreds. He had little patience with sabras who did not know their language properly. For example, in *The Seventh Day,* his response to the sensitive kibbutz reaction to the Six-Day War dealt not so much with the contents as with the "barbarous style of some of the writers."

Rosenzweig once said of him: "Scholem is here for the summer, and he is, as always, unspeakably ill-behaved, but likewise, as always, brilliant." Buber said of him: "All of us have students, some of us have even created schools, but only Gershom Scholem has created a whole academic discipline." And Scholem said of himself: "I was like a street mongrel. They said of me—there is this crazy Scholem, a Jew from an assimilated family who doesn't put on tefillin and isn't very observant, but he studies Hebrew and Judaism, wants to know everything, and is consumed by Zionism."

Behind the sometimes abrasive exterior, there was the Scholem of warmth and understanding. In the very letters of rebuke, there were also the answers. In his home, in the circle of conversation on Shabbat, there was the warm, expansive, concerned friend reflecting with wry humor about his childhood, reminiscing enthusiastically about Moroccan cooking, or displaying a genuine interest in what one was doing.

Scholem is, to my way of thinking, the *homo judaicus par excellence.* It is expressed in his scholarship, in his person, in his perceptions, in his deep awareness of the intensity and meaning of Jewish being. He has shown us the way to learn it, to experience it, to understand it, to confront it, and—above all—to live it.

This essay, a revised version of a paper delivered at the Washington Hebrew Congregation, Washington, D.C., as a part of its Scholars' Series, was originally published in the Journal of Reform Judaism, *Summer 1984.*

CHAPTER SEVEN

From Prophet to Preacher

We have thus far examined Rabbinic Judaism as a revolutionary mutation that made possible the survival of Judaism and the Jewish people in wake of the destruction of their state and their dispersion. We have seen how the rabbinic–pharisaic–scribe process developed this through the idea of the Oral Law and through midrash.

We have looked at the stages of the development of the exegetical process, and at some of the central figures that shaped it. We have examined the academies as centers for this study in the training of continuing generations of sages.

We have seen how Rabbinic Judaism and early Christianity emerged from the same stream of development, each motivated by the messianic drive and a sense for covenant survival. We have seen how this process reached out to the people and won their adherence.

To conclude this phase of the survey, it may be useful to take a brief look at another important element in the survival process. This has to do with the means of communicating all these ideas and values to the people. It has to do with the *derashah,* the sermon.

The sermon is the child of midrash. It, too, was a Jewish invention. It was the means of taking the text and bringing it to the people.

Thus we can say that the sermon, as spoken word based on sacred text, and directed toward the education of the people, grows out of the same rabbinic process, and it grows out of it in a very special way.

In a way, it can be said that the sermon and the spoken word are at the very source and origins of the Jewish experience. Even God began His intervention in the universe with the spoken word. When God said, "Let there he light," it can be said that we have the first sermon with instant result.

To be sure, historians of the Jewish sermon qua sermon situate the earliest sermons in the tannaitic period, and find at least one complete sermon, as such, so recorded. It is a sermon by Rabbi Eleazar ben Azariah, found in Ḥagigah 3a in the Babylonian Talmud.

However, it is possible to suggest that Abraham, the first Jew, began his career with the spoken word. To be sure, the inference comes from an exegetical interpretation of the text in a way that some scholars would never accept. It is my feeling that the rabbinic interpreters of Scripture had such a feel for what really went on that their comments have a dependability on which we can count. For the most part they had the right "feel" for the context, and very often it is very useful to turn to them.

Nevertheless, when we are informed that after accepting God's command to leave his home and his native land, and to go to a land that God would show him, the text records that Abraham (then Abram) took with him his wife Sarah (then Sarai), his flocks, and "the souls which he had gotten in Haran."

That last phrase cries out for interpretation. What could it possibly mean? The sages interpreted it to mean the converts he had made to the One God he had newly discovered. And how did he convert them? By talking to them, of course! By preaching to them! Hence Abraham must have been the first *darshan*!

So the sages see Abraham as the first preacher. Then how about Moses? What is the Torah that Moses receives at Sinai if not one great "Sermon on the Mount"? What is it if not a roaring, fiery sermon that sets the Jewish people on its course of destiny? Moses, in this sense, is the *darshan* par excellence. This is apparent at the beginning of his career at Mount Sinai. It is apparent throughout his career. It is especially apparent at the end of his career in those two masterful sermons in the Book of Deuteronomy written in such limpid prose and soaring poetry; I refer, of course, to his great sermon that encompasses the whole book, and that sermon-poem *Ha'azinu* at the conclusion, where he calls heaven and earth to witness, as he outlines to his people, for the last time, their story, their destiny, and their covenant obligation.

Of this poem, an early midrash says: "Great is Song, for it contains the present, the past, and the future; things of this world and things of the world to come."[1] What we deal with here, of course, is prophetic speech. Its inspiration comes directly from God, and the prophet speaks the word to the people. It is direct speech. It is not text-centered and text-oriented. The prophet does not prepare his text. He is the human vessel, divinely chosen, to project God's message to the people. It is the Mount Sinai syndrome continued throughout the period of the First Commonwealth.

As we speak of prophecy in relation to the development of preaching and of the sermon, it is well to remember the root meaning of the Hebrew word for "prophet." The root meaning

of the word *navi* is "spokesman." Moses, as we know, was a
stammerer, and when he raised this objection with God with
respect to his role, his brother Aaron was assigned to be his
spokesman, and the term used is *navi*. When we come to the
meturgeman, the first actual preacher, a little later, we will see its
first echo in Aaron.

That, indeed, is how Rashi and Ibn Ezra describe him. The
midrash to this Exodus passage tells us that Moses and Aaron
would go among the people in Egypt, teaching, instructing, and
inspiring them. In fact, we are told that "they had scrolls from
which they entertained the people, in order to persuade them
that God would redeem them."[2] You may shrug your shoulders
at this imaginative leap into the future, but the darshanic link is
clear.

The power of the spoken word in this sense emerges clearly
throughout the Bible. A few examples will suffice. When Samuel, the seer-prophet, comes upon the scene to lead the people,
it is because "the word of God was rare in those days" (1 Sam.
3:1). It had dried up and disappeared, and now it was restored.

And when Solomon, the wisest man of his time, expounded
his wisdom, and it was finally brought together in a book, that
was called Kohelet. The name *Kohelet* means "preacher." It
comes from the word *kahal,* which means "community." *Kohelet* really means "communal communicator." Let us take a
glance at a pertinent passage from Midrash Kohelet: "All the
people would gather together in the presence of Solomon to listen to the words of wisdom which God had placed in his heart.
That is why he was called Kohelet, because his words were spoken before the community (*kahal*)."[3]

King David could also be seen as preacher, communicating
with the harp through his psalms. I can just see the modern

folksinger with a guitar, speaking to the soul of the people through folk songs, speaking of their hopes, fears, and aspirations. All the ingredients for the sermon-*derashah*-folk communication are there.

We return, however, to the prophet and prophetic speech, for that is the central factor in the process of development. Prophetic speech provided the core and kernel, which the various forms of *derashah* presented. For the words of the prophets were words of insight. They were words of warning, of denunciation, of consolation. By and large the prophet is at odds with the people because he tells them what they do not wish to hear.

Who can forget Isaiah's denunciation of the selfishness and insensitivity of the people who followed their pleasures and forgot God's directions? Who can forget the intensity and power of Jeremiah's Temple sermon, which ends with the traumatic prediction of the destruction of the Temple where he was speaking?

Who can forget the fight for social justice of Amos and his cry: "Assuredly, because you impose a tax on the poor and exact from him a levy of grain, you have built houses of hewn stone, but you shall not live in them; you have planted delightful vineyards, but you shall not drink their wine" (Amos 5:11)?

Who can forget Micah's prescription for decent conduct, his "do justly, love mercy, and walk humbly with thy God" (Micah 6:8)? Who can forget Deutero-Isaiah's words of consolation, when, after the destruction and his pain, he could bind the wounds with his "*Naḥamu, naḥamu 'ammi,* comfort ye, comfort ye, My people" (Isa. 40:1)?

And who can forget those last words of Malachi, that Malachi who may be one with Ezra,[4] bridge from prophet to rabbinic-pharisaic sage: "Remember ye the law of Moses My servant, which I commanded to him in Horeb for all Israel, with the statutes and judgments" (Mal. 3:22)?

Prophecy ceases, but God can henceforth speak to the people through Torah. The task of finding what God's message is and communicating it to the people becomes the task of the sages. They train other sages by teaching them how to exegete and communicate love of Torah and what it teaches, and how one must react when it is tested; their purpose is to teach all the people through *derashah* and sermon.

The words of Malachi mark a shift in the nature of the communication of God's way to the people. Up to now it has been through prophets, directly inspired by God. The prophets did not speak out of texts. They communicated what God commanded them to say. From Jeremiah we learn how painful this could be: "When Your words were offered, I devoured them; Your word brought me delight and joy. . . . Why must my pain be endless, my wound incurable?" (Jer. 16–18).

But painful or not, that is the way it was. With the destruction of the First Commonwealth, the sacking of the Temple, and the exile of the people, something changed and changed drastically.

For this catastrophe marked the end of many things. But most of all, it marked the end of prophecy. This reality is preserved in the talmudic dictum: "When the Temple was destroyed prophecy ceased."[5] The Children of Israel had heard from God directly at Sinai, and for the next six hundred years the Word of God comes to them from the prophets. But now, with the destruction and the end of prophecy, they were another step removed. Henceforth the Divine Will would be mediated through the sacred texts, brought together and prepared for them by the sages, and mediated by the sages through the process of midrash.

Since ultimately the Jewish people were to be God's witness to the world, and the bearers of the covenant promise and heritage, the people needed to know, the people needed to be taught.

It is Ezra, and if we are to believe the Targum's comment, Malachi-become-Ezra, or prophet transformed into scribe/sage/Pharisee, who makes the crucial change. The Torah, hitherto in possession of the priests, and read infrequently to the people, is now to become part of their regular discipline. It is to be read to them regularly and interpreted to them. It is to be introduced into the liturgy.

The Babylonian Talmud records ten innovations credited to Ezra, and the first two, and clearly in their eyes the most important, have to do with this. Thus we read in Baba Kama 82a:

"The following ten enactments were ordained by Ezra: that the Torah be read publicly in the Minḥah [afternoon[service on the Sabbath; that the Torah be read [publicly] on Mondays and Thursdays; that courts be held on Mondays and Thursdays . . ."

Every Sabbath a portion from the Pentateuch is to be read, and the same portion is to be read on Mondays and Thursdays at morning prayers. And why Mondays and Thursdays? Because that was when people came to the market, so before they gathered to earn their daily bread, the Torah was read and interpreted, and the courts were to be in session.

Consider the account of this innovation as we read it in the Book of Nehemiah (8:4ff.):

And Ezra the Scribe stood upon a pulpit of wood, which they had made for the purpose; and beside them stood Mattithiah and Shema and Anaiah and Uriah and Hilkiah and Maaseiah on his right hand, and on his left hand Pedaiah and Mishael and Malchiah and

Hashum and Hashbadana, Zechariah and Meshullam. . . . And the Levites caused the people to understand the law; and the people stood in their place. So they *read in the book of the law distinctly, and gave the sense, and caused them to understand the reading.*

Here, with the reference to those "who read in the book of the law distinctly and gave the sense, and caused them to understand the reading," we have the first clue to the origins of the *darshan.*

Sometime thereafter we become aware of the structure of the *meturgeman. Meturgeman* is an Aramaic word that means "one who translates," but the "one who translates" became also the "one who interprets."

The fact that the earliest term for this craft is Aramaic and not Hebrew is very significant. Recall the destruction of the First Temple and the letter of Jeremiah to the exiles. Recall that the Babylonian community persisted and grew, always out of reach of the Roman expansion. Recall how after the destruction of the Second Commonwealth, it was Rabbinic Judaism of the long-range messianic type that moved first to Yavneh, then to the Galilee, and finally back to the Parthian Empire, out of the reach of Rome.

The Judaism that developed thus developed among Jews whose language was no longer Hebrew. Their language was Aramaic, the lingua franca of the Middle East. By the second century, even the Galilee had been Aramaicized. It was Jews from Babylonia who returned with Ezra and Nehemiah to build the Second Temple. It is doubtful that most of them by this time knew Hebrew well.

The changeover probably began with the Assyrian destruction of the Northern Kingdom, Israel, and the siege of Jerusalem, which was miraculously terminated because of a plague among the Assyrian forces. However, at the height of the siege—and a bitter siege it was, reminiscent of the later Roman siege—the Assyrian general Rab Shakeh called for surrender as he parlayed with the leaders

Here is how it is recorded:

> Then said Eliakim, the son of Hilkiah, and Shebna, and Joab unto Rab Shakeh: "Speak, I pray thee, to thy servants in the Aramean language; for we understand it; and speak not with us in the Jews' language, in the ears of the people that are on the wall." . . . [Despite this plea] Rab Shakeh stood and cried with a loud voice in the Jews' language, and spoke, saying . . .
>
> (2 Kings 18:36f.)

Language process changes do not occur overnight. Within a space of perhaps three centuries from the Assyrian invasion to the years following the confrontation with Babylonia and the destruction of Jerusalem, the change has taken place, and Aramaic becomes the language of a majority of the people. And according to tradition, Rab Shakeh, who spoke for the Assyrians, was a convert from Judaism.

Evidence of this Aramaicization is to be found in the books of Ezra and Nehemiah, as well as in the Book of Daniel, where significant portions are in Aramaic. The Kaddish prayer itself, used at the conclusion of a period of study, and in the Hebrew liturgy acting as a division between the sections of the service, and serving as a prayer for the dead, was in Aramaic.

So it becomes clear that the public reading of the Torah meant translation from Hebrew by the *meturgeman*. This was his principal role as it developed in Babylonia. The Torah would first be read in Hebrew and then translated into Aramaic. These

Aramaic translations have persisted as the Targum, and to this day are printed side by side with the Hebrew in rabbinic texts of the Bible. In fact, the custom persisted, long after Aramaic ceased to be the current language of Jews, to read the weekly portion of the Torah at home once in Hebrew and twice in Aramaic.

Although there are no collections of early sermons from this period, a careful reading illustrates that the Targumim were not simply direct translations of the texts. They were expansions and amplification, such as a later preacher or *darshan* would do. They are, indeed, an early echo of the preaching process.

Let us examine a few passages to see exactly how this took place.

In the second version of the creation story in Genesis, we read: "And the Lord formed man of the dust of the ground, and breathed into his nostrils the breath of life; and Adam became a living creature" (Gen. 2:7). The Targum to the last phrase is more than just a translation. It reads: "and it became in Adam the spirit of uttering speech." The *meturgeman* is not simply translating *nefesh ḥayah,* he is exegeting it. He is suggesting that the power of speech was the unique quality of Adam, as, by implication, the power of speech through *derashah* was a unique quality for the Jewish people in the spread of Torah.

Then we come to the story of the Garden of Eden and the expulsion of Adam and Eve because of the temptation of the serpent. Adam is told that because of this sin he will henceforth earn his bread by the sweat of his brow. Eve is informed that she will bear children in pain. And to the serpent God says: "And I will put enmity between thee and the woman, and between thy seed and her seed; it shall bruise thy head, and thou shalt bruise his heel" (Gen. 3:15). The Targum to the last phrase is not simply a translation of "it shall bruise thy head, and thou shalt bruise his heel" but an elaboration, which again has the germ of a homily, if not given in full, then at least clearly suggested: "He [mankind] will remind you of what you did to him in the past, and you will preserve your hatred for him into the future." From the beginning the serpent–human relationship had a deep and enduring psychological impact.

When Adam and Eve sinned, God had a twinge of regret for having created them. After all, He had, according to one midrash, been warned against this by a group of His angels, but He had ignored the advice. In any event we read: "And God repented that He had made man on earth and it grieved him at His heart" (Gen. 6:6). The translation to this comes out as: "He determined upon breaking their power according to His will." Quite a change, is it not? Not man's downfall, but his defeat by God through his loss of power is central. We almost hear an echo of the Prometheus myth!

Another instance deals with the moment at Mount Sinai after the people have heard the Ten Commandments proclaimed, and have cried out with one voice: "All the words which the Lord hath said, we will do" (Exod. 24:7). After which Moses, Aaron, Nadab, and Abihu go up to the mountain for a revelation of the divine, and the heavens are opened in all their radiant glory for the people to see. The people are included in this experience: "And upon the nobles of the Children of Israel He laid not his hand; also they saw God, and they did eat and drink" (Exodus 24:11). This passage troubled the *meturgeman*. The image of feasting at such a moment, an act of total self-indulgence, was not to his liking. Hence his translation reads: "They beheld God's glory and gladly offered sacrifices which were received with favor *as though they had eaten and drunk.*"

Furthermore, we find on some occasions that the variants of translation in the Targum are clearly linked to a talmudic tradition, which had by this time developed. For example, in the legal code that follows the proclamation of the Ten Commandments in Exodus, where the damages for injury are recorded, we read: "If he then gets up and walks outdoors upon his staff, the assailant shall go unpunished, except that he must pay for his idleness and for his cure" (Exod. 21:19). The Targum reads: "he shall pay him for the hire of a physician," which is exactly the formula we find in the Talmud. Similarly, in Deuteronomy, where we are told that the Levites shall have equal portions to eat except for that which is sold according to their patrimony (Deut. 18:8), the Targum reads: "They shall have equal portions to eat except for that which accrues to them from their tour of duty, for thus their fathers have decreed." What is vague in the Torah text comes out clearly as their daily wage, and it is thus specified in the Talmud (Sukkah 56a).

Here then are glimpses of how the *meturgeman* functioned, and what he did by way of not only interpreting but expounding the Torah. We have to dig for the evidence and ferret it out, but when it is put together, the portrait begins to emerge.

We watch the role of *meturgeman* grow and expand as the process of rabbinic exegesis develops and the Talmud emerges. There was a two-level process of communication. The sage taught his students in smaller groups, but as these grew in size, and because the sages were not always good speakers, they required someone who could do this for them.

This role was known as *meturgeman* or *amora*. The commentator Rashi, who in the eleventh century in the Rhineland wrote the classic commentary of the Talmud, making its study possible in the West, found it necessary to describe the role as follows: "*Amora*—the translator who stands at the side of the preaching sage while the latter quietly whispers to him in Hebrew what he wishes to say, while the former translates it into the language the people understand."[6] In another source we learn that Rav Huna had thirteen *meturgemanim,* so large were his classes.[7] They were scattered throughout the audience, and "they listened to what he said and repeated it to the assembly on either side, and from the front and rear of the audience, positioning themselves in every section of the crowd."

It has been suggested that one of the causes for Elisha ben Abuya's lapse into heresy was that he saw the martyrdom of the greatest preacher of his time, Huzpit the *Meturgeman,* whose tongue he saw devoured by dogs. That such eloquence could come to such an end was more than he could bear.

It was said of Huzpit that he studied the Book of Leviticus 170 times and was compared in brilliance to Jonathan ben Uzziel, who was one of Yoḥanan ben Zakkai's most brilliant disciples. When he spoke, "his mouth uttered pearls."

How would a lecture be stopped? If it was deemed improper it was stopped with the command: "Remove the *meturgeman!*" In our own time we would say: "Turn off the public address system!" For example, it was related that one time when Rabban Gamliel was publicly insulting Rabbi Joshua ben Hananiah, the sages put an end to it by ordering Huzpit the *Meturgeman* to halt!

We find here and there in the Talmud the names of the *meturgemanim* to various scholars. Judah the Prince, the man who finally edited the Mishnah (ca. 200), had a *meturgeman* whose name was Abba Yudan.[8] Rav, his son-in-law, who with Samuel moved the academies to Babylonia, was the *meturgeman* for his uncle Ḥiyya and for the great sage Shila.[9] We are in-

formed that he had special talent as a popular *darshan* and a very
attractive voice, and that he often acted as cantor.[10] Judah bar
Naḥmani was *meturgeman* for Simeon ben Lakish (Ḥagigah 15a),
Bar Yehudah was *meturgeman* for Abbahu,[11] and Rabbi Pedat
was *meturgeman* for Yissa.

The mere citation of these names and references shows the
wide prevalence of the *darshan/meturgeman* role. One need only
look into the Code of Maimonides, in which the whole corpus
of talmudic exegesis and development is fixed and codified as
Judaism develops in the Middle Ages to the modern era, to see
how this role emerges as a fixed institution in the process of
teaching and continuing Judaism.

In the section dealing with the laws surrounding the study of
Torah, the entire gamut of this process that is at the heart of Judaism is explored in direct and pithy statements as to what is required.

Dealing with such questions as how a teacher must teach,
how the teacher must relate to his students, and how students
must relate to their master, whether one sits or stands when a
class is in session, whether the teacher stands and the class sits,
or vice versa, who respects whom and how, the grounds for ex-
communicating a teacher and a student, when a busy person
must study, we suddenly encounter the following:

> If he [the sage] was teaching through a *meturgeman,* the [*meturgeman*]
> between him and his students, the sage speaks to the *meturgeman* and
> the *meturgeman* speaks to all the students. When they [the students]
> ask a question of the *meturgeman,* he asks the sage and the sage gives
> the answer to the *meturgeman,* and the *meturgeman* gives the answer
> to the students . . .[12]

If you think this is a strange process, let me hasten to assure you that it isn't. I cannot help, at this juncture, but recall my visit to Cracow in 1982. My book on David Darshan of Cracow was about to appear, and that year, the dean of the Pontifical Academy of Theology in Cracow, while visiting the Catholic Theological Union in Chicago, had heard about it. When he learned that I would be teaching in Jerusalem that fall, he thought it would be a good idea if I would stop in Cracow to lecture about David Darshan in his hometown!

I thought it would be a good idea too—in fact, a great idea. The only problem was that I couldn't speak Polish and the students knew no English. For my host it was no problem. He offered to act as *meturgeman,* though he didn't know the term. And he was so good and so swift in his translation that immediate rapport with the students was achieved. They even laughed at my bad jokes!

I would speak a few sentences, and he would translate them. And the questions—there were many, intense, probing, from students, some of whom were Solidarity activists who had just been freed from prison; they were asked in Polish, translated to English, answered in English, and translated back into Polish. Take my word for it, it worked, and I can assure you that it worked as well, if not better, in the process developed by Ezra and continued through the generations.

What Maimonides was here describing was clearly something institutionalized and part of the learning process. What is more, there was a whole series of mutual obligations and a whole ethic of relationship. See how he continues:

> The sage may not speak louder than the *meturgeman,* nor shall the *meturgeman* speak louder than the sage when he asks a question of the sage. The *meturgeman* may neither subtract from nor add to what

the sage has said, nor may he change anything unless he happens to be the sage's father or teacher.[13]

What we see is a carefully balanced and orchestrated relationship designed to respect the status of each. One perceptive commentator raised the question, and rightly so, that if the class was large, the *meturgeman* would have to speak louder than he spoke to the sage. And the answer comes through in the affirmative. But the mutual respect is what is really important.

The commentator invokes God to make his point, and God, in this connection, is given the role of *meturgeman*! Remember how at the beginning of this discussion I suggested that God was the first preacher?

How does the commentator make the deduction? By describing the moment at Sinai when God and Moses spoke to each other. He quotes the account from Exodus: "And the voice of the horn waxed louder and louder, Moses spoke, and God answered him by a voice" (Exod. 19:19). The question is: With what kind of voice? Being God's, was it louder and more powerful, as clearly it had to be? No, came the answer. God responded to Moses in exactly the same level of voice with which Moses spoke, just as any good *meturgeman* was required to do![14]

Thus has the road from exegete to preacher, from midrash to *darshan,* been traversed. Rabbinic Judaism and early Christianity came out of the same source, developed in the creative years of the Second Commonwealth. They emerged as reactions to the cataclysmic end of that commonwealth. They shared and developed a common basis in sacred text, spread its word, each according to its own light, through the spoken word.[15]

This essay originally appeared as chapter 9 of Siblings: Rabbinic Judaism and Early Christianity at Their Beginnings *(Mahweh, NJ: Paulist Press, 1984).*

Part III
Jewish–Christian Relations

CHAPTER EIGHT

Christianity and Judaism as Siblings

Conventional wisdom would have it that Judaism is the parent and that Christianity is the child. In considering the great religions of the Western world, we often hear both Christianity and Islam described as "daughter faiths" of Judaism. This is certainly correct on the assumption that both faiths derive from the Bible. Both Christian and Moslem vie with the Jew in claiming authentic patrimony from Abraham.

We have already seen, however, how Rabbinic or Pharisaic Judaism represented a significant mutation in the development of the Jewish experience. We have viewed Rabbinic/Pharisaic Judaism as a revolution, introducing the conception of change for the sake of continuity.

Rabbinic/Pharisaic Judaism represented a radical departure. New patterns for the organization of the Jewish people and Judaism came into being. In one way, the new was radically different from the old. And yet in another sense, it was a continuation of the old. Without the new the old would have died. In fact, in a sense, the old did die.

Both Rabbinic Judaism, the form in which Judaism survived

155

the destruction of state and Temple by the Romans, and Christianity were shaped at approximately the same time. The shaping of the emerging pattern for the survival of Judaism came out of Yavneh, at just about the same time the first gospels were written to crystallize the new Christianity.

Indeed we can look at it this way: The conflict between Rome and Judea was a struggle that lasted almost two hundred years. A friendly Rome, following its principle of *divide et impera* ("divide and rule") had befriended the Maccabean guerrillas to weaken the Seleucids and the Egyptians. That made possible the emergence of the Second Jewish Commonwealth as an independent state.

However, by 63 B.C.E., the silk gloves came off, the iron fist showed, and Pompey's troops occupied Judea. The resistance developed into a series of brutal wars, out of which Rome emerged victorious, but bloodied. Nowhere else in her military experience had she encountered such resistance.

In their confrontation with Rome the Jewish people had five options:

They could assimilate, and become Roman. Many of their predecessors had done just that during the Hellenistic period. Many did so again. In fact, the nephew of Philo, Tiberias Alexander, became thoroughly romanized, joined the army, rose in the ranks, and was second-in-command to Titus when Jerusalem was destroyed in the year 70.

They could decide to fight to the death. The slogan might have been "Better dead than Roman!" This was the path chosen by the Zealots. Betar was its grisly consequence of mass death and destruction, and Masada its somber memorial.

They could decide to withdraw from the world and resign from the struggle. They could retire to desert fastnesses, there to wait for a better and redemptive day. This was the way of Qumran.

There were two other alternatives. These were implicit in the approach of Rabbinic/Pharisaic Judaism, which had already taken shape, and which thought in terms of survival through the messianic impulse that had developed within Judaism. Both alternatives came out of Rabbinic Judaism. Both were animated by a messianic thrust, but both thought in terms of survival and not of suicide. The one believed the messianic time was at hand and should be grasped boldly. The other, having seen the messianic impulse take the form of military resistance that failed disastrously, took a long-range view.

The short-range messianic movement out of Judaism became Christianity. The long-range messianic movement became Rabbinic Judaism. The former plunged headlong into the world of the Roman Empire, and "conquered" it in less than two centuries. The latter signed a temporary "ceasefire" with Rome, and within those same two centuries moved out of the sphere of the Roman Empire, into the Parthian Empire. There perhaps a million Jews lived, where they developed Rabbinic Judaism by expanding Mishnah into Talmud, and returning to Europe as fully developed Judaism by the eighth century. It was, to quote the French, *reculer pour mieux sauter* ("taking one step back the better to leap forward").

It is in this sense that Judaism and Christianity arc clearly siblings, both responding to the same cataclysmic event as Jews, but each taking a different approach to the messianic destiny.

A word here is in place to explain the rapid growth of Christianity within the Roman Empire. For one thing, there was a spiritual crisis in all of the empire. The old ways were failing. For another, there were Jews dispersed throughout the empire.

It has been estimated by historical demographers that the total population of the Roman Empire was sixty million. Of these, six million were Jews, about half in Judea and the other half in the rest of the empire. One in ten were Jews. We have evidence from Roman sources that Judaism was beginning to make inroads among the Romans. The references to the *yir'ei adonay* ("those who fear God"), known among the Romans as *metuentes,* are an indication of this. It is estimated that the growth of the Jewish population received an impulse from the Phoenicians in North Africa and Spain after the defeat by the Romans in the Punic Wars in the second pre-Christian century. The Phoenicians were Hebrew-speaking—or, you might prefer to say, the Jews spoke Phoenician. It is surmised that after defeat and being cut off from their homeland, they merged with the Jewish communities around the empire.

In any event there were great centers of Jewish population all over the Roman Empire. The explosion of revolts all over at the time of the Bar Kochba revolt in 135 bears witness to this. By way of example, Alexandria was the first ancient city to attain a population of a million. It is estimated that that million was made up of three hundred thousand Egyptians, three hundred thousand Greeks, and three hundred thousand Jews. Evidence of Jewish influence was widespread. Juvenal, in showing how parents corrupted their children, could speak of one such who had a father who observed the Sabbath. Christian instant-messianic missionaries indeed had fertile soil to cultivate. It is no wonder that the movement spread with lightning speed. After all, the significant presence of Jews scattered through the Roman Empire constituted the primary soil from which the new seed sprouted.

A glance at the arrangement of the Hebrew Scriptures by the early Synagogue and the early Church is illustrative.

Both groups, from the matrix of Rabbinic/Pharisaic Judaism, looked on the Bible as their sacred primary resource. In the Jewish arrangement, the Pentateuch was followed by the prophetic books, which were followed by the *Ketuvim* ("Writings"). The Jewish arrangement ends with the Book of Chronicles. The Christian arrangement placed the prophetic books at the end because these ended with Malachi, and Malachi ended with the words "Lo, I will send the prophet Elijah to you before the coming of the awesome, fearful day of the Lord" (Mal. 3:23). This surely was an appropriate link between Old Testament and New, and it was an eloquent testimony of the conviction that the Messiah had come. It was an affirmation of the instant-messianic thesis within Rabbinic Judaism.

The arrangement as canonized at Yavneh by Rabbinic Judaism, the arrangement of the Sacred Scriptures for Jews, ends with the Second Book of Chronicles. Here are the concluding words:

> And in the first year of King Cyrus of Persia, when the word of the Lord spoken by Jeremiah was fulfilled, the Lord roused the spirit of King Cyrus of Persia to issue a proclamation throughout his realm by word of mouth and in writing, as follows: "Thus said King Cyrus of Persia: The Lord God of Heaven has given me all the kingdoms of the earth, and has charged me with building Him a House in Jerusalem, which is in Judah. Any one of you of all His people, the Lord God be with him and let him go up.

So here we have it. The siblings, equally impelled by their scriptural and messianic roots, blaze new trails in the highways of history, starting from a common origin and moving forward along diverse routes. But first let us sketch, with swift and rapid strokes, the common history of the siblings that represented their common background.

It will be helpful if we view the history preceding the parting of the ways between Church and Synagogue in the second century as three six-hundred-year segments. It we date Abraham at approximately 1800 B.C.E and the Exodus from Egypt at about 1200 B.C.E, we have our first segment. This marks the beginning, as our common ancestor sets out to witness to the One God of Humanity, assured of God's Promise and a Promised Land.

We have here the beginnings of nation and covenant, the period of the patriarchs, the development of the clan, and, at the very beginnings, the combination of experiences that become a paradigm for Jewish historical experience—arrival in a homeland, diaspora, success, then failure, then return home.

When you stop to think of it, this period includes a first encounter with God, beginnings, nationhood fashioned in exile, and then return. What begins with commitment to God and God's promise ends with God's fulfillment of that promise and the return of the people to the Promised Land. The result provides material for memories of that encounter, for memories of the beginnings, and for memories of the pause on the way home at Sinai to renew the covenant that was the outcome of that first encounter. And this time it is not the experience of one patriarch alone, but rather of the entire people.

What we have here, if you will, is the first struggle for freedom, the first national liberation movement, in all historical experience, and the first messianic experience, a fulfilled messianic experience for the Jewish people. These then are the beginnings, and here the basic themes of Jewish history are established.

Now for the second six hundred years, from 1200 B.C.E. (approximately) to 600 B.C.E. (approximately). This period takes us from the settlement of the land, the development of the First Jewish Commonwealth, to the destruction of Jerusalem by the Babylonians (586 B.C.E.), and the exile to Babylonia. Here Jewish covenant nationhood comes to its completest fulfillment and fruition. Here the patriarchal period of Bedouin-type wandering, tribal organization, oscillation between promised land and diaspora, individual covenant, group covenant, exile and messianic return become embodied in the physical trappings of state, of Temple, of national religious institutions.

The state grows and develops, and the covenant memories as well. This is the period that produces Temple and priesthood sanctioned by God, monarchy and kingship sanctioned by God. It produces as well something else, and something unique: the embodiment of that special kind of communication between the newly discovered one, universal God and the special vessels of the communication of His message through an Abraham, a Moses, and finally an entire consecrated God-dedicated people. This embodiment we call prophet, and that which the prophets were about we call prophecy.

Prophets are the embodied conscience of the people, the crucial means of communication between God and His covenant people. There is ample need for this communication, for the people and its leaders, despite the best of intentions, are always forgetting and always tending to go astray. It is the prophets who are the visible, ever-present, and ever-uncomfortable prod. It is the prophets whose hand guides the editing of Scripture. The historical and prophetic books are clear evidence of this. All of Jewish history up to that point is to be remembered from their point of view. The greatest events not relevant to their point of view were simply omitted. Witness the great achievements of Jeroboam II and the remarkably little space he gets in the Book of Kings, despite them!

Temple and cult attain the high and magnificent and impressive solemnity of the Sanctuary in Jerusalem; monarchy culminates in the glories of the Davidic dynasty; but after all is said and done, the legacy of the First Jewish Commonwealth is neither a Jewish-type acropolis nor a Jewish-type complex of palaces, pyramids, or soaring obelisks. It is, rather, the prophetic heritage that becomes the Bible for us. Pentateuch, prophets, some psalms, and some of the other books are products of this period. The prophets place their stamp on the spirit of these books, and on the heritage they design for the people to preserve. Simply put, if you were to add the century or so that followed the destruction of the First Temple, this is the period that provides us with the Tanakh (Old Testament, as it is named in the Christian world), the first great literary creation of this period.

When this period comes to an end, and it comes to an end with a catastrophic upheaval, it leaves the national hopes in ashes, leaves the survivors to pick up the pieces: putting together their literary heritage—the Bible; organizing their memories— Davidic dynasty and its glories; remembering the Temple and its magnificence.

This catastrophe has a numbing but not a paralyzing effect. "How can we sing a song of the Lord on alien soil?" (Ps. 137:4) the exiles asked, and yet they did. The Book of Lamentations describes the numbing trauma: "Bitterly she weeps in the night . . . there is none to comfort her" (Lam. 1:2). The people recall:

"All the precious things she had in the days of old, Jerusalem re-called in her days of woe and sorrow" (Lam. 1:7); they remember, and they do something about preserving the memories. In the aftermath of catastrophe a superhuman effort to collect and preserve the written memories of the days of glory goes forward, probably most especially in Babylonia. Out of this we get the edited Pentateuch, the histories and most of the prophetic books.

I focus on Jeremiah because, in my view, it is in Jeremiah and what he does that we see the first seeds of what becomes the flower of Rabbinic Judaism.

Jeremiah is the prophet who witnesses the destruction. He has desperately tried to prevent it. As God's reluctant spokesman he is constant—and how he suffers for it—in his message that in obedience to God and His ways, and not in pragmatic political alliances, lay the path to survival and the avoidance of destruction. But no one listens to him. Those who support regional military alliances against Babylonia, especially with Egypt, carry the day. Their failures result in the siege of Jerusalem and its ultimate destruction.

While Jerusalem is already in flames, and the end in sight, Jeremiah does two things. He buys a plot of land in Jerusalem to express the faith that there will be a future, that "houses and fields and vineyards shall yet again be bought in this land" (Jer. 32:15). And he writes a letter to the exiles in Babylonia, who are being assured by the people whom Jeremiah opposes that the exile will be of short duration, and he tells them:

> Build houses and live in them, plant gardens and eat their fruit.
> Take wives and beget sons and daughters; and take wives for your
> sons, and give your daughters to husbands, that they may bear sons

and daughters. Multiply there, do not decrease. And seek the welfare of the city to which I have exiled you, and pray to the Lord in
its behalf; for in its prosperity you shall prosper.

(Jer. 29:5ff.)

Here, for the first time, we have the expression of the long-
range messianic outlook, as contrasted with the impatience of its
short-range exponents, who were proclaiming a swift and early
redemption.

As it turned out, the restoration came neither as quickly as the
prophets opposing Jeremiah would have it nor as slowly as Jeremiah himself predicted. But he was already projecting a strategy for Jewish survival that took account of the real possibility
of destruction. In a sense, with respect to the Second Commonwealth that was to follow, he was giving the cure in advance of
the disease!

For in setting a permanent community in Babylonia, he set
up an area for developments in Judaism that looked to new possibilities for survival. And there was coming into being a great
center of Jewish life, where the long-range messianists, after the
destruction of the Second Commonwealth, could retreat, as I
have already said, and where Rabbinic Judaism could go forward and develop.

For in the period between the destruction by Babylonia and
the beginnings of restoration under Ezra, a period of a scant
century or so, we have the end of the prophetic period and the
beginning of the transition to Rabbinic Judaism.

With Ezra we get the Men of the Great Synagogue. The
reading of the Torah was introduced into the prayer life of the
Jewish people, even though the Temple was being rebuilt. The
process of midrash was introduced and there evolved genera-

tions of sages who developed the Oral Law, and transformed the teachings of the prophets and the ways of the Temple cult into new ways that could survive destruction. It was not without significance that an early Aramaic translator of the Prophets could comment: "Malachi and Ezra are one person" (Tg. Mal. 1:1) That is to say, the last prophet and the first of the scribes/sages/pharisees were one!

Now the third six hundred years: This is the period of the Second Jewish Commonwealth. This is a period of rich and seminal creativity. It is a period of extraordinary pluralism and variety. Different sects surface in Judaism—Pharisees, Sadducees, Essenes. We have gnostics and mystics, Hellenists and secularists. This is the time that the Middle East and the Greek world of Europe meet in an explosion of creativity occasioned by their encounter.

Alexander the Great's sweep to the shores of India created an encounter between two ancient worlds. The challenge of Greek thought and Greek ways forced all the ancient cultures to reexamine and reevaluate themselves, and the development of Judaism was no exception. There are many who see the rapid development of Rabbinic Judaism in this period as a response to that challenge.

Suffice to say, this period of restoration is characterized by the Jewish people's confrontation not with Egypt, Babylonia, Assyria, and Persia, as in the past, but with Greece and Rome. Out of this came the final restoration of Jewish independence with the Maccabean revolt in 163 B.C.E. But underpinning it was an immense range of cultural and spiritual development.

Judaism's transition from the biblical to the rabbinic mold is quiet and imperceptible, but inexorable. You hardly see it develop. Yet when the Maccabean revolt explodes, there is a people responding to a direction of leadership that is clearly a transition from the previous era of glory. The state is there again, but no Davidic dynasty. The Temple is there again, but not in its former glory. There are prophets no longer. Now there are rabbinic sages, their heirs, who give leadership and direction. This is the period in which the Bible is completed, the period in which it is translated into Greek and carried to the Greek world. This is the period, as the Roman threat to independence sets in, that sees an explosion in messianic and eschatological thinking and writing. This is the period when an Aristotle can look upon Jews as a nation of philosophers, and Philo interprets Judaism to a Greek world steeped in Homer, Plato, and Aristotle. This is the period when mystical groups explore the gnostic secrets, when rabbinic interpretation expands the parameters of Torah.

Above all, these six hundred years saw the kinds of developments in Judaism, with its messianic thrust and its capacity for survival, that created the subsoil out of which Rabbinic Judaism and Christianity grew. These six hundred years see the completion of the Bible, the Apocrypha, and end with the writing down of the Mishnah, the code of Oral Law, and the beginnings of the Siddur, the prayer book. The tools for survival and the crucial infrastructure were in place.

You may have noted how frequently the compound scribe/sage/pharisee has been used. This is to underscore the idea that these terms are interchangeable and represent the same thing. For it was out of the combination of scribe/sage/exegete that the type known as rabbi, and called by their enemies pharisee, emerges as the decisive developing type who shaped Judaism and the beginnings of Christianity. Already in Jeremiah's time we have the scribe Baruch. We have the scribe Ezra. Their role is to record and to teach. For Judaism is a text-bound destiny, bound to the Torah, its interpretation and expansion.

The characteristic of the scribe/sage/rabbi/pharisee model is that of teacher-exegete. The relationship and communication mode is teacher-disciple. The central principle is that the power over the text is not in an elite priesthood, but potentially available to every single Jew no matter what his status. The principle enunciated by the rabbis that "a bastard who is a scholar outranks a high priest who is an ignoramus" (B. Horayot 3a) is clearly indicative of the direction.

Before the time of Ezra, the Torah was the exclusive possession of the priests, and was read to the people once every seven years. With Ezra, the Torah is taken out of that exclusive domain, and read every week, so that by the end of the year it will all have been read. And not just read. It is read *m'forash,* i.e., interpreted, explained. The Book of Nehemiah tells us how this happened the first time: "They read from the scroll of the Teaching of God, translating it and giving it sense, so they understood the reading" (Neh. 8:8).

"Translating and giving the sense so they understood . . ." Here in a nutshell is the crux of Rabbinic Judaism. Here is seen how midrash is at the core, the process of explanation and of exegesis. The rabbinic sage was truly a "novum," a mutation in history that seized a past, made it its own, and handed it on to future generations.

Thus we see how in the turmoil surrounding the First Jewish Commonwealth this new phenomenon comes into being. We see how in the early days of the Second Commonwealth it begins to develop. We see how during the period of the Second

Commonwealth it emerges full blown, fully prepared to step into the breach when this commonwealth falls and the Jewish people enters its two-thousand-year diaspora period.

Pirkei Avot (Ethics of the Fathers) in the Mishnah captures this development, and that is why it was placed at the beginning of the handbook that presented the generations of the rabbinic leaders who were the bridge of one period into the other. Here is what it tells us:

> Moses received the Torah on Sinai and handed it down to Joshua; Joshua to the elders; the elders to the prophets; and the prophets handed it down to the Men of the Great Assembly. . . . Simon the Just was one of the last survivors of the Men of the Great Assembly. . . . Antigonos of Socho received the tradition from Simon the Just. . . . Yose the son of Yoezer of Zereda and Yose the son of Yoḥanan received the tradition from the preceding. . . . Joshua the son of Peraḥyah and Nittai the Arbelite received the tradition from them. . . . Judah ben Tabbai and Simeon the son of Shetaḥ received the tradition from them . . .
>
> (Pirkei Avot 1:1)

And so it goes, down the generations. This list takes us from the time of Ezra about 400 B.C.E. to Simeon the son of Shetaḥ, who lived approximately 100 B.C.E. And it is with this Simeon that we shall begin to examine the crucial figures who shaped Rabbinic Judaism, by developing its system and its means of communication.

This essay originally appeared as chapter 2 of Siblings: Rabbinic Judaism and Early Christianity at Their Beginnings *(Mahweh, NJ: Paulist Press, 1989).*

CHAPTER NINE

After Emancipation: Jews and Germans

The Jewish-German encounter in the post-Emancipation period can be described as a love-hate relationship that touched the heights and plumbed the depths. It can also be seen as a dialogue of the deaf across a chasm of silence. In a way it could be said that German and Jew confronted each other as related extremes, the opposite sides of the same coin, at odds and needing each other at the same time.

It is equally true to say that this encounter, at its height and at its best, produced a creative explosion in art, literature, and science that shaped and influenced our age as nothing else. One need only mention the names Freud, Einstein, Marx, Mahler, and Schoenberg to grasp the scope of the impact. Einstein in physics and the nuclear age; Freud in the discovery of new frontiers in the human soul; Marx in the contours of modern politics and economics; and Mahler and Schoenberg in the expression of the possibilities in music.

In the period of the great efflorescence and development, world Jewry lived in the German cultural sphere in Central and Eastern Europe. The operative language of this great segment of the Jewish world was a form of German written in Hebrew characters.

For some fifteen centuries before Emancipation, Jews lived among Germans as a nation in exile, apart and yet an intimate part of their life and times. This was true in the Rhineland, true in the Germany of the medieval period, even when they were expelled from a city here and a city there between 1300 and 1600. What they took with them to Eastern Europe was their deep Jewish piety and their German speech in Hebrew letters. The direct dialogue was between court Jew and noble, but at most other levels it was at once two solitudes and communication by a kind of osmosis and a fascinating symbiotic existence.

The Renaissance and the Enlightenment, which came to England and Holland as a commercial and colonial revolution, and to France as a political upheaval that turned the medieval system on its head, came to Germany as a cultural explosion. Luther in religion, Bach and Beethoven in music, Kant and Hegel in philosophy, Goethe and Schiller in literature, these were the benchmarks of that explosion.

Friedrich Schiller was the quintessential expression of universal humanism, and it was this aspect of the German spirit that most appealed to Jews as they came out of the ghettos into the mainstream of German life. Moses Mendelssohn (1729–1786), the great Jewish theoretician of the Enlightenment, represented the bridge of such possibilities in a Berlin where such ideas took root and flourished.

The rationalism of the seventeenth and early eighteenth centuries, culminating in the French Revolution and the Napoleonic wars, catapulted the German lands into a new era of development. The emancipation of the Jews was one consequence of these developments. Germany's Jews grasped at its possibilities, even though it had strings—the strings of abandoning any sense of their own national-historical identity. Even the liberal Christians who vigorously advocated emancipation did so with the feeling that it would hasten the process of the Jews' disappearance into a broader German society. There were reservations in the broader German society, and there were reservations on the Jewish side. But in the main, the process of acculturation and interaction went forward as though on the crest of a tidal wave. The creative consequences were enormous, and equally enormous was the collapse that followed the end of the Weimar period, the Nazi epoch, and World War II.

This process, in all its immense grandeur and sparkling achievement, this culmination of the impact of economic growth, national unification, and the extraordinary Jewish contribution, can be examined through the prism of cultural and intellectual development. The period between 1812 and the end of the Weimar Republic brings what can be seen through that prism into sharp focus.

Emancipation came to the Napoleon-created Westphalian Confederation in 1811, and to a Prussia that had successfully resisted Napoleon, in 1812. With the impetus of Moses Mendelssohn, Jews like Heinrich Heine and Ludwig Boerne entered the mainstream of German literature, the former giving a new elan to lyric poetry and satire, and the latter to the essay form. Gabriel Riesser led the way in the political struggle for emancipation, and in the short-lived Revolution of 1848 was actually elected vice-president of the National Assembly in Frankfurt. The suppression of the revolution in 1849 saw a period of reaction set in, but by 1870, with the unification of the German state, full equality and citizenship were given to the Jew.

The movement for reform in Judaism was part of the process of acculturation. Its leaders were Israel Jacobson, Eduard Kley, and Abraham Geiger. Neo-Orthodoxy, under the leadership of Samson Raphael Hirsch, and a middle-of-the-road liberalism led by Zacharias Frankel were two significant responses. Out of the establishment of the Verein für Kultur und Wissenschaft des Judentums (1818) came the monumental scholarly work of men like Leopold Zunz, Moritz Steinschneider, and Heinrich Graetz. This scholarship analyzed the literature and history of Judaism in German academic style and method. The task was to make Judaism understandable to the world. Zunz felt that only when Jewish studies were included in the German university curriculum would full emancipation have been achieved. Steinschneider, one of the greatest Jewish bibliographers, believed that this task needed to be done to give Judaism "a decent burial" before it was fully absorbed by the German nation. Heinrich Graetz was not of that mind. He saw the immense force and significance of Jewish peoplehood on the stage of world history.

In philosophy, among the earlier Jewish thinkers of that period, Solomon Formstecher took his cue from Schelling, Samuel Hirsch was influenced by Hegel, but Solomon Steinheim insisted that Judaism not be confused with philosophical speculation. He resisted modern rationalism and like Graetz saw a special role for the Jewish people.

As the Jew entered the age of Emancipation, there were inner differences. These ranged from a small group that opted for isolation, a middle group that may have differed on the question of continuing national identity, but on the whole went forward with the new possibilities. Finally, there were those like Rahel

Varnhagen and Henriette Herz, leaders of the Berlin intellectual salons, who were swept along by Feuerbach into the arms of Romanticism and Christianity.

In German society the promise of enlightened rationalist humanism had a wide appeal, but the new rationalism engendered by the successes of Napoleon, and by the resistance to those successes, brought into being a sense of Germanism and an intense reaction which not only set back the Emancipation, but brought in its wake a romantic, mystical Volkism that rejected enlightened humanist rationalism and its materialistic image.

Johann Gottfried Herder (1744–1803) and Friedrich Ludwig Jahn were its theorists. Volkism saw in the folk a collective romantic mystical entity that expressed and embodied the national soul. This stood in counterpoint to the rationalist humanism centered on the individual and individual fulfillment that had foreign, i.e., French, origins. Volkism turned inward, lived on myths and symbols, and saw things in terms of symbolic stereotypes. The big city, the foreigner, the Jew—all these represented forces hostile to the fulfillment of the folk's destiny.

The popular folk image of the Jew was a symbolic stereotype seen as inimical to what this movement represented. In popular literature, where ideas glorifying the peasant, the village, and homely values were adumbrated, writers like Gustave Freytag, Wilhelm Raabe, and later Jakob Burckhardt and Nathaniel Jurgen cultivated this view. The image of the Jew emerged as one bereft of spirit, excessively materialistic, and inherently un-German. Volkists looked back to the Middle Ages with nostalgia and felt that the rationalist consequences of the industrial and bourgeois revolution had to be undone.

Not all volkists were racists. Freytag, for example, who portrayed the "ugly" Jew, at the same time drew up plans for complete Jewish assimilation, because he believed that Jews were salvageable. The fact, however, is that through the volkist trend, popular antisemitism was tapped and continued as a deeply rooted, significant force in the fabric of popular German culture, waiting to be brought to the surface when the right combination of circumstances intersected.

Yet the volkist movement was not without influence on the Jews. In many cases they were involved in it, influenced through it, and shaped by it. Since its aim was to halt and even reverse the forward thrust of industrialization, materialism, and rationalist secularism, its influence ran deep. The nationalists rejected the traditional saber-rattling worship of the state. Jews rejected the ghetto, and left-wing intellectuals rejected the orthodox Marxism of their immediate predecessors. Youth movements of the Wandervogel type saw in a return to nature and soil and landscape the means of making contact with the mystical spirit of the healing national soul.

Jews seeking assimilation and rejecting their bourgeois elders and ghetto past found they could be part of volkist youth groups. German Volkism and mysticism influenced those who turned to Zionism as well. Martin Buber's Zionism and revival of Jewish mysticism can be seen in relation to the volkist interest in German mysticism. It is significant that Buber's doctoral thesis was on the works of the German mystic Jakob Boehm. A similar kind of link can be made for the left-wing intellectual movement. And so, for that matter, in its extremes, the Nazi movement. The broad streams of German history, through its rationalist, humanist thrust and its mystical, volkist thrust, underlay the whole web of mutually contradictory developments. The story is told in a wide range of reactions to them, the glorious development of the human spirit at its best, and at its worst, the sordid consequences of a mystical Volkism gone wild, hand in hand with a materialist rationalism bereft of an ethical base and conscience. It is also told in the German-Jewish dialogue, where the Jew came to exemplify a German humanist tradition which created space for Jew and German to meet. It may also be said that when the eclipse of this spirit came, between 1933 and 1945, the German-Jewish version of this cultural glory preserved Germany's better self perhaps as much as any other single group across the chasm of the Holocaust, war, and subsequent disasters for all sides.

How the German spirit at its best and the creative Jewish response could be seen as a cooperative process is made clear, for example, by the *Threepenny Opera*; this work, which so quintessentially caught the spirit of the Weimar epoch, was written by a gentile, Berthold Brecht, and a Jew, Kurt Weil. The opera *Wozzek,* continental divide for the breakthrough into contemporary music, was the product of the Catholic Alban Berg, using the twelve-tone system developed by the Jew Arnold Schoenberg.

Or, for that matter, if we look at the contemporary German scene, where Gunther Grass was among the literary giants of the postwar era, foremost among those who confronted the immediate past, we find that he was deeply influenced by the Jewish writer Alfred Doeblin. *Berlin Alexanderplatz,* Germany's analogue to Joyce's *Ulysses,* once prompted Grass to say: "I am descended from that Doeblin . . ."

The list could go on and on, and in fact does. It can be vividly summarized by a look at the wide range of creative areas that shaped Germany and the rest of the world. In the realm of music, it takes little expertise to realize what Bach, Mozart, Beethoven, Brahms, and Wagner have meant. What is perhaps not so well known is the role of Felix Mendelssohn-Bartholdy in reviving interest in an all-but-forgotten Bach, or of Jewish music critics in projecting Wagner despite his animus against Jews.

Even further, the people who wrote the psalms and sang them, later advanced the appreciation of the German classical greats, moving music forward to new horizons. Gustave Mahler advanced the frontiers with his "dissonance by collision" and his multidimensional creativity, and was a musical counterpoint to Freud in expressing the struggle between Eros and Death. Arnold Schoenberg formulated the twelve-tone method of composing, and opened the doors to the vast range of contemporary music that so accurately expressed the explosiveness and dynamism of a new world aborning.

In the world of medicine, Sigmund Freud revolutionized man's way at looking at his own psyche. He drew new maps for the geography of the soul, and led the world into the new age of psychiatry. As W. H. Auden put it at his funeral: "He changed the world . . . all he did was to remember like the old and be honest like children." In the world of science, Albert Einstein stands out at the very epicenter, with his theory of relativity, his work on the unified-field theory, and the impact of the smashing of the atom. Georg Simmel ushered in the ace of sociology, and Franz Boas the era of anthropology. Thinking of such as these, and adding Heine, Herzl, and Marx to the list, the role of German Jews in changing our world and chipping away at our old certainties stands out in bold relief. Shades of Kepler, Galileo, and Christopher Columbus! It made some people nervous, but was an extraordinary impulse for those who had no fear of new horizons and newly discovered continents of the mind.

The Jewish role in German expressionism was crucial, if not seminal. It was born in the latter years of the Wilhelmine period and flowered after the conclusion of World War I. The expressionists had a sense of the war's impending disaster and were animated by an overwhelming sense of compassion and foreboding, and a deep sense of human brotherhood. They saw in the war the apogee of suicidal self-destruction. Expressionism was at once a scream of protest and a cry of hope. In art a Kirschner, a Nolde, a Pechstein, a Franz Marc, and a Kokoschka expressed the ugliness as though lancing a boil for healing. *Der Sturm,* edited by Hermann Walden, served as the literary launching pad for their ideas. By 1920, Max Lieberman had become the first Jew to be elected president of the Prussian Academy of Arts, as though to symbolize arrival at the pinnacle.

In poetry, Else Lasker-Schueler, a bohemian and dreamer, led the search for a "city with an angel at the gate." A winner of the Kleist Prize for poetry in 1932, on the eve of the Nazi rise to power, she wrote in *Arthur Aronymus* of her dream of the possibility of brotherly love between German and Jew of whatever religion or background. And Gertrude Kolmar, for whom that dream became, as for so many others, a reality of rejection, could write as the train took her from Berlin to Auschwitz:

So wirf dich du dem Niedern hin, sei schwach, umarme das Leid
Bis einst dein mueder Wanderschuh auf den Nacken der Starken tritt!

Cast your lot with the lowly, be weak, embrace the pain
Until your weary, wander-shoe tramples on the neck of the bully!

Franz Kafka, well ahead of his time, had a sense of the oncoming doom that was to engulf Europe. He caught the spirit of the time, expressing the angst and foreboding in a way that made literature turn a new corner. Living in Prague, in the tensions of Jewish existence, on the one hand, and the emergence of Czech nationalism, on the other, he chose to be a German writer with Jewish roots. In a very deep sense he was the prophet of the crisis that was to be, and though his life was cut short in the 1920s, he left his mark on the shape of world literature. He was the peer among many, and the many include a roster of dazzling names that include Georg Steinheim, Arthur Schnitzler, Alfred Doeblin, Jakob Wasserman, Lion Feuchtwanger, and Franz Werfel; and this far from exhausts the list.

In the world of theater Max Reinhardt held sway, and directors like Josef von Sternberg, Ernst Lubitsch, and Billy Wilder gave the world of German theater and film a glow; and when they were forced to leave they brought that glow to America. In music there was Bruno Walter and Otto Klemperer, and there were essayists and critics like Karl Krause, Alfred Kerr, Theodore Lessing, Ernst Bloch, and Walter Benjamin. Merely to list them is to touch upon the glory of the age that came to such an abrupt and tragic end in 1933.

And when that end approached, the saving remnant was formidable enough to carry the heritage of the German culture they had touched and shaped westward, where a new renaissance was born. New York and Los Angeles became successors to Berlin, and the impact on science, on the arts, theater and literature, and politics was enormous. As it was with Lessing and Mendelssohn two centuries earlier, the interaction between German Christian and Jewish refugees climaxed with such works as Schoenberg's *Survivor from Warsaw,* Thomas Mann's *Dr. Faustus,* Alfred Doeblin's *Schicksalsreise,* Else Lasker Schueler's *Mein blaues Klavier,* Nelly Sachs' *O the Chimneys,* and Walter Benjamin's *Passages.*

Benjamin, an introspective, sensitive spirit who could never achieve a professorship, shaped the literature and thought of his time as few others could. A master of German, he had an incisive, critical, and perceptive eye that caught reality on the wing. Like Freud and Schoenberg, he knew deeply that he was a Jew in Germany, steeped in German culture, exponent of the German word, yet aware of the distance. While his cousin Gertrude Kolmar was trapped in Berlin, he was trapped at the Spanish frontier, where he took his own life in despair.

But it was his type, thinkers and critics who flourished on German soil, who shaped the intellectual life of the 1950s and 1960s, and are now being recovered and appreciated.

It has been suggested that the German-Jewish relationship extended beyond the frontiers of Germany to touch the Jews of Eastern Europe. The language they spoke was a German language, and the partition of Poland (1772) brought them by the hundreds of thousands under Prussian and Austrian control. From the areas of oppression Jews streamed westward to the centers of culture and hopes for freedom—Berlin and Vienna. Vienna, city of Freud, Mahler, and Herzl, was at once a center of immense Jewish creativity and a center of antisemitism; witness Lueger, its mayor, and his influence on subsequent Nazism. Berlin was similarly a mecca for Jews seeking freedom, and here too there was an antisemitic component; witness Adolph Stoecker, the Kaiser's court chaplain in the 1880s.

The Berlin of the Wilhelmine and Weimar periods was, as we have seen, the center of a great cultural renaissance. Berlin played a central role in the Jewish national renaissance as well. Here gathered a group of Zionist theorists and Hebrew writers, fugitives from tsarist oppression and eager for university training. Here, for example, before they went to Palestine, lived the

Hebrew poet Bialik, the Hebrew novelist Agnon, the Zionist theorist Shai Hurwitz, the Zionist activist Schneuer Zalman Rubashov, who as Zalman Shazar was later to become president of Israel. In the last years of World War I and in the early 1920s, this was the center of Jewish cultural creativity for a few brief shining years.

It was contact with this group that changed the life of Gershom Scholem, raised in a fourth-generation assimilated German-Jewish family. This contact brought back into Jewish life a man who was dramatically to influence the course of Jewish thought and the direction of Jewish historiography. His revolt against Jewish bourgeois existence, which had opted for full integration into German life, took the form of a turn to the study of Jewish mysticism, to Zionism, and to emigration to Palestine in 1923. It also took the course of his lifelong commitment to changing the course and direction of Jewish scholarship. Scholem confronted the rationalist enlightenment thrust of Jewish scholarship, using the very rationalist, scholarly method to do their theories in, by showing that Jewish mysticism, which had been repressed and cast aside as alien to the spirit of Jewish progress, was indeed a significant force in Jewish history. It expressed the Jewish national will to live in a very deep sense and coexisted with the national level as a subterranean force in constant dialectic with it.

The German cultural influence touched off the immense forces of Jewish assimilation and acculturation. Even those who cast aside their religious and cultural connection with Judaism transformed their Jewish ethical and prophetic roots into that part of German culture that resisted Nazism, and was in fact a survival of their Jewishness in that reincarnation.

It also touched off an intense return to Judaism, a capacity to express Judaism in forms emerging from this cultural impetus. In philosophy and theology Hermann Cohen, Franz Rosenzweig, Martin Buber, and Leo Baeck, the seminaries in Berlin and Breslau, and the Lehrhaus in Frankfurt stood in a direct line to the sages of Yavneh, Philo, Saadia, and Maimonides. The impact of Jewish life and thought transcended the borders of the Germany where they lived and worked. Buber migrated to Palestine, and Leo Baeck remained behind to stay with his people through the war; he was interned at Theresienstadt and later came to the United States, where he died.

The several hundred thousand Jews who escaped Germany and Austria before the outbreak of World War II and the subsequent Holocaust had a special impact on the Jewish community of what was then Palestine and on the Jews of the United States. The German-Jewish emigration to Palestine in the thirties brought great resources and special qualities of talent, culture, and expertise. The universities, government, banking, the professions, journalism and literature, the quality of life, the sophistication of the cities, bore their imprint. In the United States, as we have seen, together with non-Jewish emigres, the impact on the culture was unparalleled. In the rabbinate it gave the Jewish community seminary heads, an infusion of great scholars, and escaping rabbinical students who provided a meaningful corps of leadership to national Jewish organizations, to say nothing of national, political, and cultural leadership.

The agreement on reparations by the Adenauer government was a substantive acknowledgment by West Germany of the wrongs suffered by the Jews, and since a significant portion of it went to Israel, it played a not insignificant role in the development of the Jewish state that emerged after the shambles of the war.

In our own time there have been a wide range of observances

marking the fortieth anniversary of the end of World War II. In every country affected it was recalled with a special poignancy, none more so than the memories of the Holocaust survivors. In Germany it was an especially sensitive time of inner reflection and evaluation, especially in West Germany in the events that swirled around the Bitburg controversy. Old hurts, old pains were awakened, yet new hopes were aroused. The painful, traumatic immediate past cannot be forgotten. But the German-Jewish encounter in history, so rich, so variegated, so multifaceted, was indeed a dialogue, a dialogue of consequence, a dialogue still going on.

The summing up has best been made by a Jew, Gershom Scholem, and by a German, the president of the Federal Republic of Germany, Richard Weiszacker. Scholem concluded his lecture on "Jews and Germans" in 1966 with these words:

> Only by remembering a past that we will never completely master can we regenerate hope in the resumption of communication between Germans and Jews and in the reconciliation of those who have been separated.

And President Weiszacker, speaking to German students and youth perhaps the greatest words spoken after the Bitburg episode in the spring of 1985, words that confronted the past with a candor and a compassion that may well be the glory of the Federal Republic, could say:

> We seek reconciliation. Precisely for this reason we must understand that there can be no reconciliation without remembrance. The experience of millionfold death is part of the very being of every Jew in the world not only because people cannot forget such atrocities, but also because remembrance is part of the Jewish faith.

. . . Remembrance is the experience of the work of God in history. It is the source of faith and redemption. This experience creates hope, creates faith in redemption, in reunification of the divided in reconciliation. Whoever forgets this experience loses his faith.

A German translation of this essay was published in Emil Bernhard Cohn and Hayim Goren Perelmuter, Von Kanaan Nach Israel *by the Deutsche Taschen-buch Verlag, Munich in 1986.*

CHAPTER TEN

Fifty and Hundred

When I heard from Clemens Thoma, shortly after my arrival in Lucerne for a six-month visiting professor stint at the Theologische Fakultaet in the Fall of 1986, that the centenary of Franz Rosenzweig would be marked in Kassel by an international conference, I knew that I must go.

Right off I remembered that I had first encountered the *Stern* back in 1936 at the Jewish Institute of Religion. That made it fifty years ago, and it gave me a special personal stake in the observance. I may well have been the first Jewish seminarian ever to study the *Stern der Erlösung* in the United States. Who knew about Rosenzweig in the States then?

Let there be no misunderstanding about this from the beginning. There was no prescient quality about me. I hadn't the foggiest notion about the main trends in Jewish theology and philosophy at the time. I was not the "whiz kid" who read everything on his own. Like our ancestors at Mount Sinai, according to the midrash, I was dragged screaming to the task.

Two factors came together to make that encounter possible.

Henry Slonimsky was the dean and professor of theology and Midrash; and I happened to have majored in German at McGill.

It was in October, at the beginning of a new semester. I had already registered for my full quota of courses. And then I encountered Slonimsky leaving a classroom. His blue eyes flashed through his horn-rimmed glasses.

"Perelmuter," he began, "you will take a course with me!"

"I will?" came my bewildered reply.

"You will. You can read German, and I want to teach Franz Rosenzweig's recent book *Der Stern der Erlösung*."

There was no escaping, and I hardly realized then what was really happening. Here I found myself in a seminar of one, being led into the magic of the work by a man who, although he did not write many books, was one of those rare, Socratic, volcanic, brilliantly inspiring teachers. Grounded in the classics, English, American, and European literature, philosophy, and Hebrew, he taught Midrash and Jewish philosophy with a power that shaped a generation of rabbis.

Slonimsky wanted to teach Rosenzweig because he had known him at Marburg, where he had studied with Hermann Cohen and earned his doctorate. After a short period of teaching at Johns Hopkins and Hebrew Union College, he had come to New York in 1922 to become part of the faculty of the Jewish Institute of Religion, which Stephen Wise had founded. That was the year that the first edition of the *Stern* appeared.

He sent me out to buy it, and I came back with the 1929 edition, which had come out in three thin volumes. As I recall it, I didn't so much read as listen. From the reflection on the aloneness of man in death to the *"ins Leben"* at the end; the moving beyond Hegel, Schelling, and Cohen into new thought patterns that shaped a renewal of Judaism; the gripping account of the

Jewish festival cycle; the new dialogic confrontation of Judaism and Christianity; the turn back to Judaism at the apex of the assimilationist wave—all these themes poured out like a volcano in the reading that Slonimsky gave to the book. He well understood Rosenzweig's view of a text: that it was not just print on paper. It was the gesture, the theatricality of bringing the text alive that really mattered.

If ever a text really came alive for me in that year, it was that text, alive with power and passion. I must confess that I never fully understood the whole thing. But I understood enough. It was a kind of revelation. It became part of my way of thinking about Judaism.

From the *Star* I went to the *Briefe* when they came out, then to *Zweistromland* and *Das Neue Denken,* and discovered the Lehrhaus and what it had done. A year or so later, Gershom Scholem, one of the Lehrhaus people, was at the JIR giving the lectures that became *Major Trends in Jewish Mysticism.*

And not many years after that, in 1943, I encountered another important Lehrhaus person at the American Jewish Conference. There I had gone, a recently ordained rabbi, as Stephen Wise's aide. This meant I could get into all the sessions and follow all the critical debates about American Jewry's postwar aim for a Jewish commonwealth in Palestine.

The sessions were hot and heavy, and a breather was needed. Out on the street, I found myself strolling with an observer at the conference. He turned out to be Eduard Strauss, a chemist, who had played an important role in the development of the Lehrhaus. When I told him that I had read the *Stern* with Henry Slonimsky seven years previously, he reacted with amazement. He didn't think anyone in America was then paying attention to it.

There we were, walking up Fifth Avenue, with Strauss doing

the talking, about the Lehrhaus and how it had come to be, and how it had functioned, and what it had been like in those days of exciting creativity. For the third time in seven years I had encountered a living witness of that great renewal. His communication to me included a copy of *Zweistromland*, a clipping of the obituary for Rosenzweig in the *Frankfurter Zeitung*, and a clipping of his own tribute to Rosenzweig in the *Jüdische Rundschau* of 1929.

So I had to go to Kassel, but what I had not bargained for was that the stop before Kassel was Marburg. The train sat in the station for ten minutes. Opposite was a German troop train. A variety of thoughts and associations raced through my head. Marburg. Beyond the train I felt the presence of the ghosts of Hermann Cohen, Franz Rosenzweig, and Henry Slonimsky.

And then came the opening of the Conference, with Rafael Rosenzweig talking about his father, and suggesting that what his father and his associates did at the Lehrhaus could only be compared with what Yoḥanan ben Zakkai had done at Yavneh.

That night two actors from Berlin did an evocation of the dybbuk growing out of a situation of two people sitting at a Shabbat table. It was an unusual tour de force. Here, in *Judenrein* Kassel, with Rosenzweig and his work at center stage, with scholars from all over the world in attendance, there were many ghosts and some dybbuks. The ghosts carried with them memories of the past and hopes for the future. I do not know if any dybbuks were exorcised.

I went away wondering whether serendipity was just a series of accidents.

This letter originally appeared in European Judaism *20, no. 2 (Winter 1986):* *15–17.*

CHAPTER ELEVEN

Mission

Mission is central to Judaism and to its development; and evangelization, in one form or another, has been its technique. This fact has been obscured by the dramatic success and equally dramatic spread of Christianity and Islam, with their supersessionist claims. Hence this aspect of Jewish history and Jewish experience has tended to be ignored. The very fact that Rabbinic Judaism saw Abraham not only as the first Jew but as the first missionary is indicative of this. He proclaimed one God (Gen. 13:4) and brought in converts (Genesis Rabbah to Gen. 12:5).

The number of Jews who entered the Promised Land after the Exodus was, by scholarly consensus, a rather small group who made common cause with the native inhabitants who resisted Egyptian rule The latter, the so-called seven nations, were absorbed into Jewish peoplehood through the acceptance of YHWH as their God (cf. Milgrom, *Journal of Biblical Literature* 101, 1982, pp. 169–176). Evidence of this is found throughout the Pentateuch in the frequent references to mixed multitude (*erev rav*), *ger,* and *ger toshav,* and in the frequent exhortations to

188

treat the *ger* (convert) with justice and consideration. That this was an ongoing process in the growth of the nation can be seen in the fact that a figure of 153,000 is given for the time of Solomon and David (2 Chron. 2:16).

The Book of Deuteronomy has a strong missionizing undertone, as does Deutero-Isaiah. We find calls to conversion in Joel 3:1, 2, 5, Isaiah 2:2–4, Micah 4:1–3, and Psalms 47:1–2, 66:1, and others. Jeremiah (1:5) is called to be a prophet to the nations; Deutero-Isaiah 42:6 sees the Jewish people as a light unto the nations, and speaks of those who join the Jewish people as *hanilvim* (Isa. 56:6); while in Esther 8:17 the author speaks of *hamityahadim,* i.e., those who become Jews. In Tobit (13:13) we read that "many nations shall come from far away . . . to dwell close to the Holy Name of the Lord God." The same motif is found in Ruth and in Jonah.

To be sure, we find indications of opposition to this process, as in Ezra's acts of exclusion of "foreign wives," but it is always in a dialectic tension with the attitude of openness and acceptance. This tension can be seen to persist in the entire history of the process. The books of Ruth and Jonah can be seen as the other pole of the debate.

Deutero-Isaiah's call to the Jewish people to be a "light unto the nations" stimulated a renewal of growth of the mission impulse in Judaism after the destruction of the first Jewish state. When one considers that at the period of the height of power of the Roman Empire, according to the best demographic estimates of historians, one in ten inhabitants of the empire was a Jew, clearly there had been enormous growth. The Latin and Greek literature of the period testifies to this. There was, for one thing, a widespread anti-Jewish literature in the ancient world, just to mention Manetho and Apion. Seneca, Tacitus, Juvenal and Horace, Dio Cassius, and Strabo, among others, make reference to the spread of Judaism. The Emperor Claudius and later Hadrian proscribed circumcision.

There are scholars (George Rosen, Hayim Hillel Ben-Sasson) who theorize that the Phoenicians of North Africa converted en mass to Judaism after their defeat at the hand of the Romans. It is during this period that the Idumeans, Itureans, and Moabites were converted to Judaism (ca. 140 B.C.E.), and the rulers of Adiabene and their people, a small nation between Syria and Parthia, joined the Jewish people in the first century.

Rabbinic literature, as attested by the studies of Bernard Bamberger and William Braude, was full of references indicating that a structured missionizing movement had come into being. Some of the greatest of the rabbinic sages, such as Shemaiah, Abtalion, Hillel, Akiba, and Meir, were deemed to be descendants of converts. We read in Pesaḥim 87b, for instance, that "the Holy One, praised be He, dispersed the peoples of Israel in order that they might acquire proselytes." Or as in Ḥagigah 5a: "A person who oppresses a proselyte is as one who has oppressed God." To be sure, it is possible to find passages hostile to proselytism, but the sheer volume of the supporting side overwhelms them.

As the Jewish center of learning and population shifted to Babylonia, the evidence of intense proselytization continues. The Geonim (Yeshiva Heads) actually set quotas. We note (Berakhot 14b) that Rabbis Judah and Joseph, heads of Pumbeditha in the third century, and Ashi in the fourth century chided the people for not bringing in sufficient converts. There was an eschatological impulse to the missionizing movement. Idolatry needed to be eliminated, and when all were brought under "the shelter of the covenant" the messianic era would be at hand.

With the triumph of Christianity in the fourth century, and of Islam in the seventh, the pressure on the Jew to limit these activities mounted, but the activity persisted. The rise of Islam, among other things, created an immense supply of slaves. It is among slaves that proselytization was active. The six centuries following the conversion of Constantine to Christianity saw some dramatic evidences of the spread of Judaism, despite its repression within areas of Christian and Islamic power. The mass conversion of Arabs to Judaism in southern Arabia under Dhu Nowas and the conversion of the Aksunite kingdom of Ethiopia, out of which emerged the Falashas, all at the edges of Christian and Islamic expansion, give evidence of this. And then there were the Khazars, that people in the area between the Caspian and Black Seas and the Crimea, who resisted the pressures of expanding Christianity and Islam by choosing Judaism, and who figure in a dramatic correspondence between Ḥasdai ibn Shaprut, Jewish vizier to the king of Cordoba, and Joseph, king of the Khazars in the tenth century.

In medieval Europe the records of conversion to Judaism indicate that the converts came principally from the clergy and the nobility. From the Christian side, the complaints of Bishop Agobert of Lyons that Christians were attracted to Jewish preaching, the efforts to ban relations between Jews and Christians as finally formulated by the Fourth Lateran Council (1215), and the constant concerns of the Church about judaizing, point in this direction.

From the Cairo Genizah alone we have about fifty fragments that refer to conversions. Since in the medieval world there were some forty Jewish communities of equal size in Egypt, North Africa, Spain, Syria, Palestine, and Iraq, Norman Golb (*Jewish Proselytism,* p. 34) has calculated, by projection, that

there were 15,000 conversions to Judaism in the period between the ninth and eleventh centuries. Best known among
these are Bodo, a nobleman; Wecelin, a high-ranking cleric;
Andreas, bishop of Bari; and Obadiah (Johannes son of Dreux),
who corresponded with Maimonides.

A careful analysis of contemporary sources indicates that during the period of Jan Hus and the early years of Luther, Jewish
observers saw this as the sign of a messianic return of Christians
to Judaism. Earlier in the thirteenth century, the mystic Abraham Abulafia attempted to convert the pope, as did the messianic claimant in the fifteenth century, Solomon Molcho. And
although Spinoza in his philosophy is seen as attacking Judaism
and somewhat favoring Christianity, his contribution to the development of secularism turned out to be an attack on the hegemony of the Church.

The advent of the modern era, beginning with the French
Revolution and the Emancipation, created a hemorrhage of
Jewish desertions through conversion and intermarriage. But it
also resulted in the development of Reform and Liberal Judaism
as a response, with an emphasis on the Mission of Israel with its
implications for proselytization.

Baron has noted that the increase of Jewish population from
850,000 in 1660 to over 12,000,000 in 1940 was an increase of
1500 percent, as against 350 percent for Western Europe and
250 percent for the world population. Part of the growth must
have come from proselytization, he suggests.

The United States of America is the only country to which
Jews have come that had no tradition of the dominance of a previous religious culture, and the growth of American Judaism is
a response to this. Although it is not easy to detect organized
missionizing movements, the role of American Jews influencing

American culture through literature and the arts is not insignificant. There have been some efforts to create missionary movements by such figures as Israel Ben-Ze'ev in Israel and Ben Maccabee in the United States.[1] Rabbi Alexander Schindler, president of the Union of American Hebrew Congregations (Reform), has spearheaded a national movement of outreach to non-Jewish spouses in Jewish families, with considerable effect. One must also note the return to Judaism of alienated Jews, the so-called *hozrei b'teshuvah* ("penitents"). There is a vital Orthodox synagogue in Berkeley that consists of 1960s radicals who have returned.

Though some cite the growth of intermarriage as a threat to Jewish survival, the fact is that some 10,000 non-Jews convert to Judaism each year, and the statistics suggest that in intermarriage there are more gains than losses. And despite the efforts to suppress Judaism in the Soviet Union since the Revolution, the amazing surge of Russian Jews to Israel in our time needs to be noted.

One can look at the Zionist movement as it developed from the late nineteenth century to see missionary characteristics in the way it reached out for and gained adherents. There is, as the saying goes, more than one way to skin a cat, and there is more than one way to look at the question of mission in Judaism.

An edited German translation of this essay appeared in the Theologische Realenzyklopaedie, *vol. 23, (Berlin, New York: Walter de Gruyter, 1995).*

Bibliography

Bamberger, Bernard. *Proselytism in the Talmudic Period*. New York: Ktav, 1939.

Ben-Ze'ev, Israel. *Gerim v'Giyur*. Jerusalem, 1961.

Braude, William. *Jewish Proselyting*. Providence: Brown University Press, 1940.

Cohen, Steven M. *American Assimilation or Jewish Revival?* Bloomington: Indiana University Press, 1988.

Fein, Leonard. *Where Are We?* New York: Harper & Row, 1988.

Golb, Norman. *Jewish Proselytism: A Phenomenon in the Religious History of Early Europe*. Judaica Studies Program Monograph Series. Cincinnati: University of Cincinnati, 1987.

Rosenbloom, Joseph. *Conversion to Judaism*. Cincinnati: Hebrew Union College Press, 1978.

Seltzer, Robert. "Joining the Jewish Faith." In *Pushing the Faith*, ed. Frederick Greenspahn and Martin Marty. New York: Crossroads, 1988.

Silverman, Charles. *A Certain People*. New York: Summit, 1988.

Part IV
Contemporary Issues

CHAPTER TWELVE

Rabbinical Tradition on the Role of Women

It will be useful in looking at the problem of ordination and a religious leadership role for women in the Church to examine the experience of Judaism in this direction. There is much both faiths have in common on this subject and many areas in which they differ.

For the Church, priesthood was seen as a continuation of the model developed in the Old Testament. It saw itself as the successor to Israel into history in its role as elect of God, with priesthood as a central role of linkage. In Scripture, the model for the priest was male, and there was no room for a woman to function in this role.

For the Synagogue, the destruction of the Temple was a traumatic experience, an interruption to be restored only by the messianic era at the end of time. New models for leadership emerged through Rabbinic Judaism. What now became central were the knowledge of the Torah, the capacity to interpret it,

197

and the authority to deal with it—expertise that came from ordination.

The emphasis on maleness, nevertheless, was common to both Synagogue and Church, and the role for women was one that needed to be worked out in a painstaking way, with much soul-searching and inner struggle.

For the Church, priesthood was a continuing reality. For the Synagogue, on the other hand, it became a memory, preserved in a sense of awareness of descent from the priesthood. The descendants of the priestly family possessed the right of precedence in being called up to the Torah and blessing the congregation on the three pilgrim festivals: Passover, Tabernacles, and Shavuot. They were subject, if they wished to retain their status of ancestral purities, to the same laws as were their priestly forebears.

Yet for Judaism, the emphasis is plainly on the rabbinate and its role, and it is here that the struggle for the participation of women develops.

I

Leadership models for women are clearly to be found in the Old Testament and Rabbinic Judaism, but not in sufficient emphasis to qualify for the kind of role which is being sought after in our day.

Certainly Eve plays no minor role as she moves from the role of man's helpmate to the shaper of his destiny. In a way, the story of the Fall is intended as a corrective to that view. The matriarchs, each in their way, show a sense of creative independence, and Rebecca's role in achieving primacy for Jacob is a case in point (Gen. 27).

There is the mother of Moses, Jochebed (Exod. 2:1–10), and

his sister Miriam, who play significant leadership roles in the shaping of his career. There is Deborah, of course, who acts as leader and judge, clearly a figure of strength and of influence (Ju. 4–5). There is the Queen Mother Athaliah, to say nothing of Jezebel, both of whom play such a crucial part in the affairs of state. There are Bathsheba and Abigail in David's time, and the former's role in achieving King Solomon's succession to the throne would do credit to the best political manipulators of our time. We have the wise woman in the days of Samuel; the prophetess Hulda in Jeremiah's day (2 Kings 22:14–20).

In a time of Israel's history when prophets and judges were central to its national and religious formation, it is of no little significance that women could be recognized as judges and prophets. Not many to be sure, but that there were any at all is worthy of note.

There are, however, clear indications of a polarized view of woman in the infrastructure of the biblical narrative. In the creation stories the view of woman before the Fall sees her as the equal of man, as his fulfillment. Then, after the Fall, there is a change in her status because of her sin.

In the Book of Proverbs we tend to find a negative view of woman: in the Song of Songs there is a return to the "prelapsarian view" of woman, autonomous and strong.[1]

The daughters of Zelophehad, who made such a strong plea for woman's rights in inheritance, emerged in later rabbinic tradition as experts in the interpretation of Torah. "It was taught," the Talmud records. "The daughters of Zelophehad were wise women, they were expert expositors of Torah, they were virtuous."[2] Not many women emerge in rabbinic literature as experts in scholarship. Beruriah, wife of Rabbi Meir, is perhaps the best known.

She is described as an avid scholar, a perceptive student of Torah, who apparently went through the intensive three-year
course of study customary for disciples of rabbis at the time. The
Talmud relates how a scholar who came before Rabbi Yoḥanan, asking him to teach him the Book of Genealogies in three
months, is rebuked for his presumption with the words: "If
Beruriah, who studied three hundred laws from three hundred
teachers in one day could nevertheless not do her duty in three
years, how can you propose to do it in three months!"[3]

Nevertheless, into the intertestamentary period and the formative years of the development of Rabbinic Judaism, the role
of woman becomes circumscribed and limited. When Josephus,
writing about Judaism to the Roman world in the first century,
boldly expresses his defense of Judaism in response to the attacks
of Apion, he could write: ". . . for, says the Scripture: a woman
is inferior to her husband in all things, let her therefore be obe-
dient to him: not that he should abuse her, but that she may acknowledge her duty to her husband."[4]

Certainly, if we were to apply the criteria of individual human rights, the role of woman in the postbiblical, formative,
rabbinic era would have to be seen as limited, and perhaps secondary. When it came to references to rights and status in courts
of law, women were coupled with children and slaves in their
ineligibility to testify in a court of law. They could be divorced
by, but could not divorce, their husbands. A woman could never marry again if her husband were to disappear or abandoned
her. Women were not required to study Torah or to perform
most of the 613 commandments.

Yet the woman was honored and cherished in the society as
Mother and Wife. She was protected by contract. Judaism was
basically a monogamous society.

A deeper reason is seen for this special status. Rabbinic Judaism emerged as a force for Jewish survival after the destruction
of the Jewish state by Rome. Survival was its goal, through Torah and family. The role of studying Torah was given to the
man: of being the central force in developing and influencing
the family—to the woman.

In the conflict with Hellenism, in the first pre-Christian century, the stress was on the unity and survivability of the Jewish
people. Hence it became very important to ward off outside influences which could blur and dilute that identity and unity.[5]
Thus a special status develops for woman to protect her, and to
protect the structure of Jewish society.

The central fact is, whether viewed from a negative or a positive viewpoint, that the place for woman in a ministerial role
was minimal. There were virtually no women scholars, no
women rabbis, no women religious functionaries.

What we do find are women playing an economic or business
role as the husband concentrates on the study of Torah. We
find, for example, the case of an eleventh-century woman in
Babylonia, Wuhsha by name,[6] who appears in court, makes a
will, takes part in commercial transactions, heads a committee
for the repair of a synagogue building, and dedicates a Torah
scroll.

We learn that in Renaissance Italy permission was given occasionally to women to act as *shoḥet* (a ritual functionary, usually
male, who slaughtered fowl and domestic animals to provide
the community with kosher meat).

In the responsa of Isaac di Lattes, a rabbi in Mantua. we find
the formula of permission for a woman to function as a religious
functionary in this role. He writes:

Just as man fulfills his role to the highest degree by devoting himself to study [of Torah], searching after wisdom and probing into the causes of all phenomena, so it is the glory and the grandeur of woman to remain in the home to give guidance to her children and to prepare food for the household. Therefore the management of the household devolves upon her. Now since it is the woman's responsibility to prepare meals for her husband and to care for her flock, her little children, and to raise them as flower beds that they may become strong to serve their Creator, should they desire to eat dressed meat properly slaughtered, she cooks it and prepares the table. Now, in order that a stranger may not come into her house [to be with her] in performing the act of ritual slaughter as required by our holy Torah, *it has been a practice for the daughters of Israel to study the laws of ritual slaughter.* And this worthy and virtuous maiden in Israel, who is not lacking in worth and grandeur, has studied the laws of ritual slaughter [of permitted animals and birds for food], has mastered the material in the appropriate manuals, and has become proficient in them through instruction from the venerable Rabbi _____, who attests to her proficiency and validates her work as acceptable. *I therefore give her my support, and open the door to her, permitting her to perform this holy task* to feed others, provided only that she perform in the presence of an expert to determine whether she faints or not [i.e., whether she can really stand the gaff!], she must do this twice a day, morning and evening, for the first three months, then once a week for the following year, and thereafter once a month for the rest of her life, that she not forget what she has learned. Her deeds will praise her in the gates, she will eat of the fruit of her hands, and she will merit a good marriage, sons who will study Torah and perform good deeds in Israel in the lifetime of her father and her mother, her brothers and sisters, uncles and aunts, who will behold the good things that come to her, and will rejoice. Amen.[7]

I have translated and cited this episode because it reflects the subtle change in attitude to ministry by woman in a male-oriented religious culture, and within the legal framework of the accepted tradition. One must remember that the proper preparation of meat for the table was an injunction rooted in the Bible and related to the Temple cult. The animals brought to the Temple for sacrifice were, as we read in the Book of Samuel, slaughtered by the priests, who kept a small portion, returning the rest to the one who brought the offering so that he and his family could partake of it.

This priestly activity became the task of a specially trained religious functionary who had to master a tractate of the Talmud which dealt with it both from a religious and technical point of view. This functionary was usually a male, To permit a woman to do this was in reality a departure from norm, and we must note how this departure is justified by attempting to portray and defend the traditional role of woman!

II

To take a leap from the sixteenth century to the nineteenth century is not as long a leap as the years suggest. For, from the point of view of Jewish history, the Middle Ages extend from the eighth century, when the Talmud was completed, up to the eve of the French Revolution, during which time most of world Jewry lived under talmudic law.

It is with the French and American Revolutions that the ghetto walls began to fall, and opportunities for the entry of the Jew into the world of Western culture appeared. The price of the "ticket of admission to European civilization," as Heine put it, was the acceptance of individual freedom at the price of national identity.

Thus many Jews tended to see themselves a French (or German, or British, or American) Jew of the Mosaic persuasion, and Reform Judaism appeared on the scene, in an attempt to refashion Judaism in consonance with the new spirit of the new times.

Here were new views for the emancipation of men and women; new ideals of equal status; new dreams touched off by the Romantic movement. Mary Wollstonecraft Shelley dreamed of the liberated woman in England; George Sand, in France, made her claim for emancipation in men's garb! Rahel Herz and her Jewish compatriots presided over salons which were centers of literary, artistic, and political creativity.

Since Reform Judaism saw itself as a new incarnation of prophetic Judaism, reborn for a new messianic day, it declared itself emancipated from the "bonds" of rabbinic law, and could legislate freely for the future.

Early in the nineteenth century it proclaimed equal status for men and women within Judaism. By the mid-nineteenth century it had declared that women could be ordained as rabbis. The first woman rabbi was so ordained in American Reform Judaism in—1973! That it took more than a century to implement this declaration speaks volumes for the tension between legislation and custom in any religious movement, even the most liberal.

At the present time there are four or five ordained women rabbis in the American Reform movement. One of them, Sally Priesand, the first to be ordained (1973),[8] was elected in June of 1977 as the first woman to serve on the executive committee of the Central Conference of American Rabbis. Almost one-third of the enrollment in the four branches of the Hebrew Union College–Jewish Institute of Religion, the American seminary that trains Reform rabbis, are women. So in this wing of Judaism, it would appear that the breakthrough for women in the ministry has been achieved.

A closer look at the process will be helpful. For one thing, the first woman known to have filled any rabbinical function in modern times was Hannah Rachel Werbermacher (1805–1892), who was known as the Maid of Ludomir.[9] She became famous as a talmudic scholar, and was consulted by a great number of Hasidim, who regarded her as a saint. She wore a prayer shawl, put on phylacteries, said Kaddish, and attended services regularly. But she never received ordination. In the 1930s Regina Jonas was the first woman to be ordained a rabbi in Germany. However, she never led a congregation. She died in a concentration camp under the Nazis.

We must note that it took almost a century for the first woman to be ordained as rabbi in the Reform movement. For as early as 1846, the Breslau Synod passed a resolution "that woman be entitled to the same religious rights and subject to the same religious duties as man . . . that women are obliged to perform religious acts as depend on a fixed time, insofar as such acts have significance for our religious consciousness."[10] It stopped short, however, of including ordination.

It took American Reform Judaism, in the spirit of American liberalism and freedom, to take that step. In 1892, three years after its founding, the Central Conference of American Rabbis (CCAR), the central body of Reform rabbis, passed a resolution which repeated the spirit of the Breslau resolution, equal rights for women, but still no mention of ordination.

It was not until 1922 that the question of ordination was confronted head on at a session of the CCAR. Here the question was dealt with directly. Prof. Jacob Lauterbach presented a lengthy responsum on the question, and came to a cautiously negative conclusion on the grounds that it might jeopardize the authority and historical character of ordination. He was opposed in the debate by Prof. David Neumark, who argued: "You cannot treat the Reform rabbinate from the Orthodox point of view. Orthodoxy is Orthodoxy and Reform is Reform. Our good relations with our Orthodox brethren may still be improved upon a clear and decided stand upon the question." Therefore, a resolution approving the ordination of women was overwhelmingly passed, with two negative votes cast by Prof. Lauterbach and Rabbi Barnett Brickner.

So there was the resolution, but still no ordained rabbis. A few women here and there took full rabbinic courses hoping to be ordained. Between 1922 and 1932 three or four women were graduated without ordination from the New York and Cincinnati schools of the College-Institute.

In 1935, the daughter of a rabbi enrolled at the New York School (Jewish Institute of Religion) took the full course, asked for ordination, and after a faculty battle it was denied by a narrow majority. The student received a Master of Hebrew Letters degree but no ordination.

In England, in the early twenties, the Hon. Lily Montagu, one of the founders of the World Union for Progressive Judaism, was elected as "lay preacher" of her congregation and served for many years as its spiritual leader and preacher. She had no ordination from a theological seminary, although in later years she was given an honorary D.H.L. degree from Hebrew Union College.[11]

But still no ordination of women. Finally, the man who had voted against ordination of women in 1922 came out for it in 1955. In that year, Rabbi Brickner, who had by this time become president of the Central Conference of American Rabbis, called for a reconsideration in his presidential address. Acknowledging his opposition in 1922, he added: "But since then our needs have changed and I have changed my mind. Many Christian Protestant denominations have also changed their minds and now ordain women."

Earlier in 1955. Harvard Divinity School had voted to admit women to qualify for ordination, and the General Assembly of the Presbyterian Church had made a similar decision. He, therefore, recommended the appointment of a special committee to study the matter and to report at the next conference. The following year a report was brought in, giving its approval to the 1922 resolution and suggesting that the time of ordination had come. This report was received, and tabled for further discussion.

No additional resolution seemed needed, for the 1922 resolution was clear enough. All that remained was implementation. and in 1967, a woman was admitted to the rabbinic program, fulfilled the requirements, and was ordained by Dr. Nelson Glueck, who had served as a member of the 1956 committee.

The hand of custom hung heavy even over a movement that had hitched its wagon to the star of change.

III

In the traditional wings of Judaism (Orthodox and Conservative), the movement toward the religious equalization of woman's role has moved much more slowly.

The restraints in Jewish law, the paramount role for the male despite a protective role for woman, remained. The part assigned to women in synagogue worship remained secondary. They were kept separate in worship service, and in some situations even veiled from view.

Yet as one moved into Western societies, with their tendency to a more liberated view of woman. one saw evidences of changing attitudes.

The Conservative movement, although it saw itself as living under the authority of the halakhah (religious law), nevertheless conceded some change in religious practice. The elimination of separation of seating in public worship was the major change it made when it first appeared on the American Jewish scene at the turn of the century. Some Conservative congregations (but not many) went so far as to introduce the organ as an instrument of musical accompaniment in worship.

In the Conservative movement there were gradations of subtle change. The faculty of its theological seminary tended to adhere most closely to the Orthodox position; the rabbinate tended to be sensitive to constructive change within the tradition; and the laity was flexible in its own practice while insisting on the maintenance of traditional patterns by its functionaries.

But here, as in the Orthodox world, the pressures for change were constant. Many Jewish women were involved in the woman's liberation movements. Many women of Conservative and Orthodox backgrounds moved ahead in the academic and professional world, and began to press for more significant roles in their religious lives.

Responding to this pressure in the Conservative movement, the Rabbinical Assembly's Committee on Law and Standards ruled that women could be counted as members of the quorum (minyan) for group prayer.[12] This has not yet won widespread acceptance in the movement, yet it is indicative of a process of change that is not likely to be stemmed. Just over the horizon, demands that women serve as cantor and as rabbi are surfacing. Women have long been students in the Teacher's College of the Jewish Theological Seminary, but some are now knocking insistently upon the doors of the Rabbinic Division for admission.

Philip Sigal of the Law Committee put it succinctly, after giving the full measure of legal arguments for the inclusion of women in the religious quorum, when he wrote:

> To disqualify women from sharing in the right to constitute an assembly or a worship community is to offend them without reason. Even if we categorize the disqualification of women to constitute a quorum as *minhag* (custom) it is a *minhag* which has lost its reason and its appeal.[13]

The issue has surfaced and keeps reappearing. It is a constant theme in scholarly and popular journals; it emerges at assemblies and conferences of religious and law bodies across the spectrum of Jewish life.

Not even Orthodoxy is immune from these stirrings. Here, however, the emphasis is more on removing certain disabilities in legal status and in participatory roles in the synagogue. Orthodox women who have made their way in the professional and academic world are leaders in this advocacy for their advancement in religious status.

Particularly symptomatic of this is the very sober and penetrating analysis by the dean of Stern College, an Orthodox-sponsored woman's college in New York.[14] That the article was written at all is evidence of the stirrings on this question within the Orthodox camp.

Writing in *Tradition: A Journal of Orthodox Thought,* Dean Saul Berman deals with the problem in all its complexity. He examines the discontent with the role of women in traditional Judaism, analyzes the legal components which Jewish law assigns to women, evaluates the justice of complaints, and makes some "modest proposals."

The issues as Dean Berman sees them involve: a sense of being deprived of opportunities for positive religious identification; disadvantages in civil law, especially in the role of the abandoned wife; and the rabbinic perception of the nature of women and the role to which they are assigned.

There ought to be a moratorium on apologetics and a determination to do something about the most serious problems, Berman believes. He very clearly suggests a direction for Orthodoxy:

> It is vital for us to examine these laws and social practices which seem to be unjust to women. When all is said and done, those laws were the total preoccupation of centuries of Jewish sages and scholars through whose interpretative skills capital punishment was virtually abolished; through whose legal authority the task of transformation and eventual elimination of slavery was accomplished; and through whose social awareness a Jewish welfare system came into existence, which is unmatched to this day for its sensitivity to the feelings of the poor.[15]

Reform could proceed *de novo,* though it was not immune from the pressures of custom. For Orthodoxy, he sees the response to the problems in the slow and steady working out of the situation, by bending, without breaking the law to meet new situations.

What this portends for the ministry role for women, especially ordination, in the development of Orthodoxy is not promising in the long run. But what can be expected is a facing up to and gradual change of some aspects of the legal role of women, and a gradual freeing up of women for more of a role in public worship. At the very least, it may be said that the problem is beginning to be faced and discussed.

Conclusion

One thing is clear, and it would seem to be operative not only in the experience of Judaism, but in the experience of many other religious and cultural movements.

It has to do with the delicate balance between custom and law and their development. Accepted customs sometimes harden into and find their expression in law. Law, in its turn, comes under the constant pressure of newly emerging customs.[16]

You do not make a law, a rabbinic maxim once observed, unless a consensus of the people is willing to accept it![17] And when the law is in existence, if consensus rejects it, it becomes ultimately necessary to change the law.

When Rabbi Joseph Caro wrote his code of Jewish law in the sixteenth century, he did not take into account the folk practices of Polish and German Jewry. It became acceptable to them only when Rabbi Moses Isserles (1526–1571), a great rabbinic leader of East European Jewry, included them.[18]

There are now women rabbis in Reform and Reconstructionist Judaism, women ministers in many Protestant denominations. As one observer wryly put it: "While women ministers are getting the pulpits with less status, less money, and less hope for advancement, they have nevertheless made it to the bottom rung." How many palm trees await how many Deborahs to sit under them and judge, we do not know. But what we do know is that the process moves forward, the pressures are irresistible, and law and custom in their interaction will create situations where woman's drive for ministry will ultimately find its fulfillment.

This essay originally appeared as chapter 8 of Women and Priesthood: A Call to Dialogue from the Faculty of the Catholic Theological Union, *edited by Carroll Stuhlmueller, C.P. (Collegeville, Minn: Liturgical Press, 1978).*

Bibliography

Berman, Saul J. "Status of Women in Halakhic Judaism," *Tradition,* 14:2, Fall 1973, pp. 5–28.

Central Conference of American Rabbis, Year Books Vol. LXV, 1995 and LXVI 1956.

Goitein, Shelomo Dov, "Middle Ages," *Hadassah Magazine,* October 1973.

Greenburg, Blu and Irving, "Equality in Judaism," *Hadassah Magazine,* December 1973.

Hyman, Paula, "Jewish Theology: What's in It For and Against Us?," *Ms. Magazine,* July 1974.

de Lattes, Rabbi Isaac b. Imanuel, *She'elot Uteshuvot,* Friedrich Foerster Verlag, Vienna 1860.

Priesand, Sally, *Judaism and the New Woman,* Behrman House, New York 1975.

Rainey, Anson, "Woman," Encyclopedia Judaica, Vol. 16, p. 62.

Sacks, Bracha, "Why I Choose Orthodoxy," *Ms. Magazine,* July 1974.

Sigal, Philip, "Women in the Minyan," *Judaism Quarterly,* Spring 1974.

Starkman, Elaine, "Women in the Pulpit," *Hadassah Magazine,* December 1973, p. 15ff.

Swidler, Leonard, *Women in Judaism,* Scarecrow Press, Inc. Metuchen, NJ 1976.

CHAPTER THIRTEEN

"Do Not Destroy"
Ecology in the Fabric of Judaism

Two Childhood Memories

There was a "blue box" in our kitchen. It had a map of the land of Israel on it, and we regularly dropped our pennies in it. It was to purchase and redeem land through the Jewish National Fund. The goal: to transform desert into productive land, to cover denuded hills with trees. I did not know at the time that ecology was involved.

The other memory is of the visit of a leader of the Jewish National Fund in what was then Palestine to our home. I was twelve at the time. My father and he discussed the process of contacting leaders of the Canadian Zionist Movement. The goal: to win support for the project to raise $100,000 a year for ten years to purchase a huge swamp area in the middle of the country, to be drained and made useful for agriculture. I did not realize it then, but it was another lesson in ecology for me.

Forty-five years later, in the summer of 1971, I found myself in that area at a seaside dune, right at the edge of where this swamp had been, hardly twenty kilometers north of Tel Aviv. I had the occasion to see Kfar Vitkin and the Hepher Valley area, now lush, fertile, and productive, veritably the breadbasket of Israel. In the town square was a plaque recording the fact that this valley had been reclaimed by Canadian Jewry. And it all started with those conversations when I was just a stripling. The lush fields and farms, where once mosquitoes and malaria held sway, awoke those memories. Ecology indeed. Redemption of land from desert, swamp, and desolation.

This aspect of redemption, redemption of fertile and productive land from arid desert and wasteland, which came into my own childhood consciousness in the development of the movement for the national rebirth of the Jewish people, was deeply influenced, I think it fair to say, by deep currents within Judaism that had to do with accepting this world, loving it, and taking seriously its stewardship. Looked at this way, this redemption is perhaps the heart of what we see as the ecological goal.

Ecology in the Jewish Tradition

It is our purpose to examine the motif of ecology at two levels, first in the biblical and rabbinic approach, and second in what the cycle of the Jewish festival year can tell us about ecology and its central role in Judaism.

The Hebrew Bible gets a mixed review from ecologists. There are those like Lynn White, who argue that human arrogance toward nature derives ultimately from attitudes already present in the Bible's creation stories.[1] The "rule over it" of Genesis 1:29 is taken for a mandate to justify the policy of "slash and burn" and devil take the hindmost.

Arnold Toynbee echoes this view. He reads the "rule over it" verse of Genesis as a "license and an incentive for mechanization and pollution."[2] And if one were to believe landscape architect Ian L. McHage, it was the sanction and injunction "to conquer nature, the enemy of Jehovah."[3]

There is a long and sorry tradition of this kind of view. It is part and parcel of the approach that tended, almost on reflex, to negate Judaism and its biblical roots. Here, from the hindsight of triumphalist Christianity with its supersessionist motifs, "Old Testament" Judaism was seen as vengeful, legalistic, under a somber divine authority, in which humankind, in the image of a vengeful, angry God, was similarly vengeful and angry in relationship to nature. Robert Hamerton-Kelly's description of biblical Judaism as violence incarnate is a recent example of the extremes, wittingly or unwittingly, to which these views can be taken.[4] The earth and its produce was to be exploited by humankind. Such virtues as compassion, gentleness, caring, love of fellow human, and forgiveness were "New Testament virtues" foreign to the hard-hearted "Old Testament." Jewish law was mean, violent, nasty. Scholars like Wellhausen, Harnack, Bossuet, and Bultmann, just to mention a few, nurtured this negative view.

The other view is getting its day in court. One has only to name George Foot Moore, E. P. Sanders, J. G. D. Dunn, Albert Schweitzer, W. D. Davies, Krister Stendahl, David Flusser, and Samuel Sandmel, to see the subsoil for that approach. More and more the perception that a careful reading of the Jewish Scriptures, particularly as read and exegeted by rabbinic sources that gave us Mishnah, Talmud, and Midrashim, yields a totally different picture. It is a reading that enabled Bernhard Anderson to observe that "the biblical motif of human domination over nature, when understood in the full context of Israel's creation theology, calls into question the present practices of exploitation and summons people to a new responsibility."[5] Theodore Hiebert could add: "Israel's world view, which did not labor under the dichotomies between nature and history, between matter and spirit . . . may once again provide some models and symbols for more integrative ways of understanding the relationship between human society and its environment."[6]

It comes to this. Perhaps now is the time for the theologians of today once again to affirm a few simple truths: it was not we who created the world, it is not we who control it. It is our responsibility to learn to live with all other creatures, human and otherwise, within the limits of the world. What we should least wish to do is to complete the opening sentence, "In the beginning God created the heavens and the earth," with "In the end we choked the heavens and destroyed the earth."

This becomes possible when it is recognized that, so far as Judaism is concerned, the essential meaning of the Bible is not simply on the surface of the text, but in how the compilers and editors read it and understood it. When we want to understand what the Bible really has to say on an issue, we look at its texts as they are refracted through rabbinic commentary. The way in which the rabbis understood Scripture gives us a clue as to where the essence of the Jewish theological position is to be located.

What we know now as Rabbinic Judaism, innovative, imaginative, and immensely creative, grew up within Second Commonwealth Judaism, and as though to "anticipate the cure before the disease," developed that crucial change which shaped a Judaism that could survive the destruction of the second Jewish state with a normative Judaism and an evolving Christianity.[7] It shaped Jewish life and Jewish tradition through the hermeneutic process of Torah interpretation and commentary. Here the attitude of Judaism can be discovered and decoded. It is to the rabbinic reading of Scripture that we turn for the Jewish position.

Let us begin with the already-cited Genesis 1:28: "God blessed them and said to them: 'Be fertile and increase, fill the earth and master it (*u'r'du va*); and rule the fish of the sea, the birds of the sky, and all the living things that creep on earth.'" What an indignant ecologist sees as a mandate to rule or ruin is understood quite differently in rabbinic commentary. The crux lies in the verb *r'du,* usually translated as "rule." Rabbinic commentary depends on a pun to interpret the passage. To be sure, there is a Hebrew root *rada* that means "rule." But there is also a root *yarad* which means "to descend," and whose imperative form is also *r'du.*

Here the pun comes to the rescue of ecology. Both the Midrash to this passage and the Rashi commentary tell us: "If man is deserving, he rules; if not, he is diminished." The ultimate test for humankind therefore comes in its attitude to ecology and stewardship.

Nor is this the only interpretation of *r'du* that is not obsessed with the idea of mastery. In the Talmud (Yebamot 65b) we read that in the context of this passage, "rule" suggests "procreation" and not "mastery." At bottom the rabbinic conviction is that "the earth is the Lord's" and that we are not so much its masters as its stewards.

From this point of view, Genesis 1:28 is clearly associated with Genesis 2:18, where we learn that God "placed him [Adam] in the garden to till it and guard it." Clearly stewardship rather than mastery seems to be the guiding principle and supports the rabbi's pun.

Jeremy Cohen, in a thorough study of how Genesis 1:28 was read and interpreted in both Jewish and Christian commentaries, points out that the post-Reformation negative conclusion proceeded from a "flawed methodology. Scholars simply assumed that their own understanding of the verse matched that of the author, that this understanding characterized Jewish and Christian readers of the Bible throughout the intervening centuries. . . . Hence it was perfectly permissible to link the verse directly to social and scientific tendencies of our own day and age."[8]

Another important building block is to be found in Deuteronomy 20:19–20: "When in your war against a city you have to besiege it a long time in order to capture it, you must not destroy the trees, wielding the axe against them. You may eat of their fruit, but you must not cut them down." Indeed a crusading ecologist in Oregon would enthusiastically seize upon this verse. One is reminded of Astroff in Chekhov's *Uncle Vanya,* who could say:

> Well, I admit you can cut woods out of some need, but why destroy them? Russian woods are creaking under the axe, milliards of trees perish, dwellings of beasts and birds are emptied, rivers go shallow and dry, wonderful landscapes vanish, never to be brought back again, and all because lazy man hasn't enough sense to bend down and pick up fuel from the ground. . . . He must be a reckless barbarian to burn this beauty in his stove, destroy what we cannot create again . . . [9]

The rabbis took that verse from Deuteronomy to represent a principle of ecological responsibility and concern. They extended the prohibition of cutting trees to all wanton acts of destruction (B. Kiddushin 32a). They extended the prohibition to matters of peacetime concern, including air pollution, restrictions on where tanneries could be located, and the placing of cemeteries near cities (Mishnah, Baba Batra 2:8–9; B. Baba Kama 82b). They extended its application from objects of nature to human artifacts. "Whoever breaks vessels or tears garments or clogs up a fountain or does away with food in a destructive manner, violates the prohibition of *bal tashḥit* [you may not destroy]."[10]

Underlying this principle is the clear recognition that what we are wont to call our property is really God's. It is a misreading of Scripture to suggest that the Bible is person-centered, that the human bestrides the world like a colossus and can do anything with nature. The "image of God" in us does not make us God. It does make us God's agent or steward, and God wants God's world hallowed and preserved. That is what mitzvot (divine commands to humans) are about, and doing ecology is a supreme mitzvah!

Even when it comes to animal sacrifice as a means of worshipping God, this principle comes through clearly. We learn in Leviticus 22:28 that "no animal from the herd or from the flock shall be slaughtered the same day with its young." The vegetarian would shrug his or her shoulders and ask, "Why not spare them all?" But when we read the commentary of Naḥmanides on Leviticus 22:28, which says that "Scripture will not permit a destructive act that will bring about the extinction of a species, even though it has permitted the ritual slaughter of that animal for food," the ethic that translates itself into environmental awareness emerges clearly.

Samson Raphael Hirsch and Umberto Cassuto further corroborate this classical Jewish perspective. Hirsch, a great nineteenth-century theologian, insists that the prohibition of purposeless destruction of fruit trees around a besieged city is only to be taken as an example of general wastefulness. Under the concept of the principle of *bal tashḥit* ("do not destroy"), the purposeless destruction of anything at all is taken to be forbidden, so that our text becomes the most comprehensive warning to human beings not to misuse the position which God has given them as masters of the world.[11] And according to Cassuto, "legal cases recorded in the Torah . . . show important points in which Israel's conduct was to be different and superior to their contemporaries in this regard to emphasize the importance of the protection of the environment in a civilization where such considerations were not accepted."[12]

Ecology in the Jewish Liturgical Tradition

Applying the rabbinic principle of scriptural hermeneutic to the cycle of festivals of the year yields similar results.

Let us begin with the Sabbath, the keystone of the arch of the festival cycle that shapes Jewish life. Of the Sabbath, the Hebrew thinker Ahad Ha'am once said, "The Sabbath has kept the Jew more than the Jew has kept the Sabbath."[13] It is the analogue to God's resting after the process of creation. It is a recurring day in a seven-day week, in which there is an opportunity to stand back, reflect, and achieve a taste of the messianic fulfillment at the end of time, to catch a glimpse of a world at peace. How significant that this command includes your "manservant and maidservant, your ox and your ass": it extends to all creatures of creation.

More than this, it extends to the environment itself. How else can we understand the Sabbath of the cycle of years, the sabbatical year, the command that every seventh year the land itself enjoy a Sabbath? The land is to lie fallow, to rest, to restore itself, to reinvigorate itself—an instinctive insight into how things ought to be. What a profound insight, in a prescientific era, of how what is taken from the land must be allowed to return to the land.

And what about the Sabbath of Sabbaths every seven sabbatical years, that fiftieth year that is to recur to the end of time, the year to which we give the name Jubilee, when everything returns to its original owner, all bets are off, all slaves freed, all land returns to its original owner? Surely this is a signal to us, placed at the very heart of the religious cycle, that we are not masters of everything, that we are in fact stewards at best, stewards at risk in our stewardship if it is a flawed, destructive stewardship.

Abraham Joshua Heschel was right on target when he wrote of the spirit of the Sabbath, which he saw as the spirit of Judaism and vice versa: "There are three ways in which we may relate ourselves to the world—we may exploit it, we may enjoy it, we may accept it in awe."[14] Accepting the world in awe is good advice in an approach to ecology, and it comes straight out of the spirit of Judaism.

Furthermore, Rosh Hashanah and Yom Kippur, the New Year and the Day of Atonement, manifest an ecological concern in cutting the human species down to size. Hubris is taken to the woodshed and we spend much introspective time coming to understand that God rules, that we do not run the show, that we are not quite the masters of our fate that we think we are. We stand in judgment for our human frailties and sinfulness, and only prayer, penitence, and acts of justice/charity (one word in Hebrew, *zedakah!*) can avert the evil decree. And in the penitential prayers our ecological sins are placed alongside the catalogue of our other misdeeds for consideration.

In the main symbol of these days of awe, the shofar (ram's

horn) and its shrill, primitive call to repentance, there is a hidden ecological note. We have in our past, in the ancient Temple service, animal sacrifice. But when it comes to the main symbol of atonement and the remembering of the sparing of Isaac on the mountaintop, it is not the whole animal, but an expendable portion, that we use, the lack of which does no harm to the animal.

Ecology is involved in the basic reason for Rosh Hashanah. According to tradition, this time of the year represents two beginnings: the creation of Adam and the creation of the cosmos. Human and cosmos share the same birthday; the one does not dominate the other. Somehow their destiny is linked, and part of the repentance/return (*teshuvah*) has to do with our understanding that how we deal with our environment is directly involved in the case on our behalf in the heavenly court of judgment.[15]

Yom Kippur, the great fast-day of intense introspection and self-evaluation, is a day on which we shut ourselves off from the world to prepare to return to that world a better and more caring person. It is on this day that we read the Book of Jonah as the prophetic reading that follows the afternoon Torah reading. As the day mounts to its climax, it is an ecological model that remains with us. For God reminds Jonah that the gourd, the cattle and the sheep, the fish of the sea, and the world of nature are a central concern. Jonah swallowed by the fish is indeed a somber warning. The reminder is well worth remembering: "You cared about the plant, for which you did not work and which you did not grow, which appeared overnight and perished overnight. And should I not care about Nineveh, that great city, in which there are more than a hundred and twenty thousand persons who do not know their right hand from their left hand,

and much cattle as well?" (Jonah 4:10). Indeed, the gourd is the Bible's "spotted owl," held out as a warning to us to be ecologically responsible.

Just five days after Yom Kippur come the eight days of Tabernacles, of Sukkot, the ecological festival par excellence. The bridge from the God-intoxication of the Day of Atonement back into the everyday world, the transition from holy to profane, comes through the sukkah, the frail booth in which we live for the eight days of the festival. We leave our houses of brick and mortar, our urban milieu, to live in a setting redolent with autumn's beauty, roofed with thatch, through which the stars can be seen. We carry the palm, willow, and myrtle tied together in one hand, and the citron in the other. We remember the wandering in the wilderness after Sinai, and just as we were brought closer to the divine in the days of awe, we are brought closer to nature around us and its needs.

When winter closes its grip on us, a little minor festival—but how precious to children, and pregnant with ecological implications—comes to remind us of new years: a new year for trees. This festival is Tu B'Shvat, designated by its date, the fifteenth day of Sh'vat. In Israel and its Mediterranean setting, the almond trees began to bud in mid-January. So the trees have their festival. There is the talmudic story of a sage meeting an old man planting a tree. When asked why he was doing something the fruits of which he would never live to enjoy, he replied: "Just as my grandparents planted fruit trees from which I have eaten, so I plant them for my grandchildren" (BT, Ta'anit 23a). And so it is a happy celebration, and in northern climates it comes in midwinter as a welcome harbinger of spring.

How important this is, is seen in a statement made by Yoḥanan ben Zakkai about the Messiah: "If a man is planting a tree, and someone comes to him and says that the Messiah has come, let him finish planting the tree and then go to greet the Messiah!"

Passover comes with its message of exodus and freedom in the spring. The Seder table uses greens, and the reading of the Song of Songs highlights a sensitivity to spring and its hopes of rebirth, a rebirth as much for the environment as for us. Through the winter months, up to Passover, the core of the daily prayer includes a prayer for rain, reflecting the climate of the land of Israel, where the winter rains are important to the spring and summer crops. From Passover through the summer, the prayer for rain shifts to a prayer for dew: always a concern for the right conditions for good crops.

Fifty days after Passover, the festival of freedom, comes Shavuot, the Feast of Weeks, also known as Pentecost. Something of ecology lies hidden in that fifty-day link. For the fifty days between these two festivals represent the fifty years of the Jubilee, the culmination of the seven sabbatical years with everything that this means for ecological healing. What applies to nature, on the one hand, applies to the link between freedom and Torah, on the other.

Indeed, the three pilgrim festivals form a significant sequence in this sense. First come Passover and freedom: the newly freed slaves journey fifty days through the wilderness, come to Mount Sinai, and receive the Torah. Then comes Sukkot to remind them of the forty years of wandering in the desert until the entry to the Promised Land. And so we are bidden to count the days (*sefirat ha'omer*) from Passover to Shavuot, fifty of them, jubilee-preparing days, ecologically significant days.

On the thirty-third day we have Lag B'Omer—another great favorite of the ghetto-captive schoolchildren. This was the day they left their dingy classrooms and their dingy ghetto surroundings, and went out into the woods to be one again with nature. It was a happy, carefree time for them. It was also a special day for the mystics, for it was the day their sage and teacher, fleeing from the persecutions of the emperor Hadrian, emerged from the cave where he had hidden for seven years. It is on this day that we remember this sage, Simeon bar Yoḥai, who resisted the Romans, fled for his life, and hid in a cave, where, tradition tells us, he was sustained by a fruit tree that sprouted at its mouth. When he finally emerged from the cave, he saw an old man (was it the man who planted the tree?) walking with myrtle branches in his hand. Asked where he was going he replied: "To greet the Sabbath." The myrtle branch and the Sabbath, Adam and cosmos, ecology and ethics! (BT, Shabbat 33b).

When the celebration of Shavuot, the birthday of the Torah, comes, it is celebrated by all-night study of the Torah, by confirmation, by eating only vegetarian meals, and by decorating the synagogue with foliage. "Greens for Shavuot" was a slogan deep in the consciousness of many generations. A story with that title by the Yiddish writer Sholom Aleichem burns brightly in my own memory of childhood.[16]

Moses de Leon, author of the *Zohar,* that great classic of kabbalism, in the thirteenth century spoke of the triad God, Torah, and Israel; and Franz Rosenzweig in the twentieth century spoke of creation, revelation, and redemption as the three basic principles of Judaism. Creation is at the beginning, and links humankind with cosmos. God's world and humankind's place in it: the human person as part of the cosmos, on the one hand, and God's steward, on the other, has profound implications for locating ecological concerns at the very heart and center of Judaism.

Conclusion

This chapter began with a blue box, a telephone call, and a later visit to the Valley of Hepher, now the breadbasket of Israel. It began with childhood memories that had to do with salvaging deserts, replanting forests, and making for a habitable world. The planting of a tree, the fragrance of the sukkah, the greens in the synagogue, the romp in the woods, the ram's horn, all woven in the fabric of memory, seem symbolically to have everything in common with what ecological issues are all about.

This two-pronged effort to enlist the rabbinic hermeneutic of biblical references and the cycle of the Jewish year is intended to suggest that Judaism is deeply connected with ecological values. It seems to come down to the tree. Do not destroy it. Make it a paradigm for everything that has to be done to protect the delicate ecological fabric that surrounds our world, so that we can save the world. As our "forefathers planted trees for us, may we plant trees for our grandchildren" (BT, Ta'anit 23a).

This essay originally appeared in The Ecological Challenge: Ethical, Liturgical, and Spiritual Resources, *edited by Richard N. Fragomeni and John T. Pawlikowski (Collegeville, Minn.: Liturgical Press, 1994).*

Part V
Epilogue: Celebration Tributes

Hayim Goren Perelmuter: A Tribute

Donald Senior, C.P.

For Rabbi Perelmuter's colleagues at Catholic Theological Union, this book is both a tribute and a labor of love.

For more than a quarter of a century, Hayim Perelmuter has been a charter faculty member at the largest Roman Catholic school of theology in the country. Few rabbis, I imagine, can make a similar claim! His presence on our faculty has never been a token or even merely a dramatic ecumenical symbol. Hayim has been for us a revered colleague, a wise and beloved teacher, a respected scholar, and an essential part of our educational commitment.

CTU began its history in 1968 as a direct result of the Second Vatican Council. Several religious orders decided to pool their resources and begin a new venture in preparing students for ministry. They closed their own individual seminaries, which, for the most part, were located in remote rural settings, and took up residence in the Hyde Park area of Chicago, in proximity to the University of Chicago and to a number of important Protestant divinity schools. The conviction was then, and still is, that

229

students preparing for ministry would be better and more realistically prepared in an urban, ecumenical, and university setting.

Right from the start, that sense of openness extended to the richness and power of the Jewish heritage. Rabbi Hayim Perelmuter, then rabbi at the important K.A.M.–Isaiah Israel congregation in Hyde Park, joined the faculty in CTU's first year, offering courses in Rabbinic Judaism and becoming an essential part of the life of a Roman Catholic school of divinity.

Because of Hayim's presence on our faculty, literally hundreds, even thousands, of graduates have experienced first-hand both the depth of Jewish tradition and thought and the living embodiment of Jewish faith. I can only believe that these Catholic graduates and the people they serve will never be the same. How many teachers can have such satisfaction as to know that they have touched in a profound way a whole generation of religious leaders, and in a tradition not their own!

Now Hayim celebrates eighty years of life, a number deserving respect in its own right, besides having biblical sanction! Of course, only a part of Hayim's professional life is defined by his relationship to CTU. He has served as a distinguished rabbi for several congregations, exercised civic and national leadership on behalf of the Jewish community, and been recognized for the excellence and creativity of his scholarship. What a blessed life!

But for those of us who have been with Hayim as colleagues and friends all these years, even these accomplishments take second place to the treasure of friendship with a warm, gracious, wise, and noble man. It is a privilege, and a joy, to know him.

On the occasion of announcing this book and welcoming Hayim's student and distinguished colleague, Professor Michael Walzer, to a symposium in Rabbi Perelmuter's honor, I had the occasion to survey the remarkable gathering of people who came to offer birthday tribute: faculty and students from Catholic Theological Union and from the Hyde Park cluster of divinity schools; faculty and students from the University of Chicago divinity school; members of the long-standing Roman Catholic–Jewish Dialogue; religious leaders from the Jewish and Christian communities of Chicago; friends and congregants from K.A.M.–Isaiah Israel; and, of course, Hayim's dear wife, Nancy Perelmuter, and members of his family.

How often does such a gathering take place in a spirit of peace and common exuberant joy? In a time of growing ethnic violence, when nurtured memories of old wounds seem to erode tolerance, when the wisdom of religious faith is often ignored, such a gathering becomes not simply a tribute to the graceful man who gave us reason to come together but a sign of hope for the future of humanity.

In this volume, the intelligence, the conviction, and the dedicated scholarship that have nourished the religious spirit of Hayim Perelmuter become apparent. Catholic Theological Union and the many friends of Hayim Perelmuter dedicate this work gratefully to this remarkable and beloved man.

Reflections on a Man and His Dialogue

Michael Walzer

I have been asked to address a large subject today—the impact of the Jewish-Catholic dialogue—but my own idea about this occasion, and about my participation in it, has from the beginning been cast in rather different terms. Here I am with my teacher, remembering the old days: it is a chance to feel young again—like a boy delivering his bar mitzvah speech. Were speeches required in 1948? I don't recall what I said or whether I said anything at all. Maybe I didn't thank Rabbi Perelmuter enough, and so I have been given another chance.

I do remember my Torah portion, Ki Tissa from the Book of Exodus, which includes the story of the golden calf; and I remember my response to the slaughter of the idol worshippers after Moses came down from the mountain (how could he order the killing of so many people?); and I remember Rabbi Perelmuter's response to my response. He talked to me as if I really were an adult Jew whose opinions on the interpretation of Torah had to be taken seriously—for which I am everlastingly grateful. But the day is a blur; my clearest memory is focused on the crucial physical sign that I wasn't an adult Jew at all: the box that I had to climb onto so that I could see over the pulpit. With what an odd combination of humiliation and pride did I stand before the congregation that day: I was certainly too short, but thanks to my teacher, I knew my text!

Before there can be a Jewish-Catholic dialogue, there have to be Jews and Catholics. I can testify today to Rabbi Perelmuter's extraordinary talent for turning American Jewish children into knowledgeable and committed Jews. This is not so easy in these latter days, when we live with an uneasy sense of the thinning out of Jewish culture, a growing textual illiteracy. Another memory: when I was fourteen or fifteen, I studied the Book of Joshua with Rabbi Perelmuter. Joshua is one of the more problematic of biblical books, with its triumphant accounts of conquest and extermination. The moral difficulties posed by those accounts have stuck in my mind; I have written about them more than once, and been forced each time to go back to the texts and the commentaries. The only cure for illiteracy is reading.

But the reading will only be sustained in a community where the issues it raises are discussed and debated. I learned in those Johnstown years that one didn't read in order to learn this or that established *doctrine*; one read in order to learn what to worry about—and how to worry together with other people within a tradition of discourse. The Jewish tradition, or the part of the tradition on which I want to focus today, which encompasses the debates about law and politics and the temporary, prescriptive resolutions, is called halakhah. It includes the legal portions of the Talmud, the later codifications, and the immense litera-

ture of rabbinic responsa. One of the distinctive, defining features of this tradition is that its written texts incorporate not
only the authoritative prescriptions but also the dissents—the
opinions of minorities or even of lone rabbis. When no prescription is necessary, the arguments are often left unconcluded:
there is this view, held by the majority of sages, and then there
is "another view," equally legitimate. The decision to preserve
dissenting views is recorded in tractate Eduyyot of the Mishnah,
and the reason is familiar from our own judicial practice: today's
minority opinion may be picked up later on by a majority. Every opinion is potentially authoritative; the debate is ongoing,
permanent. When Maimonides omitted the arguments and the
dissents from his great code, the *Mishneh Torah,* he was bitterly
criticized: how could a scholar make up his mind for himself if
he could not see the reasons of his predecessors? The only
change that the Messiah will bring to the life of the halakhah is
this: in the society that he initiates, all of us, and not only a small
elite, will have time to study and argue.

Halakhah today is largely the preserve of Orthodox Jews,
who have made it into a narrow and constricted affair; its creative moments lie in the past. The Reform Judaism in which I
grew up was biblically, not talmudically, focused. I have come
to believe that this is a mistake, another example of narrowness.
Reading Rabbi Perelmuter's *Siblings* with its sympathetic and
persuasive account of the creation of Rabbinic Judaism, I conclude that he has come to feel the same way. My own reasons
for taking a new interest in Jewish law derive in part from an
encounter with American Catholicism—and it is that encounter, rather than the larger issues suggested by my title, that I
want to describe to you today.

Some years ago, I watched with great interest while the Bishops' Conference worked on its pastoral letter on nuclear deterrence. Brian Hehir, one of the major intellectual figures involved in drafting the letter, knew my book *Just and Unjust Wars* and sent me successive versions of the work-in-progress. I was very impressed (as I was again with the later, equally or perhaps more controversial letter on economic justice). Father Hehir and the other drafters drew on a specifically Catholic tradition of natural-law theorizing, quoting texts the way the rabbis do. Their work was aimed in the first instance at the Catholic community; the resulting letter was a teaching document for the Church. And at the same time, it was a policy statement for all Americans. It had a useful doubleness; it provoked a debate among Catholics and among Americans generally. There were interesting revisionist and dissenting opinions in both audiences. The same thing happened with the letter on economic justice, where a critical campaign against the bishops' arguments (or the arguments of the majority of the bishops) was led by Michael Novak, who grew up in Johnstown, and who must have been studying with a local priest in the same years that I was studying with Rabbi Perelmuter. We did not meet until many years later and didn't agree on much when we met; I was far more sympathetic to the bishops than he was.

Jews have a lot to learn from the bishops. We will never have a central conference like theirs (the Central Conference of American Rabbis, characteristically, includes only some American rabbis). Jewish life is radically decentralized; it is congregationalist in form—as it was, indeed, long before the Protestant Reformation made congregationalism one of the options for Christians. So when I try to imagine—and the attempt seems to me important—a Jewish "letter" on nuclear deterrence or economic justice, reflecting the specific legal and moral wisdom of

our tradition, I can never come up, even in my mind, with just
one letter, with whatever accompanying dissents. There are always competing letters, reading the tradition differently—and
none of them authoritative. Our authorities, since the end of
prophecy and the decline of the priesthood, are simply learned
individuals, without any hierarchical position, who must win
their way by their learning, by the persuasiveness of the arguments they make, and by the sense they convey in making them
of moral seriousness and attentiveness to the texts. (But you
should know about Jewish "authorities" of this sort, since you
have had one working here among you at CTU.)

Still, the effort to produce even a set of letters by a number of
different authorities would be immensely valuable, for Jews and
for anyone else who cared to watch, as I watched the bishops.
The result would be speculative halakhah—which, with reference to issues like war and peace, might have to be long on
speculation. The centuries of Jewish statelessness did not provide many occasions for addressing the hard questions that
Catholic casuists faced again and again: who should fight and
who should refuse to fight, who can be attacked and who cannot be. But statelessness doesn't mean the absence of politics.
Even in the long centuries from the time of Bar Kochba to the
time of Ben-Gurion, there was a Jewish polity, and one of great
interest today when the world is full of wanderers, minorities,
stateless refugees. The Jewish polity was constituted by a set of
dispersed, autonomous, or semi-autonomous communities,
without sovereign power, without territory, without an army
or police force, but managing nonetheless to sustain a common
life, a common identity, and a common law.

The legal discussions among the sages and scholars of these
communities, though they did not extend to such "high" mat-

ters as war and peace, did extend to taxation, welfare, education, membership, and political organization. What was said about these everyday matters at meetings of the *kahal* ("community") is lost to us. But the arguments and rulings of the sages, who were regularly consulted, are in print (or in manuscript) and can still be, and ought to be, recovered, studied, criticized, revised, elaborated, and applied, when they are applicable, to contemporary issues.

If we were to do all that, we would have at the end the basis for a new kind of Jewish-Catholic dialogue, concretely focused on issues and cases. We could see where we differ, or where we have differed, and where the two traditions overlap or even coincide. Maybe this can't be done: Emancipation and reform divided Jewry as profoundly as the Reformation divided Christendom, and the halakhah was left on one side of the divide; maybe it can't be recovered on the other side. But the value of the effort is made clear, I think, by the success of Catholic intellectuals in sustaining a tradition of speculative argument and case-by-case application in the circumstances of modernity. I would be happy here to benefit from the long experience of our younger sibling—to learn from the bishops as you, perhaps, have learned, with the mediating help of Hayim Perelmuter, from the rabbis.

Siblings: A Jewish and a Roman Catholic Scholar

Dianne Bergant, C.S.A.

"Walk with a wise man and you will become wise" (Prov. 13:20).
Hayim Goren Perelmuter is an unusual scholar. I can say this
about many people, but not in the way I say it about Hayim.
We have been colleagues in the Department of Biblical Literature and Languages at Catholic Theological Union since 1978,
where he preceded me by several years. I have walked with him
and, as have many other people, I have learned from him. He is
unusual in at least three ways: (1) He launched a full-time career
of scholarship upon his retirement as rabbi of K.A.M.—Isaiah
Congregation in Chicago; (2) He is a rabbi who teaches rabbinic studies in a Roman Catholic school of ministry; (3) He has
developed an understanding of the relationship between Rabbinic Judaism and Early Christianity that respects the integrity
of each without undermining the claims of either. Each of these
three features will be expanded in what follows.

238

"A wise man will hear and will increase learning" (Prov 1:5). At a time in life when most people eagerly await retirement and the leisure that it normally brings, Hayim resumed the rigors of the doctoral studies that had been cut short by the Second World War. This bespeaks not only the degree of his physical vitality but the keenness of his intellectual gifts. The tenacity with which he committed himself and the enthusiasm that directed his dedication were an inspiration to faculty and student alike. Here was a man for whom age was an asset that brought insight and perspective rather than a liability that limited the horizon of possibility or justified inactivity.

The conferral of his doctoral degree in 1979 was celebrated by students, who, though themselves struggling with the complexities of academic theology, could not fail to be inspired by the accomplishment of this energetic learner. Hayim would probably have been unable to embark on this demanding undertaking had he not been continually challenging his own intellectual development over the years. This is another lesson to be learned by the aspiring ministerial student who might eagerly anticipate the time when serious study can be happily relegated to the past and all of one's energies be devoted to the projects at hand. In contrast, Hayim's life is characterized by ongoing creative ministry grounded in astute comprehension, deliberation, and decision.

The vitality that motivated his return to a life of scholarship is evidenced in the range and volume of the publications that have sprung from his computer. While it is true that this kind of work is expected of one committed to study and writing, we should not forget that this man began anew at a time when many of his contemporaries were retiring. Hayim is a constant reminder to us of the perduring youthfulness that intellectual inquiry fosters and the dogged persistence that scholarly endeavor rewards.

"The teaching of the wise is a fountain of life" (Prov 13:14). The celebrated Vatican II document *Nostra Aetate,* "Declaration of the Relationship of the Church to Non-Christian Religions" (1965), begins its statement regarding the relationship between Christianity and Judaism on a very positive note. Dependent upon the biblical tradition, it recognizes the fundamental spiritual bond linking two of the religious traditions that claim Abraham as their forebear. The document states: "Since the spiritual patrimony common to Christians and Jews is thus so great, this sacred Synod wishes to foster and recommend that mutual understanding and respect which is the fruit of all biblical and theological studies"[1]

When CTU was founded the following year, it took a bold yet fateful step in response to the recommendation, inviting this well-respected rabbinic scholar to join the faculty. From the beginning Hayim has been an integral part of the school, not only teaching but also participating in policy development through departmental and committee discussion and decision-making. He has heightened the CTU community's awareness of post-Holocaust Jewish self-consciousness, both political and religious.

The curricular offerings of the biblical department at CTU have been enhanced by the courses in rabbinic studies taught by Hayim. For students preparing for ministry in the Roman Catholic Church, he has provided an overview of the worship forms in the contemporary American synagogue, carefully tracing the common threads as well as the variations in the Jewish denominations: Orthodox, Conservative, and Reform. He has introduced many students to the liturgy of the High Holy Days of

Rosh Hashanah, Yom Kippur, and Sukkot, even providing them with an opportunity to participate in the Sabbath celebrations of a neighboring Jewish community. His course in Jewish mysticism and messianism has proven to be an invaluable complement to the study of Christology. His courses for Roman Catholic students have successfully contributed to the atmosphere of mutual understanding and respect.

"Interpreting it so that all could understand" (Neh. 8:). 8:8). Hayim's return to scholarship might be perceived as a personal fulfillment, and his energetic and innovative participation in the life of the school is certainly an interreligious success. Without diminishing the importance of either of these accomplishments, his most far-reaching achievement may well be the contribution he has made to both Jews and Christians in their understanding of their interrelationship. His thoughts on the subject are developed in his book *Siblings: Rabbinic Judaism and Early Christianity at Their Beginnings*. The book furthers both Jewish and Christian scholarship, offering a way of understanding the origins of the Christianity and Rabbinic Judaism that respects the religious integrity of both.

Christians who study the history, culture, and religion of ancient Israel frequently do so from one of two points of view. They might regard it as the religious history of a believing community to which they do not belong and, consequently, in which they have great interest but to which they have no personal commitment. On the other hand, they might consider it a part of their own religious history, but a part which eventually finds its fulfillment in the Christian experience. Those who espouse the first position come dangerously close to the intellectual errors associated with Marcion; those who hold the second view may also be endorsing some form of supersessionism. Unfortunately, both points of view have been used to justify religious bigotry.

Other Christians who study the First Testament[2] maintain that the religious message found there has inherent religious significance independent of any subsequent Early Christian reinterpretation. However, they still face a twofold problem: Can one relate the two testaments in a way other than the promise-fulfillment approach so prominent in the Second Testament itself? If so, how then can one be faithful to the Christian theology embedded within that interpretive approach?

Reading rabbinic interpretation or teaching with a rabbinic scholar does not necessarily assist Christians in answering these questions. It might merely result in better understanding and deeper respect, attitudes admittedly necessary for harmonious living in a pluralistic society. The importance of interfaith dialogue cannot be overestimated, especially at a time like the present when we are trying seriously to rectify earlier anti-Semitic and/or anti-Christian attitudes. However, when apparent commonalities are not understood within their respective and quite diverse religious contexts, genuine differences can easily be blurred. For dialogue to be authentic, it must acknowledge dissimilarities as well as similarities.

At various times in history, each of these two religious bodies has justified its own existence by challenging the authenticity of the other. Their respective views of the original relationship between the two traditions often engendered and supported this alienation. Both traditions insist on their own integrity and claim some of the same history and religious documents. Hence honest investigation demands that the reason for both the similarities and the differences be understood in a way that respects each religious body. The work of Hayim Goren Perelmuter does just that. He has very carefully traced the historical and re-ligious reason why these "siblings" interpreted their common tradition in such very different ways.

"Be attentive that you may gain understanding" (Prov 4:1). The way one perceives the various religious movements that made up the Jewish community at the end of the Second Common-wealth (the beginning of the common era) will influence the way one understands the religious literature that was edited, compiled, and newly fashioned at that time, literature that even-tually became the Sacred Scriptures of each of the communities. For example, the Sadducees, the favorite party of the priest-hood, accorded exclusive authority to the Written Law. The Pharisees, on the other hand, argued that the Oral Law was its legitimate interpreter. Politics being what it is, each party would most likely criticize the other's religious beliefs, accusing it of error and unfaithfulness. The criticism was often quite fierce and served as a personal defense as well as a condemnation of the other.

Criticism of both of these parties abounds in early Christian writings and probably stems from the same source, that is, dis-agreement over the correct interpretation of a religious tradition held in common. The Jewish community seemed able to sustain a high degree of diversity and disagreement until the Roman occupation of Judea became intolerable and Jews had to decide on some course of action. Their options included: assimilation into Roman society (apostasy); military resistance (the Zealots); withdrawal from society (the Qumran community); or survival through some messianic fulfillment of the religion of ancient Is-rael. *Siblings* maintains that Christianity and Rabbinic Judaism are both, in very different ways, messianic religions born of an earlier form of Judaism. This view does not deny Christianity's messianic character, but it does call for a revised understanding of it. Furthermore, it gives us insight into the origin of some of the exclusive claims made by Christian theology and the role they played in the earliest communities.

A second insight gleaned from this new perspective deals with the polemical character of some of the early Christian writings. If we believe that much of the controversy is waged between parties within the same religious community who are divided over matters of interpretation, we might perceive the denunciations in a different light and be less apt to dismiss the views of the opposing party as obtuse, self-serving, or false-hearted. This is not intended to throw into question the revelatory value of the Second Testament. Instead, it is meant to appreciate the historical conditioning of some of its assertions. The adversarial character of its polemical statements must be taken into consideration if one is to grasp the import of its religious testimony.

These new insights do not resolve religious controversy, they merely redirect it. However, to characterize the relationship as that of siblings rather than one of supersession is to acknowledge the inherent integrity of both traditions. With this attestation as the starting point, we can begin to develop our respective theologies in cooperation with each other rather than in contention. Our fundamental differences will remain, but they need not be seen as fraudulent. They are, instead, contemporary developments of distinct religious traditions that sprang from different interpretations of a common faith. Through his scholarship and his companionship, Hayim Perelmuter has shown how Christians and Jews can be siblings.

A Response

Hayim Goren Perelmuter

Although I began my association with the Catholic Theological Union in 1968 as a lecturer, the career shift from active rabbi to active academician took place in 1970–80 with the completion of my doctorate and the publication of my work on David Darshan of Cracow. This opened new worlds of possibilities broadening from the Chicago base to the West Coast, to Europe and to Israel.

There have been many highlights, some of which I touch upon here:

There was, first, the student turmoil of the Vietnam War era and the Kent State tragedy, and it engulfed CTU. The faculty found it necessary to deal with student revolt and a demand that the school be shut down. It was exam time, and many faculty members were violently opposed to this and were ready for a confrontation. Our own two sons were deeply involved in the tumult about the war, one as a seminarian, and the other as an undergraduate. I was able to convey to the faculty, through their experiences and reaction, how our students felt, and succeeded in encouraging a compromise that honored their wishes but left a door open to those who wished to come and write their exams. It was a healing experience for us all.

Then there was the Israel Program, which has since become one of the glories of this school. I recall how Carroll Stuhlmueller, who conceived the idea, discussed with me how it might be implemented. Together we contacted the Israeli consulate and various sources in Israel, and the project began. Humbly and modestly it has grown into one of the school's major programs. Carroll's creative imagination lives on in this project, as his presence does with us generally, although the pain left by his recent passing hangs heavily over all.

And then, because of circumstances beyond our control, the housing of the project shifted from Ein Karem in Israel to Bethany in the West Bank, and the need to be sensitive to the refraction of the Israel-Arab struggle through our students, the efforts to create the proper levels of understanding through appropriate debriefings became an important task. It was an example of our dialogue at its most sensitive point. And now, thankfully, there is a peace process and the mutual recognition of Israel and the Vatican.

And then there was the episode of the papal visit to Chicago in 1979, the year that my term as president of the Chicago Board of Rabbis began. In that capacity I found myself as part of a small delegation of non-Catholic religious leaders in Chicago who were to greet the Holy Father on behalf of the general community.

At the same time the entire faculty received an invitation to meet privately with Pope John Paul in a session with the faculties of Catholic theologates in the Chicago area. Our faculty included four women (sisters in religious orders), one Lutheran, and one Jew. As I recall it, the invitation included the spouses, and there was much excitement in anticipation of the visit. All security preliminaries were complied with, including the providing of Social Security numbers.

Then suddenly came word from the inner circle surrounding the Holy Father that only faculty members who were priests would be permitted to go. This ruled out the woman faculty members and the two non-Catholic members of the faculty.

How well I recall the special faculty meeting called to consider this unexpected turn of events. The sense of disappointment and shock was palpable. The president ruled, and the faculty concurred, that under these circumstances no member of the faculty would attend, and that he himself would not travel to Washington for the meeting of seminary presidents with the Pontiff. I recall saying with the greatest sadness: "How ironic it is that I, as a rabbi, will be the only member of this faculty meeting the Holy Father personally!"

An extraordinary serendipity characterizes these wonderful years at CTU. Not only did they make possible the incredibly enriching experiences with students and faculty, but they broadened the scope that took me to Berkeley for ten creative winter quarters at the Graduate Theological Union and Pacific Lutheran Theological Seminary; teaching in Jerusalem for the Israel Program; a seminar in Louvain and an opportunity to contribute to the healing of a Catholic-Jewish rift in Antwerp; several lectures at the Pontifical Academy of Theology in Cracow, where I was the first Jew to teach qua Jew in the 650 years of that institution; a week's seminar at the Catholic University of Lublin on the theme of "Non-Christian Religions in Transition; and a half year teaching at the Institut für Jüdisch-Christliche Forschung in Lucerne, and the Theology Faculty of the

University of Bern. In every instance these possibilities developed from contacts and encounters at CTU.

It was at CTU that my doctorate was completed, and the book on David Darshan published. It was as a result of my teaching the history of Rabbinic Judaism here that the idea of the sibling relationship between Christianity and Judaism germinated, and the book *Siblings* resulted. It was here that *This Immortal People* was born out of one of the team-taught courses with Franklin Sherman and the links between Paulist Press and CTU faculty.

It was here (and in Berkeley) that the idea of a reading of Paul's letters as a source for the study of Rabbinic Judaism and the significant conference on that subject was held. Indeed, CTU has served as a creative leaven for intellectual and scholarly growth which was shaped by the Christian-Jewish dialogue and which at the same time shaped the dialogue.

As I speak of the impact of the dialogue at this level on my own development, I think that it needs to be said that it sharpened and clarified my perception and understanding of myself and my Judaism. At every step along the way it was required of me to be precise in my definitions of where I stood, and where I thought Judaism stood on a host of issues. It came at all levels, on the extent of the Jewishness of Christianity; the attitudes of Judaism to Christianity, and vice versa; the readings of the roles of Jesus and Paul; church attitudes, synagogue attitudes.

In this respect, perhaps the greatest benefit to me was how I perceived my own Judaism and my relationship to it. It left me, I must confess, with a deeper understanding and a more self-assured capacity to relate to the other, which, I can only hope, has turned out to be helpful and useful to the other.

Equally important, perhaps crucial, was the relationship with the faculty. It has been a heavily traveled highway in both directions, a rich and rewarding field of mutual cross-fertilization. I would frequently deal with the "What is the Jewish (or rabbinic) position on . . ." question that happened to be germane to research and writing that was going on, whether in the biblical field, medieval history, contemporary ethics, or sociology.

The reverse held true as well. Not long ago I was called upon by the editor of the Lutheran journal *Dialog* to respond to a book by Robert Hamerton-Kelly on Paul and religious violence. It was a very difficult issue that seemed to me, as it did to a whole range of Jewish scholars in the field, to call for a sharp and pointed response. Yet it had to be controlled and civil. I could turn to several colleagues in the field of Bible, liturgy, and theology for reactions to the article, especially monitoring the tone as it might be read by Christian readers. Their input was invaluable, but despite it Hamerton-Kelly responded with great anger. Not long after we met at a meeting of the Society for Biblical Literature. The personal chemistry between us was good, and he invited me to his seminary in Stanford with Rene Girard, where we talked it out.

And then there is the relationship with students over the years. To see where students have gone all over the world, and to hear from them in their positions of influence in Japan, Africa, Ethiopia, the United States, and Canada, and to learn from them that what they have acquired here continues to help sustain them, is a heart-warming validation.

Most recently, in connection with a national conference on Afro-American studies and seminary studies, a doctoral candidate at CTU from Detroit came in to see me and tell me about his thesis on the theme of racism and a pathology of the racist. My response was that I found his thesis interesting, and that it reflected a pamphlet written in Hebrew in Russia, in 1881, on just that subject, a pamphlet that had contributed to the birth of the Zionist movement. He had never heard of it and was excited to learn that something like that existed. So when, someday, Leo Pinsker's pamphlet *Autoemancipation,* a classic in the history of Zionism that posits antisemitism as Judeophobia, a disease of the hating community, appears in his dissertation, it will be thanks to this aspect of the dialogue!

Does all this matter? Does the dialogue make a dent? Will it change things radically? Do minds really change? No one can tell for certain, but I believe very deeply that it does matter, and that it does make a difference.

Judaism and Christianity emerged from a common womb, and as siblings broke sharply from each other. They talked past each other, or at each other, but rarely with each other. The consequences of the alienation were deep and daunting, indescribably and inexpressively painful. Their views of each other were blurred and distorted through the cataracts of misprision.

The change that has come, especially since the end of World War II, has lowered the decibels, and made rational understanding and communication possible. Growing forces with Christendom hunger to restore their Jewish roots; growing forces within Judaism are more relaxed and open in expressing where Judaism stands.

Perhaps the best we can expect is what the shapers of the Talmud finally decided upon, to encompass differing views under a broad umbrella of diversity within common goals. The Hillel-Shammai differences remain, but they remain within a more universal discourse. "These and these are the words of the living God." Perhaps that is the best we can expect for the Christian-Jewish dialogue, and I think it is a lot. There is much to be said for pluralism and loving dialogue that leaves room for dissent. It is perhaps the best insurance we have against fanaticism and extremism, and we know with painful certainty where they can lead.

The Catholic Theological Union has a noble and significant role in this dialogue process, and it is a matter of great pride for me to have been part of it.

Notes

Chapter 1: Transcendence in Context

1. Eliezer Berkovits, *With God in Hell* (New York: Sanhedrin Press, 1979), pp. 20ff.

2. Gershom Scholem, *Major Trends in Jewish Mysticism* (Jerusalem: Schocken, 1941), p. 8.

3. Yehezkel Kaufmann, *The Religion of Israel* (New York: Schocken, 1972), p. 21.

4. Emil Fackenheim, *Encounter Between Judaism and Modern Philosophy* (Philadelphia, 1973), p. 4.

5. Gershom Scholem, "Tradition and Commentary as Religious Categories in Judaism," in *Arguments and Doctrines*, ed. Arthur Cohen (New York: Harper & Row, 1970), pp. 307ff.

6. The effort to know God and bridge transcendence is expressed by the mystics in this way. The reference, of course, is to Ezekiel's chariot vision.

7. Zvi Werblowski, "Kabbalism and the Lurianic Community" (Paper given at the Conference on Transcendence, University of Chicago Divinity School, April 10, 1972).

8. Scholem, *Major Trends in Jewish Mysticism*, p. 2.

9. Scholem, *The Messianic Idea in Judaism* (New York, 1971), pp. 27ff.

10. An early Arabic school of philosophy opposed to Aristotelianism. See Isaac Husik, *History of Mediaeval Jewish Philosophy* (Philadelphia, 1948), pp. xxiv, 248.

11. Clermont-Tonerre, at the National Assembly in Paris, Dec. 23, 1789. See the *Encyclopaedia Judaica*, vol. 6, col. 702.

12. Rabbi Gustavus Poznanski, at the dedication of the new building of Temple Beth Elohim, Charleston, South Carolina, in 1841. See Charles Reznikoff and Uriah Engelman, *The Jews of Charleston* (Philadelphia, 1950), p. 140.

13. David Biale, *Gershom Scholem, Kabbalah and Counter-History* (Cambridge, 1979), p. 1.

14. Eugene Borowitz, "The Changing Form of Jewish Spirituality," *America*, April 28, 1979, p. 347.

15. Ibid., p. 379.

16. Harry J. Cargas, *In Conversation with Elie Wiesel* (Paulist Press, 1976), p. 6.

17. Ibid., p. 52.

18. Ibid., p. 56.

19. Ibid., p. 110.

20. Richard Rubenstein, *After Auschwitz* (Indianapolis, 1960), p. 46.

21. Ibid., p. 152.

22. Ibid., p. 128.

23. Jacob Neusner, "On Transcendence and Worship," *CCAR Journal*, Spring 1978, p. 15.

24. Fackenheim, op. cit., p. 166.

25. Ibid.

26. Ibid.

27. Biale, op. cit., chap. 4, passim.

28. Elie Wiesel, *Night*, trans. Shelly Rodway (New York, 1969), p. 76.

29. Saul Friedlander, *When Memory Comes* (New York, 1979), p. 79.

30. Ibid.

31. Ibid., p. 137.

32. Ibid., p. 135.

33. Ibid., p. 28.

Chapter 2: American Judaism in Transition

1. See Hayim Goren Perelmuter, *David Darshan, Shir HaMa'alot L'David* (Cincinnati: Hebrew Union College Press, 1984).

2. "Population," Encyclopedia Judaica (MacMillan, 1971), vol. 13, p. 866.

3. *Christianity and Judaism as Siblings* in Studies in Formative Spirituality, Feb. 1987, p. 71ff.

4. BT, Megillah 13b.

5. Joseph Blau, *Judaism in America* (Chicago: University of Chicago Press, 1976), p. 20.

6. Nathan Glazer, *American Judaism* (Chicago: University of Chicago Press, 1957), p. 13.

7. Blau, p. 23.

8. Masserman and Baker, *The Jews Come to America* (New York: Bloch Publishing Co., 1932), p. 22ff.

9. Glazer, p. 22ff.

10. Emil Bernhard Cohn and Hayim Goren Perelmuter, *Von Kanaan Nach Israel* (Muenchen: Deutscher Taschenbuch Verlag, 1986), p. 106ff.

11. Robert Seltzer *Jewish People, Jewish Thought* (New York: MacMillan, 1980), p. 580.

12. Ibid.

13. Ibid., p. 648.

14. Ibid., p. 748.

15. Samuel Karff, ed., *Hebrew Union College-Jewish Institute of Religion at One Hundred Years* (Cincinnati: Hebrew Union College Press, 1976).

16. Glazer, Introduction.

17. Cf. *World of Our Fathers*, Irving Howe, Simon & Schuster Inc. New York, 1976.

18. Cf. Leonard Fein. "The Issue is Conversion," *Moment* 4:4, March 1979, p. 17ff.

19. Cf. Eugene Borowitz *A New Theology in the Making* (Philadelphia: Westminster Press, 1968).

20. Harry J. Cargas, *In Conversation with Elie Wiesel* (Mahwah, NJ: Paulist Press, 1976), p. 6.

21. Cf. Gershom Scholem, Introduction to *Sabbatai Sevi*, Bollingen Series, (Princeton: Princeton University Press, 1973).

22. Ibid.

23. Carl Herman Voss, *Rabbi and Minister* (New York: Association Press, 1964), passim.

24. Emil Bernhard Cohn and Hayim Gorem Perelmuter, *This Immortal People* (Mahwah, NJ: Paulist Press, 1985), p. 149ff.

25. Cf. Pinchas Lapide and Juergen Moltmann, *Jewish Monotheism and Christian Trinitarian Doctrine*, trans. by Leonard Swidler, (Philadelphia: Fortress Press, 1981).

26. This course was given by the writer with Professor Wuellner, and selected papers by the students and an introduction by Professors Wuellner and Perelmuter were published by the Graduate Theological Union in Berkeley, California, in 1990.

Chapter 3: When Prayer Became Sacrfice

1. H. G. Perelmuter, *David Darshan, Shir HaMa'alot L'David* (Cincinnati: Hebrew Union College Press, 1984), p. 39.
2. Avot d'Rabbi Nathan 20a.
3. Cf. Rashi's comment on Shabbat 116b.
4. BT, Rosh Hashanah 17b.
5. Joseph Hertz, ed., *Authorized Daily Prayer Book*, rev. ed. (New York: Bloch, 1948), pp. 116–129.
6. Ibid., p. 13.
7. Lawrence Hoffman, *The Canonization of the Synagogue Service* (South Bend, Ind.: Notre Dame University Press, 1979), p. 68.
8. J. Adler and N. Davis, *Service of the Synagogue: Day of Atonement* (New York: Jewish Premium Publishing Co., 1902), p. 134.

Chapter 4: Once a Pun a Preacher

1. Immanuel M. Casanowitz, *Paranomasia in the Old Testament* (Boston, 1894), pp. 1ff.
2. Edwin Good, *Irony in the Old Testament* (Philadelphia, 1950), passim.
3. Samuel Sandmel, *The Hebrew Scriptures* (New York, 1963), p. 341.
4. Robert H. Pfeiffer, *Introduction to the Old Testament* (New York, 1941), p. 441.
5. Ibid., p. 431.
6. A. Guillaume, "Paranomasia in the Old Testament," *Journal of Semitic Studies* 9 (August 1964): 282–290.
7. Ibid., p. 282.
8. Casanowitz, *Paranomasia in the Old Testament*, pp. 14ff.; Good, *Irony in the Old Testament*, pp. 121ff.
9. Simon Jacob Glicksberg, *HaDerashah b'Yisrael* (Jerusalem, 1940), p. 31.
10. Maimonides, *Guide of the Perplexed*, Pines, Strauss ed. (Chicago, 1963). He quotes Bar Kappara in Ketubot 15a as stating that the verse "and thou shalt have a paddle (*yated*) upon thy weapon (*azaneka*)" teaches us that when a man hears a reprehensible thing he should put his fingers in his ear.
11. Gershom Scholem, *Sabbetai Sevi* (Princeton, 1973), p. 163.
12. David Darshan, *Shir HaMa'alot L'David* (Cracow, 1571), *hakdamah*.
13. Berechiah Berekh b. Eliakum, *darshan* of Cracow up to 1648 and later a follower of Shabbetai Zevi. See Scholem, *Sabbetai Sevi* and *hakdamah* to *Zera Berakh* (Amsterdam, 1666).
14. Glicksberg, *HaDerashah b'Yisrael*, p. 39.

15. *Sha'arei Orah* (Jerusalem: Mosad Bialik, 1970), p. 118.

16. See above.

17. Joseph Sarachek, *Don Isaac Abarbanel* (New York, 1938), p. 68.

18 . Ibid., p. 67.

19. The first effort, several years before, proved fruitless when the Helez brothers, who introduced it, converted to Christianity.

20. *K'tav Hitnazzelut*, par. 4.

21. Ibid.

22. Ibid., par. 7.

23. This technique passed into Jewish preaching in the early Middle Ages and is found in the sermons of Baḥya ben Asher (12th cent.).

24. Rabbi Hayim ben Bezalel (a brother of the Maharal of Prague) was an active leader in this tendency. See H. H. Ben-Sasson, *Hagut V'Hanhagah* (Jerusalem, 1959).

25. *Shir HaMa'alot L'David, hakdamah.*

26. Ibid. For the meaning of *novev* in the sense of "gadfly," see Zech. 9:19 and its interpretation in Baba Batra 12b.

Chapter 5: Introduction to the Writings of David Darshan

1. Copies of *Shir HaMa'alot l'David* (Cracow, 1571) are to be found in the Bodleian, British Museum, and Jewish Theological Seminary libraries, The Bodleian copy has the title page (torn and repaired) but is missing pages of the text; the British Museum copy lacks the title page, but the rest of the text is complete; the title page of the Jewish Theological Seminary copy is torn at the top, as is the last page. *K'tav Hitnazzelut l'Darshanim* (Lublin, 1574) is in the British Museum. The Juedische Gemeindebibliothek of Vienna had a copy which disappeared at the time of the Nazi occupation.

2. L. Zunz, *Die gottesdienstlichen Vortraege der Juden* (Berlin, 1832), p. 428.

3. Naphtali Herz ben Menaḥem of Lwow, *Perush al haMidrash Rabbah meHamesh haMegillot* (Cracow, 1569).

4. David Werner Amram, *Makers of Hebrew Books in Italy* (Philadelphia, 1909), pp. 139–143 and 217–223.

5. Cf. part 4 of the introduction.

6. Jeremiah 29:1ff.

7. BT, Megillah 13b.

8. Ezra 8:1–8.

9. Psalms 111:5.

10. Midrash Genesis Rabbah 40:2.

11. BT, Gittin 35b.

12. BT, Pesaḥim 117a; Song of Songs Rabbah 15:3.

13. BT, Horayot 48b; Mishnah Eruvin 3:5.

14. JT, Yevamot, chap. 12.

15. S. Glicksberg, *HaDerashah b'Yisrael*, pp. 14ff.

16. Maimonides, *Mishneh Torah*, Hilkhot Teshuvah 4:2.

17. Maimonides, in the introduction to his Mishnah commentary on tractate Zera'im.

18. Moses Isserles, *Torat haOlah* (Prague, 1569), chap. 4.

19. A. M. Haberman, *Gezerot Ashkenaz v'Zarefat* (1945), p. 166.

20. Moses of Coucy, *Sefer Mitzvot Gadol* (Rome, 1470), introd. 1, 2; 111:11.

21. Venice, 1577.

22. For a brilliant exposition of this period, see H. H. Ben-Sasson, *Hagut v'Hanhagah* (Jerusalem, 1959).

23. Cf. Israel Bettan, *Studies in Jewish Preaching*, pp. 273ff.

24. Ben-Sasson, *Hagut v'Hanhagah*, pp. 46ff.

25. David Darshan, *Shir HaMa'alot l'David*, p. 7a.

26. David Darshan, *K'tav Hitnazzelut l'Darshanim*, par. 17.

27. Ben-Sasson, *Hagut v'Hanhagah*, p. 38.

28. For the student of this field, such works as L. Zunz, *Die gottesdienstlichen Vortraege*, J. Heinemann, *Derashot b'Zibbur biTkufat haTalmud*, I. Bettan, *Studies in Jewish Preaching*, S. Glicksberg, *HaDerashah b'Yisrael*, and H. H. Ben-Sasson, *Hagut v'Hanhagah*, are indispensable.

29. *Shir HaMa'alot l'David*, title page.

30. Ibid., p. 10a.

31. Ibid., p. 12a.

32. Ibid., p. 13a.

33. *K'tav Hitnazzelut l'Darshanim*, par. 14.

34. Moses Isserles, *Mekhir Yayin* (Cremona, 1559), pp. 2a and 24a.

35. Ben-Sasson, *Hagut v'Hanhagah*, passim.

36. Asher Ziv, *She'elot v'Teshuvot haRema* (Jerusalem, 1970), notes to responsa nos. 61 and 71.

37. S. Dubnow, *A History of the Jews in Russia and Poland*, vol. 1, p. 66.

38. M. Balaban, "Italienische und spanische Aerzte," in *Heimkehr* (Berlin, 1912), pp. 173, 177.

39. Cf. Israel Heilperin, *Pinkas Vaad Arba Arazot* (Jerusalem, 1947), p. 17.

40. On the title page of *K'tav Hitnazzelut l'Darshanim*, David is referred to as "the son of the martyred Gaon, Rabbi Manasseh, may God avenge his blood."

41. This was the first stage of yeshiva study in the Middle Ages. The next stage was *meshuḥrar*, corresponding to *licentius* in the universities. The highest level, preceding ordination and the title rabbi, was *ḥaver*. Cf. M. Breuer, "HaYeshivah

haAshkenazit b'Shilhei Y'mei haBeinayim" (doctoral diss., Hebrew University, Jerusalem, 1962).

42. *New Cambridge Modern History,* vol. 2, *The Reformation* (1965), pp. 186ff.

43. Cf. Breuer, "HaYeshivah haAshkenazit b'Shilhei Y'mei haBeinayim."

44. *K'tav Hitnazzelut l'Darshanim,* par. 14.

45. Ibid., par. 31.

46. I. Zinberg, *Geschichte fun der Literatur bei Yiden* (Vilna, 1935), vol. 5, pp. 58ff.

47. Moses Isserles, *She'elot u'Tshuvot haRema* (Cracow, 1640), responsum 7.

48. Ben-Sasson, *Hagut v'Hanhagah,* pp. 13ff. and 39ff.

49. Isserles, *Responsa,* responsum 81.

50. See above, n. 34.

51. This version of the MS is listed in G. Marigoliouth, *Catalogue of Hebrew and Samaritan Manuscripts in the British Museum,* vol. 3, no. 829. Two other versions of this commentary by the kabbalist Reuven haZarfati (14th cent.) are in the Bodleian Library. Cf. A. Neubauer, *Catalogue of Hebrew Manuscripts,* nos. 1949 and 2429.

52. *Shir haMa'alot l'David,* p. 16b.

53. Ibid., p. 15b.

54. Ibid., pp. 12a and 15b.

55. Cf. Breuer, "HaYeshivah haAshkenazit b'Shilhei Y'mei haBeinayim," passim.

56. *K'tav Hitnazzelut l'Darshanim,* par. 14.

57. M. Shulvass, *Jews in the World of the Renaissance* (Leiden, 1973), pp. 19, 20.

58. S. Simonsohn, *A History of the Jews in the Duchy of Mantua* (Jerusalem, 1977), p. 211.

59. Cf. H. D. Friedberg, *Toldot haDfus haIvri b'Poloniah* (Antwerp, 1932), pp. 1ff.

60. Cf. Isserles, *Responsa,* nos. 10 and 69.

61. Zinberg, *Geschichte fun der Literatur bei Yiden,* vol. 5, p. 40.

62. Ibid., p. 19. See also vol. 4, p. 69.

63. Ibid.

64. Amram, *Makers of Hebrew Books in Italy,* pp. 253ff. See also Isserles, *Responsa,* nos. 31 and 69.

65. S. Simonsohn, "Sefarim v'Sifriot shel Yehudei Mantua," *Kiryat Sefer* 37, no, 1 (Jerusalem, 1961–62), p. 103.

66. For a fine detailed account of this controversy, see I. Tishbi, "HaPulmus al Sefer haZohar b'Me'ah haShesh-esrei b'Italiah," in *Mehkarim b'Kabbalah, in Honor of Gershom Scholem* (Jerusalem, 1968).

67. Cf. *Shir haMa'alot l'David,* p. 12a

68. Cf. note 18.

69. *Shir haMa'alot l'David, hakdamah,* p. 1a.

70. Ibid., p. 12a.

71. Ibid., p. 1a.

72. Simonsohn, "Sefarim v'Sifriot shel Yehudei Mantua," pp. 103ff.

73. *Shir HaMa'alot l'David,* p. 8a.

74. Ziv, *She'elot u'Tshuvot haRema,* p. 285.

75. Cf. Andrea Balletti, *Gli Ebrei e Gli Estensi* (Reggio-Emilia, 1930), pp. 96–97.

76. *Shir HaMa'alot l'David,* p. 1a.

77. Ibid., p. 12b.

78. Isaac di Lattes, *She'elot u'Teshuvot* (Vienna, 1860), pp. 141ff.

79. Manuscript, *Sefer haProzesso.* The original is in the Leningrad Library. A microfilm version is to be found in the Hebrew University Library, where it was consulted.

80. *Shir HaMa'alot l'David,* p. 12b.

81. M. Balaban, *Yiden in Polen* (Vilna, 1930), pp. 183ff.

82. Ibid.

83. Ibid. This is one of the first inventories of printed Hebrew books on record.

84. Friedberg, *Toldot haDfus haIvri b'Poloniah,* p. 3.

85. Ibid.

86. *Shir HaMa'alot l'David,* p. 15a.

87. From the last page of *Perush al hamidrash Rabbah mehamesh hamegillot,* by Naphtali Herz ben Menahem of Lwow (Cracow, 1568).

88.

דרשו ספר. אמרי שפר. בלתי חפר. עושה פירות.
ודאי גלה. בכל מילה. הפלא פלא. תיבות זרות.
דרך דרך. אין לו ערך. התיר פרך. שורות שורות.
דבר דבר. עתיד עבר. יישב חבר. כל אפשרות.
ראה קלות. ה׳ מגלות . מצד מלות. דרש חמורות.
שם רב הו״א ר״ק. גאון הירק. גודר פרץ. ראש החבורות.
נגמר אומר. כ״ף ט״ת אב צר. חדווה יצר. לפרט קטן.

89. Ibid. first line of Hebrew text.

90. This line is based on a *yozer* for Shabbat Shekalim. Note how the poem is based on the form and content of the *piyyut:* ואפר. היותם נוהגים כופר. כלי היפי וחפר. דבר בזה ספר. וקים באמרי שפר. למשולי עפר

91. This is a pun on Herz.

92. The Hebrew phrase חדוה יצר has the numerical value of 329, which in this case is the beginning of the Hebrew year 5329, i.e., 1568. The book was published the following year.

93. *Shir HaMa'alot l'David,* p. 2b.

94. Ibid.

95. Ibid.

96. *K'tav Hitznazzelut l'Darshanim,* par. 25.

97. Cf. Friedberg, *Toldot haDfus haIvri b'Poloniah.* Note especially the sections on Cracow and Lublin.

98. *K'tav Hitznazzelut l'Darshanim,* title page.

98. Ibid., par. 16.

100. Ibid., title page.

101. Ibid.

102. Isaac Duran, *Sha'arei Dura* (Lublin, 1574).

103. Cf. Saul Lieberman, *HaYerushalmi kiPshuto* (Jerusalem, 1935), p. 8.; Cf. Talmud Yerushalmi, Nazir 54c.

104. *Shir HaMa'alot l'David,* p. 16b.

Chapter 7: From Prophet to Preacher

1. Sifrei to Deuteronomy 32.
2. Exodus Rabbah 80:5.
3. Yalkut Shim'oni 2:965.
4. See Targum to Malachi 1:1.
5. BT, Sanhedrin 11a.
6. Rashi to Yoma 20b and Ketubbot 106a.
7. BT, Ketubbot 106a.
8. JT, Berakhot 1:1.
9. BT, Yoma 20b.
10. *Teshuvot haGeonim,* Sha'arei Teshuvah 178.
11. BT, Megillah 11b.
12. Maimonides, *Mishneh Torah,* Hilkhot Talmud Torah 4:3.
13. Ibid.
14. Numbers Rabbah 14:3.
15. For much of the material in this chapter and for a guide to many of the quotations, I am indebted to Shimon Yosef Glicksberg, *haDerasha b'Yisrael,* (Jerusalem: Mosad HaRav Kook, 1940).

Chapter 11: Mission

1. See Israel Ben-Ze'ev, *Gerim v'Giyur* (Jerusalem, 1961).

Chapter 12: Rabbinical Tradition on the Role of Women

1. Leonard Swidler, *Women in Judaism* (Metuchen, NJ: Scarecrow Press, 1976), pp. 25, 33.
2. BT, Baba Batra 119b (Soncino).
3. BT, Pesaḥim 62b.
4. Josephus, *Against Apion*, Whiston ed. (Philadelphia: Lippincott, 1895), vol. 2, p. 515.
5. Swidler, *Women in Judaism*, p. 54.
6. Shelomo Dov Gotein, "Middle Ages," *Hadassah Magazine*, October 1973.
7. Rabbi Isaac ben Immanuel de Lattes, *Responsa* (Vienna, 1860), p. 140.
8. Elaine Starkman, "Women in the Pulpit," *Hadassah Magazine*, October 1973.
9. Ibid.
10. Central Conference of American Rabbis, Year Book, vol. 66, (1956), p. 91. See also CCAR Year Book for 1955, p. 13, the Presidential address of Rabbi Barnet Brickner which placed the issue on the agenda.
11. Universal Jewish Encyclopedia, vol. 7, p. 626.
12. Philip Sigal, "Women in the Minyan," *Judaism,* Spring 1974.
13. Ibid., p. 182.
14. Saul Berman, "The Status of Women in Halakhic Judaism," *Tradition,* vol. 14, no. 2, Fall 1973, p. 5ff.
15. Ibid. p. 10.
16. BT, Baba Kama 79b: "You do not make a decision for the community unless the majority of community can endure it."
17. Chaim Tchernovitz, *Toledot Ha-Poskim* vol. 3 (New York, 1947), p. 47.
18. Efthaliah Walsh, "Ever-more Women in the Pulpit," *New York Times,* Sept. 27, 1977.

Chapter 13: "Do Not Destroy": Ecology in the Fabric of Judaism

1. Lynn White, "Historical Roots of the Ecological Crisis," *Science* 155 (1967): 1203–1207.
2. Arnold Toynbee, in *International Journal of Environmental Studies*, 1971.
3. In "Theology for a Small Planet," *Harvard Divinity Bulletin* 14:3 (Fall 1991), p. 8.

4. Robert G. Hamerton-Kelly, *Sacred Violence* (Minneapolis: Fortress Press, 1992), p. 8.

5. In "Theology for a Small Planet," op. cit., p. 7.

6. Ibid., p. 9.

7. Hayim Goren Perelmuter, *Siblings* (Mahwah, N.J.: Paulist Press, 1989), p. 5.

8. Jeremy Cohen, *Be Fertile, and Increase, Fill the Earth and Master It* (Ithaca: Cornell University Press, 1989).

9. Anton Chekhov, *The Works of Anton Chekhov* (New York, 1929), p. 84.

10. Robert Gordis, *Judaic Ethics for a Lawless World* (New York: Jewish Theological Seminary, 1986), pp. 119–121.

11. Ralph Pelkowitz, *Danger and Opportunity* (New York: Shengold, 1976), p. 102.

12. Eric G. Freudenstein, "Ecology and the Jewish Tradition," *Tradition*, Fall 1970, p. 407.

13. Ahad Ha'am, *Al Parashat Derakhim* [The parting of the ways] (1921), 3:79.

14. Abraham J. Heschel, *God in Search of Man* (New York: Farrar, Straus, & Cudahy, 1955), p. 97.

15. Bernard Mandelbaum, *Pesikta d'Rav Kahana* (New York: Jewish Theological Seminary, 1962), vol. 2, chap. 3.

16. Sholom Aleichem, *Collected Works* [in Yiddish] (New York, 1925), p. 15.

Siblings: A Jewish and a Roman Catholic Scholar

1. Walter M. Abbott, S.J., ed., *The Documents of Vatican II* (New York: Guild Press, 1966), p. 665.

2. The appropriate name for this part of the Bible is disputed. Many who feel that "Old Testament" is pejorative have adopted the designation "Hebrew Scriptures." Since the Roman Catholic canon does not follow the order found in the Tanakh, that name seems imprecise. Furthermore, since this section constitutes the first of a two-testament Bible, it can rightfully be considered Christian Scripture. Therefore the term used here is "First Testament."

Selected Bibliography of Writings by Rabbi Hayim Goren Perelmuter

Compiled by Kenneth O'Malley, C.P.

Books

Jewish History in 1000 Questions and Answers, translated from the Yiddish of A.S. Zacker. Montreal: Eagle Press, 1937.

Paul the Jew: Jewish/Christian Dialogue. Edited by Hayim G. Perelmuter and Wilhelm Wuellner. Berkeley, Calif.: Center for Hermeneutical Studies, 1990.

Shir haMa'alot l'David (Song of the Steps) and *K'tav Hitnazzelut l'Darshanim (In Defence of Preachers),* by David Darshan of Cracow. With translation, introduction, and photographic reproduction of the two books published in Cracow, 1571 and Lublin, 1574. Hebrew Union College Press, Cincinnati 1985.

Siblings: Rabbinic Judaism and Early Christianity at Their Beginnings by Hayim G. Perelmuter. Mahwah, N.J.: Paulist Press, 1989.

266	Harvest of a Dialogue

Song of the Steps, and In Defense of Preachers, by David Darshan of Cracow. Translated by H. G. Perelmuter. Ph.D. Diss., Hebrew Union College, Cincinnati, 1984.

This Immortal People: One Hour of Jewish History, by Emil Bernhard Cohn. Translated by H. G. Perelmuter. New York: Behrman House, 1945.

This Immortal People: A Short History of the Jewish People, by Emil Bernhard Cohn. Translated by H. G. Perelmuter and updated with supplement. Mahweh, NJ: Paulist Press, 1985.

Von Kanaan nach Israel: Kleine Geschichte des Jüdischen Volkes, by Emil Bernhard Cohn and H. G. Perelmuter, Munich: Deutscher Taschenbuch Verlag, 1986.

Articles

"Judaizm Amerikanski w Procesie Przemian" [American Judaism in transition].In *Religie Pozechrzescijanskie w Procesie Przemian* [World religions in transition], edited by Henryka Zimonia, S.V.D., pp. 13–26. Materialy i Studia Ksiezy Werbiston, no. 35. Warsaw: Verbinum, 1990.

"A Brief History of Preaching." In *Complete Library of Christian Worship,* vol. 3, edited by Robert Webber, pp. 279–285. Nashville: Star Song Publishing Group, 1993.

"Burden of Gog" (poem), by Y. Golah. Translated from the Hebrew by H. G. Perelmuter. *Central Conference of American Rabbis Journal* 1 (June 1963): 48–49.

"A Chicago Lady and a Hebrew Writer: A Note on the Recent Death of Abraham Kariv." *Central Conference of American Rabbis Journal* 24 (Winter 1977): 92–93.

"Christianity and Judaism as Siblings: Historical Sweep Leading to Pharisaism," *Studies in Formation Spirituality* 8 (Fall 1987): 71–81.

"Do Not Destroy." In *The Ecological Challenge: Ethical, Liturgical, and Spiritual Responses,* edited by J. Pawlikowski and R. Fragomeni, pp. 129–138. Collegeville, Minn.: Liturgical Press, 1994.

"Ever Hear of Lag B'omer?" *Jewish Digest* 13 (April 1968): 78.

"Geluebde." In *Theologische Realenzyklopadie,* edited by Gerhard Muller and Horst Robert Balz, vol. 12, pp. 304–305. New York: Walter de Gruyter, 1984–.

"Gershom Scholem, Jewish Revolutionary." *Journal of Reform Judaism* 31 (Summer 1984): 72–84.

"Gewohnheit/Gewohnheitsrecht II—Judentum (*minhag*)." In: *Theologische Realenzyklopadie,* edited by Gerhard Muller, vol. 13, pp. 245–248. New York: Walter de Gruyter, 1984–.

"Hannukkah Lights and Shadows." *Bible Today* 25 (March 1987): 87–93.

"Henry Slonimsky." *Central Conference of American Rabbis Journal* 16 (June 1969): 40–44.

"Impact of Bigness on the Life of the American Jew." In *Yearbook of the Central Conference of American Rabbis,* edited by Sidney L. Regner, pp. 172–173. Philadelphia: Maurice Jacobs Press, 1960.

"J.F.K. and the Hasidic Rebbe." Condensed in *Jewish Digest* 9 (June 1964): 17–18.

"Jesus the Jew: A Jewish Perspective." *New Theology Review* 7 (May 1994): 27–36.

"Jonah—Astronaut or Aquanaut?" *Bible Today* 23 (July 1985).

"Judaism and Transcendence: From Abraham to the Late Middle Ages." *Spirituality Today* 41 (Spring 1989): 18–29.

"Judaism's Missionary Tradition." *Sh'ma* 24 (Feb. 4 1994): 5–6.

"Letters of Paul Viewed as Responsa" (with Wilhelm Wuellner). Proceedings of a Conference at Catholic Theological Union, November 1991. (Unpublished manuscript).

"Masada: Fact or Fiction." *Bible Today* 19 (July 1981): 272–276.

"Memoir of an Exile from Spain." *New Theology Review* 5 (November 1992): 66–68.

"Mission–II. Judentum." *Theologische Realenzyklopödie,* Berlin: Walter de Gruyter, 1990. Vol. xxiii lfg. 1/2. pp. 20–23.

"Mission in Judaism." *Bible Today* 30 (May 1992): 112–115.

"My Heart Is in the East" (poem by Judah Halevi). Translated from the Hebrew by H. G. Perelmuter. *Central Conference of American Rabbis Journal* 11 (April 1971): 2.

"New York: A Letter from H. G. Perelmuter on the Centenary of Franz Rosenzweig," *European Judaism* 20 (Winter 1986): 15–17.

"NFTY after Fifty Years." *Journal of Reform Judaism* 37 (Spring 1990): 69–70.

"Once a Pun a Preacher: A Study in Paranomasia in Biblical and Rabbinic Literature." *Journal of Reform Judaism* 27 (Spring 1990): 61–75.

"Practicum on Judaism for Christian Theology Students." *Journal of Ecumenical Studies* 22 (Winter 1985): 201–202.

"Rabbinic Tradition on the Role of Women." In *Women and Priesthood,* edited by Carroll Stuhlmueller, pp. 111–120. Collegeville, Minn.: Liturgical Press, 1978.

"Sabbetai Sevi: The Mystical Messiah." *Sidic* 9 (Nov. 3, 1976): 23–27.

"The Strength of the Elders." *Bible Today* 30 (November 1992): 347–352.

"To Hug or Not to Hug." *Jerusalem Report* 3 (April 22, 1993): 2 (Letter).

"Transcendence in Context: A Contemporary Jewish View." *Spirituality Today* 39 (Spring 1987): 5–21.

"What Is Hidden in Jonah's Gourd? (A Yom Kippur Midrash)." *Journal of Reform Judaism* 35 (Summer 1988): 53–55.

"When Sacrifice Became Prayer (Prayer in the Rabbinic Tradition)." In *Scripture and Prayer,* edited by Carolyn Osiek and Donald Senior, pp. 88–103. Collegeville, Minn.: Liturgical Press, 1988.

Reviews

Bursting the Bonds? A Jewish-Christian Dialogue on Jesus and Paul, by Leonard Swidler et al. *Catholic Biblical Quarterly* 54 (July 1992): 591–592.

The Canonization of the Synagogue Service, edited by Lawrence A. Hoffman. *Currents in Theology and Mission* 14 (June 1987): 204–205.

The Changing Face of Jewish and Christian Worship in North America, by Paul F. Bradshaw and Lawrence A. Hoffman. *Worship* 67 (January 1993): 86–87.

Chariots of Fire (motion picture), by William J. Weatherly. *Bible Today* 20 (July 1982): 244–245.

Die Gleichnisse der Rabbinen: Erster Teil Pesigta de Rav Kahana, by Clemens Thoma and Simon Lauer. *Journal of Reform Judaism* 37 (Winter 1990): 87–88.

Give Us a King: Legal-Religious Sources of Jewish Sovereignty, by David Polish. *New Theology Review* 4 (November 1991): 98–99.

The Gospels and Rabbinic Judaism: A Study Guide, by Michael Hilton and Gordian Marshall. *Catholic Biblical Quarterly* 52 (July 1990): 558–559.

Hear, O Israel: The History of American Jewish Preaching, 1654–1990, by Robert V. Friedenberg. *Central Conference of American Rabbis Journal* 39 (Summer 1992): 76–78.

The Heavenly Kingdom: Aspects of Political Thought in the Talmud and Midrash, by Gordon M. Greeman. *Currents in Theology and Mission* 15 (October 1988): 456.

Jewish Perspective on Christianity, edited by Fritz A. Rothschild. *New Theology Review* 5 (August 1992): 114–115.

Jewish Spirituality: From the 16th-Century Revival to the Present, edited by Arthur Green. *Worship* 62 (Summer 1988): 467–469; *New Theology Review* 1 (November 1988): 97–98.

The Jewish Way: Living the Holidays, by Irving Greenberg. *Worship* 64 (January 1990): 89–91.

Judaism: Between Yesterday and Tomorrow, by Hans Kung. *Worship* 68 (January 1994): 83–85.

Judaism: An Introduction for Christians, edited by James Limburg. *New Theology Review* 1 (Fall 1988): 134–135.

Liturgical Foundations of Social Policy in the Catholic and Jewish Traditions, edited by Daniel Polish and Eugene Fisher. *Spirituality Today* 36 (Summer 1984): 181.

Middle Judaism: Jewish Thought 300 B.C. to 200 C.E., by Gabriele Boccaccini. *New Theology Review* 7 (May 1994): 105–107.

Parable and Story in Judaism and Christianity. by Clemens Thoma and Michael Wyshogrod. *New Theology Review* 4 (Fall 1991): 81–82.

Paul and the Jewish Law, by Peter Tomson. *New Theology Review* 6 (May 1993) 115–116.

Paul the Convert: The Apostolate and Apostasy of Paul the Pharisee, by Alan F. Segal. *New Theology Review* 2 (May 1991): 110–111.

La preghiera di Israele: alle origini della liturgia cristiana, by Carmine di Sante. *Worship* 71 (Summer 1987): 476–477.

Sabbetai Sevi: The Mystical Messiah, 1626–1676, by Gershom Scholem. Review essay. *Central Conference of American Rabbis Journal* 22 (Winter 1975): 21–29.

Understanding Scripture, by Clemens Thoma and Michael Wyschograd. *New Theology Review* 1 (May 1988): 122–124.

Von Kanaan nach Israel, by E. Bernhard-Cohen. *European Judaism* 20 (Winter 1986): 48.

About

Morgan, F. Review of *Paul the Jew: Jewish/Christian Dialogue* by H. G. Perelmuter and Wilhelm Wuellner. *Catholic Biblical Quarterly* 54 (January 1992): 168–169.

Contributors

Hayim Goren Perelmuter, Rabbi Emeritus of K.A.M.–Isaiah Israel Congregation in Chicago, currently serves as Professor of Jewish Studies at the Catholic Theological Union. He has also taught at the Pacific Lutheran Theological Seminary, the Graduate Theological Union in Berkeley, the Pontifical Academy of Theology in Cracow, Poland, the Katholiek Universiteit Leuven in Louvain, Belgium, and the universities of Lucerne and Bern in Switzerland. He is a past president of the Chicago Board of Rabbis, has served on the board of governors of the Hebrew Union College–Jewish Institute of Religion, the executive board of the Central Conference of American Rabbis, the Social Action Commission of the Union of American Hebrew Congregations, and the board of the Jewish Federation of Greater Chicago. He is currently a member of the Academic Advisory Committee of the American Jewish Historical Society, a member of the Chicago Catholic-Jewish Scholars Dialogue, and sits on the board of the Jewish Council on Urban Affairs.

Dianne Bergant, C.S.A., is Professor of Old Testament studies at Catholic Theological Union. She is a member of the North American Conference on Religion and Ecology and has written several articles on issues of the Bible and ecology. Her major publications include *The World Is a Prayer Place, Collegeville Bible Commentary* (Old Testament editor), and "The Wisdom Books," in *The Catholic Study Bible* (New York, 1990).

Kenneth O'Malley, C.P., has been Director of the Library at the Catholic Theological Union since 1969. He has a Ph.D. in Library Science from the University of Illinois and has held important positions in the American Theological Library Association, the Catholic Library Association, the Illinois Library Cooperative Association, and related organizations. He regularly contributes book reviews to professional and theological journals.

John T. Pawlikowski, O.S.M., a Servite priest, is Professor of Social Ethics at the Catholic Theological Union. He is the Editor of *New Theology Review* and serves on the editorial boards of *Shofar: An Interdisciplinary Journal of Jewish Studies,* the *Journal of Ecumenical Studies,* and the *Journal of Holocaust and Genocide Studies.* He is a prolific writer in the area of Jewish–Christian relations and a presidential appointee to the United

States Holocaust Memorial Council. His books include *Christ in the Light of the Christian-Jewish Dialogue* and *Jesus and the Theology of Israel.* He has collaborated with Rabbi Perelmuter on many projects at the Catholic Theological Union for the past quarter-century.

Donald Senior, C.P., recently completed an extended tenure as President of Catholic Theological Union, where he also serves as Professor of New Testament. He holds a doctorate in New Testament studies from the University of Louvain in Belgium. He was the founding director of the school's overseas study program in Israel, and has written and lectured extensively on biblical topics.

Michael Walzer is currently a scholar in residence at the Institute for Advanced Study in Princeton, New Jersey. He is a noted author and lecturer on issues of political philosophy, and has also had a continuing interest in the sociopolitical dimensions of biblical teaching. His books include *Exodus and Revolution* and *Just and Unjust Wars.* He did his bar mitzvah under Rabbi Perelmuter in Johnstown, Pennsylvania.